The Judds

Other Books by George Mair

Oprah Winfrey: The Real Story
Bette: An Intimate Biography
Under the Rainbow: The Real Liza Minnelli
Rosie O'Donnell: Her True Story (with Anna Green)
*The Barry Diller Story: Life and Times of America's Greatest
    Entertainment Mogul*
Family Money: Inheritance Battles of Rich and Famous
Star Stalkers: Those Who Stalk and Murder Celebrities
Bridge Down: America's Collapsing Infra-Structure
Lethal Ladies: Women Who Kill for Love
Inside HBO: Billion Dollar War Between HBO and Hollywood
How to Write Better in One Hour
*Natural Born Winner: America's Hottest NASCAR Race Driver,
    Jeff Gordon*

The Judds

The True Story of
Naomi, Wynonna, and Ashley

George Mair

A Birch Lane Press Book
Published by Carol Publishing Group

A Birch Lane Press Book
Published by Carol Publishing Group
Birch Lane Press is a registered trademark of Carol Communications, Inc.

Editorial, sales and distribution, rights and permissions inquiries should be
addressed to Carol Publishing Group, 120 Enterprise Avenue, Secaucus, N.J.
07094.

In Canada: Canadian Manda Group, One Atlantic Avenue, Suite 105, Toronto,
Ontario, M6K 3E7

Carol Publishing Group books may be purchased in bulk at special discounts
for sales promotion, fundraising, or educational purposes. Special editions can
be created to specifications. For details, contact Special Sales Department,
Carol Publishing Group, 120 Enterprise Avenue, Secaucus, N.J. 07094.

Manufactured in the United States of America
10 9 8 7 6 5 4 3 2 1

Library of Congress Cataloging-in-Publication Data

Mair, George, 1927–
    The Judds : the true story of Naomi, Wynonna, and Ashley / George
Mair.
        p.   cm.
    Includes index.
    ISBN 1–55972–459–5 (hc)
    1. Judds (Musical group)   2. Judd, Ashley.   3. Country musicians—
United States—Biography.   I. Title.
ML421.J82M35   1998
782.421642′092′2—dc21
    [b]   98–3943
                                                                       CIP
                                                                       MN

With love to
Jordan, Megan, Shannon, and James

Contents

24. The Farewell Tour   219
25. From the Queen of Everything to the Queen   228
    of Quite a Lot
26. Turning Country Music Into a Money Machine   236
27. Wynonna Alone   240
28. A Stunning Confession   244
29. Finding the Fun in Dysfunctional   252

    Sources   267
    Index   269

Prologue

It was an event that was symbolic and mystical to the Judds. Christina Claire Ciminella, now known simply as Wynonna, was born on May 30, 1964, at King's Daughters Hospital in Ashland, Kentucky. Helping in the birth was the same nurse who had assisted bringing another baby into the world on January 11, 1946—18 years prior—in the very same room of that hospital. That other baby, Diana Ellen—whom we know today as Naomi—was born to Charles Glen Judd and Pauline Ruth Oliver Judd.

Diana Ellen gave birth to her firstborn daughter thirty-four years ago and in the process crossed the threshold from childhood to adulthood before graduating from high school, without a job and with a husband she didn't love. Yet Diana had what would be one of the two most precious things in her life: She had Christina. The two of them would be the wind and the sea together, the fire and the smoke, heaven and hell.

"Christina and I plunged headlong into an epic, lifelong search for harmony that would alternately unite and divide us a thousand times," said Diana Ellen, "a journey that would see us grow up together...and embrace the elusive rhythms of a unique mother-daughter relationship." This is their story as well as the story of a second, younger daughter, Ashley, who would become a star, too.

The Judds

1

The Judds'
Old Kentucky Home

IN 1946, DIANA ELLEN was the first child born to Polly, as Pauline was nicknamed, and Glen Judd, as Charles Glen Judd was called. The Judd clan was indigenous to the Kentucky bluegrass country, located at the rim of the Appalachians. The hospital where Diana Ellen first arrived, King's Daughters', was only two blocks from the Judd home. They lived in the little town of Ashland, with its ten thousand souls and a Mayberry RFD air about it. The river and its banks bustled with such industrial activities as the refining of oil and the extracting of coal and cement, the refineries and docks a backdrop to the barges that carried the region's wealth downstream to the rest of the world. Besides hearing and seeing the extraction, refining, and movement of minerals, the people of Ashland could also smell it wafting from the tall oil-refinery stacks.

Diana's middle name comes from her grandmother, who was called Ellen Judd. Later, when Diana Ellen changed her own first name to Naomi, she clung romantically to her middle name because of her deep sense of family. The original Judd homestead, located in Louisa, Kentucky, about twenty-six miles up the Sandy

River before it runs into the Ohio, was purchased by Elijah Judd (Diana's great-great-grandfather) with his pension at the end of the Civil War. Elijah, a Yankee sergeant in the mounted infantry, settled down with his wife, Fanny, to begin a simple farming and family life with their seven children.

Their eldest daughter, Mary Jane, had an affair with the local doctor, but her father refused to let her marry him for reasons that have been forgotten. She bore a baby boy, Roy Ogden, who was Diana's grandfather. When Mary Jane was in her early twenties, she died of an unspecified ailment, a situation that was not uncommon in those frontier days. Grandfather Roy was raised by his grandparents, Elijah and Fanny.

Another one of their daughters, Margaret Ann, Diana's great-aunt, took over the Judd homestead and lived as a single woman along with her cousin Zora. The two women, though different in temperament, seemed to complement each other. Zora worked in the garden, building and mending fences and doing other outdoor chores, while Margie did a lot of the handiwork. Both were eccentric and carefree enough to live and dress the way they pleased, a tendency that seems to have resurfaced with Wynonna and Ashley. Zora would wear layers of mismatched clothes and position eyeglasses on the bridge of her nose until she would get the magnification she needed in order to see clearly. Zora also helped Margie run the Judds' general store, which sold everything from farm implements to candy bars. Together they lived out their lives in a somewhat primitive home with neither indoor plumbing nor electricity. Heat was provided by a coal-grate fireplace in the living room and a wood cookstove in the kitchen. Although a modest home, it was the kind of place where children could roam about and dream.

Diana also loved to visit her grandparents, Roy and Ellen Judd, at their home on Little Cat Creek, near the small community of Louisa. Diana remembers: "I'd go out in the woods by myself, and I was like a wild animal," exploring the Kentucky wilderness, its wild flowers, embracing trees, and a wide array of animals and birds.

It would later be a place where Diana would nurture her own

sensibilities and commune with nature—a growing experience that would shape her view of life and the world. She loved the woods— the sunlight and shadows dancing through the trees' branches— surrounding the old house. "I felt the most incredible sense of freedom there, and my rich imagination soared. I roamed or prowled like an animal. I was free to become my alter egos: the Indian princess Skydancer or an alien from a far galaxy..."

Glen Judd, Diana's father, was the only boy among five sisters (Pauline, Evelyn Watseka, Mariolive, Ramona, and Faith), who were all born in the same one-room cabin on a hill across from the main house. Within walking distance, they could visit the one-room schoolhouse, the log church, and of course the family cemetery. Glen's sister Pauline moved into the second farm, which was built close to the original homestead.

Diana describes this simple, sparsely furnished house as "decorating takes a holiday." There were no photos or pictures on the wall, no living room, and certainly no indoor plumbing. Still, Diana loved being there. Pauline was a keen observer of her natural surroundings and had become adept at predicting the weather by noting the thickness of an animal's fur or testing the coldness of well water. "All these were full-on country people with a natural, endemic Appalachian wisdom," said Diana. She grew up with the herbs, people, and life that flowed from her family and everyone they touched.

One of Diana's earliest lessons consisted of the "two-finger rule," which told her when it was time to stop wandering in the woods. When the space she could see between the bottom of the sun and the horizon was two fingers wide, she knew it was time to go home. It meant there was enough sunlight left for her to get there before dark. Such natural lore was part of her growing up and shaped her subsequent view of the world.

This knowledge did not insulate the Judds from hard times and the hard life. Glen Judd, Diane's father, although emotionally remote, was a hardworking, honest man, dedicated to raising his family. He would show love to his children by putting in extra hours at work so he could afford to buy them braces or piano lessons or school clothes. His hard work paid off, because his gas station offered the cleanest place to stop, the fastest service, and the lowest prices. His shop was Ashland's Oil Filling Station of the Year—every year. He was a typical fifties father, and the family rarely saw him. He would leave for work early in the morning and return home at around 9:00 P.M. He would wash up, eat dinner, then sit down and either read a Mickey Spillane novel or watch boxing on TV.

Diana never saw any display of affection between her parents. She thought the lack of visible love was completely normal until she visited her friends' homes and saw their parents touching each other or stealing a kiss. Years later, she learned that love is one's greatest gift, but she never saw evidence of it in the Judd household.

Her parents never went out to dinner together or to see a movie. Glen Judd rarely gave his wife, Polly, presents for her birthday or at Christmastime. If he did, they were usually inexpensive. Although Diana sensed that there was some secret shared by her parents, she didn't understand what it was until years later.

Polly Judd was a private woman, keeping her emotions to herself, like her hardworking husband, and never whining about her life. She did her chores, took care of her family, and never demanded anything for herself. Diana always wondered why her mother seemed to put up with so much and demand so little. She was deeply religious and very protective of her children, particularly during this time, when America's households were haunted by poliomyelitis, or simply, polio, a mysterious, incurable illness that struck children everywhere. Parents constantly watched their youngsters and kept them clean in order to avoid the disease that had already paralyzed President Franklin D. Roosevelt.

Perhaps Polly's reclusive nature can be explained by her mother's side of the family. Polly's family was decidedly darker and more troubled than Glen's, with a cast of characters whose histories would make afternoon soap operas seem tame. Cora Lee, Diana's great-grandmother, was abandoned at age 11. Her father, an itinerant carpenter, couldn't earn a living and gave Cora to a childless couple who lived on Tygart Creek in Greenup County. Her new father was the local doctor, and while Cora didn't get past the seventh grade, she was naturally bright and became so self-reliant that she was able to assist her father with medical chores. Cora Lee was very much like Glen Judd emotionally—distant and self-possessed. To Diana, Cora Lee was different from her paternal grandparents in a way, even though she was also withdrawn. Diana figured out in later life that Cora Lee was afraid to tell anybody she loved them or to express her inner feelings openly for fear that someone close to her would abandon her again.

Diana's great-grandfather, Edward Burton, was even more withdrawn. Whenever the Judds went to visit, Edward would sit off by himself, rocking in a chair and wearing the same hardened expression that signaled others to keep their distance. Although a palpable chill hovered throughout the house, Diana noticed that while her grandparents seemed to display no affection, they did have six children, so obviously they did come together at times.

Cora Lee's first daughter, Edie Mae, became Diana's grandmother after she married Howard Oliver, a young man who grew up in a troubled family. When Howard was only seven, he and his brother, Norman, watched their father commit suicide by hanging himself from the rafters. Before he put the rope around his neck, he turned on the gas to take his two sons with him. Norman never really recovered from that emotional trauma. For years he would not talk and became an extreme introvert. Howard, on the other hand, appeared to be well adjusted and lived a normal life. That is, until he met up with Diana's grandmother, Edie Mae. Their marriage was troubled from the start, and Edie began to have affairs. However, they had three children together: Norman; Diana's mother, Polly; and Martha Lee.

The bizarre tragedies and family mysteries continued, and when Polly was nine years old, Howard Oliver was found dead in the bathroom, shot in the head. Officially, his death was ruled a suicide, but a lot of people thought it was murder. The rumor was that Edie Mae and her lover murdered Oliver, and when Edie Mae left the children at Cora Lee's and suddenly left town, the rumors ripened into a certainty that haunted Edie Mae for the rest of her life.

Before Edie Mae deserted her children, including Diana's

mother, Polly, it was clear she was bereft of a maternal instinct and emotionally vacant. Diana tells how her own mother was raised. "Edie Mae was a dreadful parent who gave little, if any, attention to her children." Her daughter Polly became a surrogate mother, raising herself and her brother and sister, for Edie Mae preferred partying to parenting and couldn't be bothered. She spent most of her time chasing men or being chased by them, and child care didn't fit into her equation of life, all of which emotionally scarred the three children she bore.

In time, Diana's mother, Polly, lived at Cora Lee's and worked at the family restaurant, called the Hamburger Inn, in Ashland. She later said she was practically raised there, where she learned to make all sorts of dishes. Cora Lee's house was filled with characters: Great-aunt Ruth, a bisexual stigmatized by the outside world; Great-uncle Leroy, a homosexual hairdresser with bleached-blond hair who ran the local beauty salon and owned a poodle; then there was Great-uncle George, an alcoholic and gambler; Great-uncle Carl, who had retired from the air force and owned a local bar; and Uncle Harry, a drunk. Diana recalled that the house was simply furnished and the shades drawn to screen out the world. Cigarette smoke tainted the air. Diana later described her relatives from that side of the family as a "menagerie that was a tangled web of secret lives and hushed truths."

Understandably, life for Polly, her mother, was not easy, either. She worked at the Hamburger Inn as a cashier but was teased and disliked by her brother, Norman, and sister, Martha Lee because they knew Polly was Cora Lee's favorite. The only person that Polly could relate to was Leroy, the gay hairdresser.

Polly led a monotonous life, too, until she met a young man at the local gas station. His name was Glen Judd. He was equally smitten with Polly. She hung around until Glen finally worked up the courage to ask her out, and they began to date. Dating for Polly was actually more like a rescue mission, and she was falling hard, for Glen turned out to be everything she had dreamed of in a man. He was an honor student in high school, held a full-time job, and had a stable home life.

Soon Polly and Glen were married by a justice of the peace.

Glen had turned eighteen and Polly was only fifteen. Two years later, on January 11, 1946, Polly gave birth to Diana in King's Daughters Hospital. That summer, in August, Glen bought the gas station where he worked and renamed it Judd's Ashland Service. Shortly thereafter, they purchased a two-story home on Hilton Avenue. Eventually, Polly and Glen purchased his parents' home at 2237 Montgomery Street for twenty thousand dollars.

Diana has fond memories of 2237 Montgomery and those early years. She developed an understanding of men early in life by hanging out at her father's gas station and listening to them talk. Diana was well served by her exposure to male society so early. She was young, so they weren't a threat, but old enough and female enough to gain a sense of how they acted, talked, and thought. The exposure would give her poise and control in later years that more sheltered women didn't enjoy.

She drank in the attention the men gave her and the security of the quiet love from her father. One of her favorite memories is that her father kept cellophane-wrapped pictures of his children taped to the cash register. This is how Diana knew her dad loved her even though he wasn't a demonstratively affectionate man.

A mark of his reserved personality still lingers in Diana's memory. She recalls that she would hug him and tell him how much she loved him, but Glen never reciprocated in the same way. He kept his feelings private, but Diana knew of his love for her and from time to time would even catch him boasting about his little girl to others when he didn't know she could hear him.

When things got too busy at the station, Glen would send her home, where she would hang out in the kitchen with her mother or roller-skate on the front porch. The kitchen was where everything happened, where everyone gathered to eat and talk and the air was thick with mouth-watering aromas. Polly was famous in the neighborhood for her cooking skills, and one of her specialties was making meat-loaf sandwiches for the kids to take to school. These sandwiches were so popular that the Judd children could trade them for any food the other youngsters brought to school that day. Sometimes neighbors would drop in for coffee, cigarettes, and gossip. Memories of the sounds and smells of that kitchen would stay with Diana her entire life. Even to this day she can remember the atmosphere of that kitchen and has tried to incorporate it into her recently published cookbook.

Since he was in business for himself, Glen had to be financially careful and tightfisted with money, and Diana's mother used her ingenuity to entertain the children. The living room would become a fortress zone, with sheets and blankets hanging every which way, and the children would crawl among them. When the fortress game got boring, everyone would hang out on the porch and play Monopoly. In the evening, Polly would make some popcorn and entertain the children with jokes and stories.

They were a middle-class family with a comfortable home. Diana could walk wherever she wanted—her father's gas station, the Paramount and Capital movie theaters, all the schools she would attend in Ashland, and the big green Central Park. Mother was always there after school with cookies and milk and to talk about her day. Diana appeared to be smart and very pretty as well as physically active in her two favorite sports, softball and swimming. Off the playing field, Diana took piano lessons from Elizabeth Johnson, who later would be surprised when Diana emerged as a country-music star, because Mrs. Johnson was sure she would become an actress. Russell Powell, editor of the *Ashland Daily Independent* and Noah Adams, of National Public Radio, were childhood friends. They remember her as outgoing, with a quirky sense of humor, and good at playing different roles.

Another important legacy Diana inherited from her mother was the love of books and reading that prompted Polly to take out library cards just as soon as her children were old enough to read. Polly harped on reading as a means by which to develop a strong mind; she even insisted that the kids read the printing on cereal boxes at the breakfast table. She also managed to get her penny-pinching husband to buy the family a set of encyclopedias. Polly understood the importance of knowledge, and if she wasn't able to be a strong role model in other ways, she was at least able to instill in her children the importance of an education. One of Polly's mantras was: "Reading is to the mind what exercise is to the body."

Glenn Brian was born two years after Diana, in 1948, and they were not just brother and sister, they became best friends. He had flaming red hair and freckles and was always made fun of at school because of his resemblance to Opie Taylor (Ron Howard) from *The Andy Griffith Show*. Diana and Glenn Brian did everything together. When they were old enough, one of their favorite activities was visiting the downtown movie house, the Capital Theater. Diana remembers the time they went to see *Fiend Without a Face*. It became one of those frightening childhood memories that would linger forever in their minds. The black and white film had a typical B-formula plot about aliens with disembodied brains attached to long stems that could enter one's skull. Diana and Glenn Brian held hands and shrieked every time one of the brain monsters appeared on screen.

When the movie ended, Diana and Glenn Brian had to return home in the dark. They had to pass through the park, where a brain monster lurked behind every rock and tree, ready to pierce their skulls and possess them! They walked hand in hand through Ashland's Central Park, comforting each other, but the long shadows and strange night sounds were too much for Glenn Brian, and he began to cry. Diana watched helplessly as her little brother sobbed. She was able to coax him along until they finally made it safely home, never to speak of the incident again.

Glenn Brian was the most sensitive of the Judd children, and he showed it by being moved by tragedies that either he heard about or saw on TV. The next sibling was Christopher Mark, born when Diana was four. When he was old enough, he shared a room with Glenn Brian, and soon the two became inseparable. The last child Polly and Glen had was Margaret Victoria, who arrived two years after Christopher Mark, which seems consistent with what apparently was Polly and Glen's pattern of having a child every two years until they reached the number and gender mix they wanted—two boys and two girls, each two years apart. Diana and Margaret enjoyed a healthy competitiveness and tried whenever they could to get the better of the other in a sisterly way.

As Diana grew into her mid-teens, she was very popular with boys and had lots of friends. Some called her "China Doll" because she had such a clear and delicate skin, often the envy of girls in her class. The sisterly rivalry became more intense when Diana began to date boys, for it gave Margaret Victoria a chance to create mischief. One of her favorite tricks was to greet Diana's dates at the door when they came to pick her up. Then she would delight in giving the poor boy graphic details of Diana padding around upstairs in robe and curlers while putting on her makeup to impress her date. She would tell the nervous young man that Diana had been in the bathroom all afternoon fiddling with her hair, lips, eyes, skin, and other parts of her anatomy.

Of course, none of this behavior is so unusual in normal families. Nor was it unusual that Dad was away working much of the time to pay the bills and Mom was home to see that everyone was properly fed, clothes were washed, and rooms were cleaned—all in all, in outward appearances a fairly typical family of the fifties and sixties in small-town America. However, there existed suppressed feelings, postponed dreams, unspoken fears, and emotional instability simmering below the surface that would not be revealed unless there was a breach in the veneer that insulated each one from the real world. For some the breach would come further down the road.

The journey of the three Judd women began in this small town on the Ohio River in one of the first states west of the Appalachians. The Judd family settled, grew up, and raised families in a mountain wilderness of rivers and hardwood forests.

When the Civil War came, the state was divided but stayed in the Union, its families split and its sons fighting on both sides. In fact, both the president of the Union, Abraham Lincoln, and the president of the Confederacy, Jefferson Davis, were born in Kentucky. Just to the east of Kentucky, in the state of Virginia, the people were so divided over the question of slavery that the state split politically into two states, with Virginia joining the South and the newly formed state of West Virginia remaining with the North.

Just at the point where the West Virginia, Kentucky, and Ohio boundaries touch the Ohio River, early settlers decided to start a town because of the nearby iron and coal deposits. That town, Ashland, founded in the early 1800s, would become Naomi and Wynonna's birthplace. There the Judd clan would settle and propagate, as had European immigrants for almost two hundred years.

In spite of the settlements, the territory contains enormous expanses that are unchanged from the days when the Indians inhabited the land before the arrival of the white man. The region boasts an aggressive national-park-preservation system that has protected the trees and streams, black bears, wild boar, red and gray foxes, raccoons, skunks, chipmunks, and an enormous population of birds, from warblers, hawks, and grouse to golden eagles and wild turkeys. This is the forest Naomi loved so much and would wander through as a child by herself, making friends with trees, birds, and animals.

Across the Ohio River from Ashland, near Coal Grove, the area's first charcoal furnace was started, in 1826, and began turning out some of the strongest, purest pig iron. Ashland is situated on one of the largest working rivers of America, the Ohio, a twenty-mile stretch of coal manufacturers and metalworks, and petroleum operations from which the Ashland Oil Company gets its name. This is the company whose petroleum products Glen Judd would sell in his gas station. This was the early world of Naomi and her two daughters.

2

Diana's Childhood

WITH ITS BEAUTY, MYSTERY, AND GRACE, Kentucky has inspired many poets, painters, and musicians. It has also broken many spirits. From the day that Daniel Boone first breached the Cumberland Gap, life in Kentucky could be harsh, impassioned, and ruthless. Diana and her brothers and sister learned this firsthand as she was entering her teenage years when her mother fell ill with a serious kidney disease and nearly died. Polly was rushed to a clinic, where she would remain under the watchful eye of doctors while the children were farmed out to relatives and friends.

Diana was sent to the farm at South Shore with her grandma and grandpa. It was a bleak time, the middle of winter, with no school, no friends, and no brothers and sister—a frightening and lonely period for Diana. Conditions were primitive to young Diana, who had to use the outhouse and do without television because her grandfather was opposed to it. The farmhouse was so cold and drafty that soon Diana became sick, too. It was here, on this lonely farm in Kentucky, that Diana realized that the love of her mother and family could not protect her from the world, that anything could happen to any of them at any time. Eventually, that harsh winter passed, and her mother recovered, but the world would never look the same to Diana.

The scenes that had played out in front of her day in and day out suddenly took on a different form. When Diana started to attend movies with friends, she became aware that her parents were not all that happy together. That troubling revelation partially resulted from her spending time with friends in their homes, where she saw their parents kissing and smiling and touching one another casually—an open display of easy, caring communication that was wholly absent in Diane's parents. At around this time, Diana became aware that her mother had little use for pretty dresses and high-heeled shoes. She needed comfortable clothes and a big car for the kids. Besides, her husband never took her out, so what would be the point of wasting good money? Down deep Diana understood, but as a teenager you want your mom to be queen of the ball.

Church became a constant in the Judd household; it provided spiritual guidance and a balm for the soul. Polly Judd would prepare the family Sunday dinner, then go to the First Baptist Church and supervise the nursery during services. It was something Polly knew how to do well and she found it fulfilling to give something to her community and to put her natural talents to work in the service of others. Polly Judd tried to live by the rule of Proverbs 22:6: "Train up a child in the way he should go: and when he is old, he will not depart from it." She was a deeply religious, introspective woman. Her family saw her lose control only once in her life, although she may have, before they were born, on that fateful day when her own father finished eating at the family dining-room table, got up and walked into the next room, and put a bullet in his brain. Polly was nine.

As she learned of her mother's childhood and the experience of being abandoned by an uncaring mother, Diana realized that Polly needed love and reassurance and care by her own children. She understood the panic and heartbreak of being an abandoned and neglected child and didn't want to see the same hurt in the eyes of other children, particularly her own. Diana, having learned compassion from her mother, would try to bring that expression of love to the next generation.

Polly Judd's compassion was limited to her own children and to those in the church, but she also offered it as a result of the more difficult circumstances of her alcoholic brother, Norman, who deserted his family. Polly helped his wife, Roberta, and their three small children by feeding them or handing out toys on birthdays or holidays. In addition to her irresponsible brother, Polly's sister, Martha, wanted to give away her illegitimate son. She took her sister's son, Eddy, into the Judd home and treated him as her own. Looking back on her childhood, Diana says, "I've come to the conclusion that mothers give us our consciences."

Diana's years at Crabbe Grade School in Ashland were fairly typical. Diana took a fancy to tap-dancing, so her mother, who had had a secret desire to be a dancer herself, shipped her off to tap-dancing school. Mrs. Nancy D. Holmes, her teacher, prepared the students for their first recital at the Paramount Theater. Diana was already getting a taste of something she loved, show business. In the fourth grade, at the age of ten, she played the lead in *Pilgrim's Progress*, which her favorite teacher, Mrs. Mildred Rigsby, directed. Diana was beginning to feel the exhilaration of a live performance and loved it. Perhaps she loved it all the more because Mrs. Rigsby would tell her over and over again that she could do anything she wanted.

Down in the basement, out of public view, Crabbe Grade School conducted a program for mentally challenged children. Every so often Diana would run into one particular girl in that group who, when she saw Diana, would stop and stare. Somehow Diana felt a bond with the girl. When she told her mother about her, she added that she also had a strange name: Naomi. Polly told her that the story of Naomi, from the Old Testament Bible, was one of devotion and loyalty and that Naomi was the widowed mother-in-law of Ruth.

As Diana entered her teenage years, she became painfully aware of her appearance. She saved up her baby-sitting money and struck a deal with her father, who agreed to pay half the cost of the clothes she bought. Like many teenagers, clothes and appearance became so important to Diana that she sometimes lost her good sense, thinking she could get her way by being difficult with her parents.

One night, she had carefully styled her hair and was all dressed up but unhappy about a new party dress that she wanted and couldn't have. She decided to argue about it with her mother just before her date arrived and burst into the kitchen complaining about her lack of clothes. Polly said nothing; she simply dumped a big jar of pickles on Diana's head, which had a very sobering effect on future complaints.

Still, not surprisingly, as Diana matured into her teenage phase, communication between her and her parents grew worse. Neither seemed able to get through to the other, although both had many questions that were troubling them. Diana, in particular, felt she couldn't connect with her parents or, for that matter, even with some of her contemporaries. She had thoughts she could not share, and her heart was filled with unexpressed emotions.

While Diana attended Coles Junior High, something happened that jolted her and the whole town of Ashland. Two boys were convicted of murdering a young couple who had parked in a lovers' lane. The two boys admitted that they killed the couple "just for kicks." What sent a chill through Diana was that the two boys had regularly sat next to her in study hall and had often talked dirty to her. She ignored them but after the murders realized that she could just as easily have been their victim as the hapless couple.

As time passed, Diana matured, at least to the point that she and her girlfriends were talking about boys and love and matters that were important to them. Diana had a large group of friends but always felt a bit on the outside because she seemed to view life a little differently, perhaps a little more maturely, or so she thought. She noticed that some things, such as relationships with boys, seemed more urgent and immediate to her girlfriends than they did to her. It was 1960, and while Diana had good friends, she would also spend time by herself, gathering walnuts from the backyard, reading Nancy Drew books, or learning a new song on the piano. It was a confusing time for the fourteen-year-old Diana. She was on the verge of womanhood, and strange new feelings and yearnings were beginning to take over.

Linda Ann McDonald, who lived across the street from Diana, introduced Michael Ciminella to Diana; that meeting would become a very important event in Diana's life. Michael was best friends with Linda's boyfriend, and both boys went to Fort Union Military Academy in Virginia. Linda had a reputation for dating only "country club" boys and felt no reason to hold back her stash of rich, eligible young fellows from her good pal Diana. Besides, Linda was pushing Michael on Diana. He was sixteen years old but was already driving around in a brand-new Chrysler Imperial. He was also high-diving champion at the Bellefonte Country Club and came from a well-to-do family. Although Diana wasn't impressed with all the fancy accoutrements, she agreed to go on a blind date with him.

Diana's parents were very strict about whom their daughter dated, but after the requisite interrogation, Michael was given their stamp of approval, and the two began seeing each other. To Diana, Michael was a dream come true; he had money, he was articulate, handsome, charming, drove a great car, and came from a stable family. In some ways their meeting was a replay of Polly and Glen's. Michael would take Diana to the Bellefonte Country Club, where the well-to-do gathered. It was Prince Charming taking Cinderella to the ball. Except there were no ugly stepsisters waiting at home, only Mom, who enjoyed hearing all about her daughter's adventures.

Diana was smitten, not only with Michael but with his lifestyle. She subscribed to *Seventeen* and *American Girl* and paid close attention to the latest fashions. Every penny Diana could get went on cosmetics and clothes. She sensed that she was poised to become a woman, and men—spell that M-i-c-h-a-e-l—had suddenly become the most important thing in her life. Michael's parents, however, were not all that enamored of Diana; her social standing was not as elite as they wanted for their son. Michael senior was the owner of Ashland Aluminum Products and considerably more wealthy than the Judds.

Although they dated throughout the school year, Diana was never sure that she was falling in love with Michael. She was only fourteen (of course Polly married Glen when she was fifteen) and there were some striking differences between them. Michael was an only child who couldn't wait to get away from his family and go back to school. His mother, Bernadine Ciminella, spent her days playing golf at the country club or getting her hair styled at the beauty parlor, and the Ciminellas had a maid who kept their house spotless.

One odd thing struck Diana: The Ciminella house was quiet, like a museum or library, which contrasted with the Judd household, always filled with people running in and out. Polly was the one who cleaned the house and made the meals and the only family member who could sit back at the end of the day and feel she had accomplished something meaningful for her family. Polly Judd took pride in her work and would never allow a stranger to take care of her family.

Besides the disparate backgrounds, Michael was also a loner who didn't have many friends. This bothered Diana, who had many pals, like Carolyn Murphy, Mary Martha, Pat Bailey, and Diane Sinnette. Michael and Diana stopped seeing each other for a time when he graduated from the military academy (Diana was a junior) and went off to Georgia Tech as a science major in 1962. That school affiliation only lasted a year. Michael transferred to nearby Transylvania College, a prestigious private academy in Lexington, Kentucky. During the summer break, Michael returned home, and he and Diana resumed dating frequently. He told her of his altered plans to get a degree in business management and pursue a career like that of his father.

Diana had been dating a number of boys while Michael was away at school. Her other boyfriends didn't have Michael's money or nice shiny car, but they knew how to carry on a conversation and have a good time. During high school Diana felt things changing. She kept thinking about her approaching womanhood and adult responsibilities and opportunities, and the prospects both excited her and made her apprehensive. She began thinking about what she was going to do with her life and was determined it should be something of value, something that would make her family proud of her. Obviously, she assumed she would marry and have children, but she wanted to accomplish more. However, she was not sure what that would be. She was at a time and place we have all found ourselves, when the old adage that life is what happens to us while we're making other plans is borne out.

The summer of 1963 brought two devastating events that illustrate that adage. They would change the direction of Diana's life as she could never have imagined. The first happened when her brother, Brian, noticed a lump on his shoulder. When Brian was examined, the family physician, Wayne Franz, thought that it might be leukemia. He suggested that the Judds take Brian to a leading hematologist who practiced at Ohio State.

It was while Diana's parents were away on this trip that the second event would take place. Some of Diana's girlfriends at school were experimenting with sex, and while Diana had not ventured into that area, she, too, was curious. Diana suddenly found herself alone in the house for the first time in her life, and it was easy to invite Michael over to keep her company. Naturally, one thing led to another, and they ended up having sex that night. Every young girl dreams of the time she gives her virginity to that someone special in a quiet, romantic evening filled with candles and soft words of love. However, more times than not, a young girl's innocence is lost on someone unworthy or played out in an atmosphere that is less than romantic.

Diana recalls her first time: "It wasn't what I'd expected and dreamed about; there was no tenderness, mystery, or romance. When I awakened the next morning to begin that first day of high school, I felt ashamed, guilty, and cheated. I could barely smile or be myself." Things were not going to improve in the immediate future.

Polly and Glen returned home with bad news: Brian had Hodgkin's disease, a form of cancer. The family was devastated, and everyone focused their prayers and attention on Brian, except for Diana, who had her own private hell to endure. She suspected that she was pregnant. As she says in her autobiography, *Love Can Build a Bridge*. "I was petrified, not just for myself but for my entire family, who were about to be put to a terrible test. A nightmare of doctors and disease was about to hit the Judds in gale-force proportions, and I had no business adding to their woes. I imagined Mom and Dad could see through me and knew what a stupid, cheap thing I'd done."

While the family was away at the hospital so that Brian could have his chemotherapy treatments, Diana told her doctor about her problem. He confirmed her worst fears. There was a new life growing inside her, and it would change her world completely. Abortion was out of the question, but she gave suicide a long, hard consideration. Diana didn't really want to kill herself. She just wanted to take back what had already happened, and she didn't want to burden her already stressed out family with another tragedy. The more Diana thought about the life inside of her, the more she drew comfort from it, as mothers have from the beginning of time.

Michael was raised in the same fashion as Diana, and an abortion was unacceptable to him. As soon as she told him who the father was, Michael insisted they get married. In fact, Michael wrote her a letter saying that he loved her and truly wanted to get married and raise their child together. Diana slipped it under her pillow and decided to think about it, only to have her mother find the letter and confront her. Polly couldn't believe that Diana would do such a thing and add to the burdens of the family. Looking back, Diana vividly remembers her state of mind. She was seventeen years old, hadn't graduated from high school, in another room her brother was vomiting from his chemotherapy treatments, and she was pregnant out of wedlock. She was still a teenager living at home, getting a $1.50-a-week allowance, and her life suddenly wasn't a Nancy Drew novel anymore.

Of course, the worst part for Diana was facing her father. She was his pristine, virgin daughter who would someday make him proud by marrying the right man after she had graduated from school and was all grown up. Diana could see the dagger she had thrust through her father's heart when she told him. She had taken away his last dream, and they were both heartsick. Then she made it worse—if that was possible—by telling him the truth. He quietly stood in her room and asked if she loved Michael. When she said no, the silence that followed seemed unbearable, and she quickly retracted her answer and changed it to yes.

She looked at her father as if for the first time. He looked smaller than she remembered, as if he had shrunk inside the clothes that hung loosely from his body. He didn't yell or scream or hit her. He quietly hugged Diana and then went into his own bedroom. Diana knew that her childhood was over.

3

A Brother's Death, A Daughter's Birth

AS BRIAN'S ILLNESS PROGRESSED, he was transformed into another, sadder person. He lost his hair, grew thin, and became very pale. It was heartbreaking for the family when they would catch a stranger gawking at Brian or whispering about his condition. Thirteen-year-old Mark, in particular, was having a terrible time coping with his brother's illness; they shared a room, and Brian was the first and last person Mark saw every day. He didn't understand what was going on, and everybody else was so consumed with grief that they didn't take the time to explain anything to him. Theirs was the typical pioneer posturing: Look tough and you'll be tough. Unfortunately for a young boy like Mark, that attitude neither worked nor helped him deal with what was happening around him.

For many people death is one of those subjects that no one wants to approach. Adults don't want to be reminded of their own mortality and are afraid of it, while children can't comprehend it. Diana, halfway between both states of mind and conscious of her own changing condition, might not have understood the entire scope of Brian's ordeal, but she did understand the most important

thing: He needed her, and she was there for him. It was a difficult
time for all of the Judds, and even Brian was becoming more and
more impatient not only with his condition but also with the
therapy and its side effects. "I don't want to go to the hospital
anymore," he confided in Diana. "I just want to be at home. Why
can't I lie on the couch in the living room?" Diana didn't know the
answer and just tried to comfort him as best she could, which often
involved just being with him and letting him talk. Brian wanted to
settle things and say goodbye, and Diana was patient and loving
enough to help him do so.

As the Judds awaited the death of one life, they also anticipated
the birth of another, for Diana's pregnancy began to show. No one
ever mentioned that Diana was pregnant, and it was assumed that
she and Michael would get married soon in spite of the fact that no
one in the family really cared for Michael anymore. Sadly, that
included Diana; nevertheless, a marriage would take place. That's
how such problems were handled in Ashland, Kentucky, in the
early 1960s.

Diana fared no better in school than at home. She was put
through the torture of mindless teenage ridicule and cruelty. In that
era, getting pregnant without a husband while still in school was
considered the number-one scandal, except for murder, as
happened with the two boys who had once sat next to Diana. Of
course, Diana hated being the object of such teasing and cruelty
and just wanted to be accepted for what she was.

Not that the funereal atmosphere at home was pleasant either.
The Judd household went through a traumatic change. What had
been a home filled with life was now as silent as a tomb. Diana's
social life crashed as she got invited to fewer and fewer parties.
Who wants some pregnant girl around as a reminder that it might
happen to any of them? Just thinking about how some fun isn't all
that free of concern destroys having a carefree time. Diana's world
was growing smaller, and she and Michael knew that the time had
come to do what they had to do according to the mores of the time,
place, and people.

There are two stories about the marriage. One suggests that the
young couple did not want to flaunt their shame before more

people than necessary and in some ways were both embarrassed by what they had done to their families. They decided to pretend that they were going to a movie but instead drove to nearby Jericho, Tennessee. They figured that if they got married in Tennessee they wouldn't need a guardian older than eighteen to sign for them and they could return home having relieved their families of the embarrassment of enduring a classic Kentucky shotgun wedding. As they were in the middle of taking their blood tests, however, they learned that Kentucky law regarding underage marriages applied in Tennessee, and they couldn't legally get married in Tennessee, either. They had to go through the double embarrassment of postponing the wedding and driving back home to discuss the wedding with their parents, which is exactly what everyone had tried to avoid doing.

A few days later, Diana and Michael tried again, except this time their parents accompanied them. They all piled in the car and drove to Pearisburg, Virginia, to a small Baptist church in what was a tense, silent journey, with everyone left to his or her own devices and no one wanting to be in that car that day. Diana wore her mother's royal-blue wool suit, for she could no longer fit into her own dresses. A corsage that her father bought was pinned to her dress. The six of them stood in front of the preacher as the parents witnessed their children repeat the vows of eternal fidelity and love.

Diana recalls the scene as bizarre and gloomy, with the half dozen of them numbly going through the motions of the ceremony in a mockery of what she had once dreamed her wedding would be like. We know what was really swirling around in Diana's head because she has told the world later, and we can imagine what Michael and the two sets of parents were experiencing. Diana said she was thinking, I can't believe I have to say what I'm saying! This is preposterous! Am I the only one here who sees this is insane?

The ceremony was followed a quiet wedding dinner and an announcement in the *Ashland Daily Independent* in a pathetic attempt to keep up appearances. It was what had to be done by way of penance and setting things right, all in conformity with Appalachian tradition. Everybody wore a smile on the outside and cried in despair on the inside, still hoping that it would all work out somehow, someday.

According to the other story of the wedding, Diana and Michael eloped on January 3, 1964, by driving over the mountains to the east to the tiny town (twenty-one hundred residents) of Pearisburg, Virginia (spelled incorrectly as Parisville in Naomi's autobiography), and the office of the circuit-court clerk, O. G. Caldwell, where an assistant county clerk did the paperwork and issued them a license. The clerk told them they could be married right there in the courthouse by a judge, but Diana wanted a preacher. According to this version, the two of them drove around the little town and finally located the Reverend D. N. McGrady, a Baptist minister on Church Avenue, who married them.

Then, in a gloomy frame of mind, the two drove back to Ashland as husband and wife. A few days later, Michael went back to school in Lexington, leaving behind a seventeen-year-old wife and some unhappy parents. The Judds were unhappy because of the shame, and the Ciminellas didn't regard them as married, since the ceremony was not performed by a Catholic priest and Diana, a non-Catholic, hadn't signed the traditional agreement to raise the children in the church. Chances are, even at that young age, she wouldn't have signed it, anyway, since she had a low opinion of Catholics.

The wedding legally changed the young couple's status, and Diana was now Michael's wife and was required to live with him. At the beginning of 1964, when he returned from school, Diana moved into his parents' home at 1515 Morningside Drive. Actually, it was in the attic of the Ciminella home. They slept together in a space whose sloping ceilings kept anyone from standing upright anywhere but in the middle of the room. Nor was there very much light or air in the attic, and in the summer the space became a suffocating hotbox that was the antithesis of the beautiful, open woods near her grandparents' house that Diana so loved.

The months that followed were strange in many ways. Diana was completing her senior year of high school by studying with Ada Brown, a tutor; she couldn't bear the shame of showing up at Paul G. Blazer High School in the early sixties with a distended belly. She would have been an embarrassment to her family and all her friends and acquaintances. At the same time, Ms. Brown also tutored Brian Glenn at home and served as a messenger between him and Diana. Diana recalled: "It was if we were both hostages and this was the only way we could communicate."

This didn't mean that Diana couldn't visit what had been her home all these years; it was just that she was now required to make her home with her husband. The house in which she grew up was now a place that belonged to her past. However, she didn't quite grasp the significance. She did feel estranged when she went back there. She would quietly slip upstairs and into her room, close the door, and long for the feeling of safety, now lost, that she once had. After a few minutes, she was thrust back into her present reality and had to return to the cell-like quarters she shared with Michael, his trophies from diving, and pictures of him at military school.

When Diana reached her seventh month of pregnancy, a small shower was held for her. It was a somber and mundane affair, unlike the fun parties she had previously attended at which the young women, filled with expectation and excitement, reveled in the good times to come, suggested by gifts of lacy panties, décolletage bras, sexy lingerie, and perfume. At Diana's shower she was given housewares—an iron, some dishes, and other practical domestic items. Instead of anticipation, the tone at her shower was one of resignation and depression. It was as if the door were coming down on her future, but deep down, that wasn't Diana, and she would ultimately refuse to accept such a fate. She would do what was expected of her for now, but time would change her circumstances. Diana ultimately was going to have that life she dreamed of no matter what. Tomorrow would be a different story.

Michael's mother, Billie (short for Bernadine), dutifully initiated Diana into the role of housewife, teaching her the domestic chores of washing dishes, ironing shirts, dusting, vacuuming and cooking. Diana was grateful for the guidance and instruction, but she still felt as if she were living somebody else's life. Her pregnancy was normal, and she gained exactly twenty-three pounds. She approached the coming birth with no fear and three prayers. She prayed to God to spare Brian, to forgive her, and to make her baby healthy.

Because everything seemed to be moving along well, Diana assumed that the birth would be simple and relatively uncomplicated until Dr. Williamson surprised her with the news that she would have to undergo a cesarean section and that she had CPD, or cephalopelvic disproportionment. That is, the baby's head was too large to get through the birth canal; they would have to cut her open to take the baby. But that's not the way the information was conveyed to Diana. As a result, she thought she had some horrible disease, like syphilis, and that her life and that of her baby might be in danger.

She sought out her mother but received little sympathy, for Polly knew it wasn't that big a deal when her frightened daughter told her in she was going to have a C-section. Polly Judd had to cope with a dying son and wasn't moved by her daughter's getting in a snit about having the procedure. Unfortunately, poor Diana was terrified. All she was seeking was a comforting embrace and some knowledge about what was to happen to her and her baby. She remembers thinking that she was frightened about going to the hospital for an operation she didn't understand and had never had before. She thought about her mother and said to herself, I'm afraid that I might die and something will go wrong with the baby, and I want you to take me in your arms and say you'll stop all this madness.

That didn't happen. On May 30, 1964, eighteen-year-old Diana Ellen Judd gave birth to a healthy, happy baby girl whom she would name Christina Claire Ciminella. Suddenly, Diana's life opened up again as she stared into her daughter's eyes. She saw a new hope and a new life, and for the first time in months, Diana was truly happy. With the arrival of the baby, life improved, because people will do things to make babies happy and comfortable that they won't do for grown-ups. The Ciminellas had turned a small room near the kitchen into a nursery complete with bassinet and rocking chair as well as some other items whose purpose Diana didn't understand, such as giant cans of disinfectant, surgical face masks, gloves, and the like.

It soon dawned on Diana that her mother-in-law—who loved Christina Claire as much or more than anyone—was a clean-freak determined that no bug or draft or speck of dirt would threaten her granddaughter! When Christina started to crawl, Billie would use thermometers to ascertain whether the floor was warm enough.

Diana and Michael tried to be patient with Billie's housecleaning habits, but things were getting a little tense when, fortunately, Michael had to return to school. So fall came, and Michael, Diana, and Christina Claire moved into their own apartment in Lexington, Kentucky. It was not much different from student apartments near school campuses the country over: cramped, with thin walls, no washing machines, and weirdos living on either side of them. Their finances were tight, and Diana was constantly cutting coupons and looking for creative ways to spend less. Almost every weekend the Ciminellas would visit, often bringing steaks or hamburgers, a common practice among families with children away at school.

Diana, at eighteen, was beginning her grown-up life. Just a year before, she was filled with dreams of a life of excitement and exploration; a year later, she hadn't had a single adventure. Would she ever get the chance to be what she had hoped and dreamed she could be, or would she forever be consigned to living in a small town in a tiny apartment with a child that needed constant attention and a husband she didn't love? Things looked bad, but Diana hadn't even begun to fight the battle that would last for the next twenty years. She knew she needed to go to college, but when she told Michael, he reminded her that she was his wife and that her role was to nurse their baby, keep their clothes clean, and have dinner ready on time.

Michael didn't understand Diana then or in the years that followed. She ignored him and enrolled at the University of Kentucky after she and Kay, a lady across the hall, worked out a trade-off of baby-sitting chores. Unfortunately, after one semester, the full school load proved to be too much for Diana, and she quit. She could not continue with school then, but life in the small apartment was suffocating, and there always seemed to be a dull, cold chill in the air when she and Michael were together. Diana felt as if she couldn't carry on a normal conversation with her husband.

Diana understood that while they were marginally civil to one another, neither one was happy. Each felt duty-bound to endure their predicament for the sake of appearances and the child, but even those two reasons were beginning to fade in importance. Diana understood men well enough to know that Michael felt tied down, saddled with a wife and baby at a time when he wanted to be out chasing leggy cheerleaders and enjoying college beer parties and poker games. Diana was also frustrated in her way. She was caring for both a man and a baby—one who didn't want her and whom she didn't want and the other, who was becoming more important to her every day.

Back in Ashland, fourteen-year-old Brian's condition worsened as tumors painfully invaded every region of his deteriorating body. As always, the emotional pain permeated the lives of Glen and Polly Judd, who were willing to grasp any wisp of hope they could find that might save their son. When they got wind of a new drug being used at Bowman Gray Medical Center in Winston-Salem, North Carolina, they immediately took Brian there to see if it would help. Diana came home immediately, and she, with the rest of the family, was there to watch the ambulance take Brian away. The whole clan followed in their cars and drove to the medical center to check Brian in and be there to comfort him.

Everyone had left Brian's room for a time except Diana, who shared a quiet moment with him reminiscing about their childhood. It wasn't that long ago, was it, Brian? Diana thought. Childhood? She was barely out of hers, and now she had a child. It was a teary moment of remembrance, and suddenly Brian's eyes turned dark and serious as he almost pleaded with her to get him out of this sterile place and take him to Aunt Pauline's farm, where the sun danced through the trees, the leaves sounded crisp underfoot, and the smells were clean and tantalizing. That's where life was real and true, not here amid sterile walls and starched professionals scurrying in and out and a institutional chime on the intercom punctuating the somber, incomprehensible messages intoned by disconnected voices from an unknown place.

Diana recalled that Brian's voice was like a stake to her heart. His pleas were pathetic, and Diana was helpless to do anything for him. "He wasn't just asking me to get him out of this hospital; he wanted out of the illness, out of the painful procession of the days that had sapped his soul." All she could do was avert her face from his and cry in despair. On November 6, 1965, shortly after his family returned home to Ashland, Brian Glenn passed away. He had just turned seventeen. He was buried in Rose Hill Cemetery, and the funeral procession stretched for miles.

Diana, Michael, and Christina returned to Lexington to play out their own dreary soap opera of lost dreams and desperate hopes. Diana remembers sitting in bed reading her sixteen-month-old daughter rhymes when she broke down and started to cry. Mommies aren't supposed to cry. Christina stared at her mother in alarm and asked what was wrong. Diana looked sadly at her daughter and gave her an answer that she surely didn't understand and perhaps even Diana didn't fully comprehend, "Oh, honey, everything's broken now. All the king's horses and all the king's men could never put us back together again."

4

A Housewife in Hollywood

WITH THE DEATH OF BRIAN, Diana had lost someone very precious to
her. God did something else for the young mother from Ashland:
Christina, such a demonstrative and vivacious little girl with an
energy of her own, now added a new dimension and meaning to
Diana's life.

Time began to pass more quickly in those lean years. Christina
was soon dancing and singing and even performing with a toy
microphone. For a treat, Diana and Christina would go to the only
place they could afford, the local hot-dog diner. They would also
return to Ashland to visit the Judd home. Mark and Margaret were
pleased to see Diana and their niece, Christina, but it was different
with Polly and Glen. They were each still trying to recover from
their son's death in their different, uncommunicative ways, and
Diana knew that her parent's marriage was now filled with sorrow
and apathy. Ironically, Diana saw obvious similarities to her own
marriage with Michael.

When Michael graduated from college and immediately landed a
salesman's job in Broadview, Illinois, the little family packed up its
scant possessions and moved on not only to another small
apartment but to a world different from the one Diana knew, loved,

and grew up in. Now they were in the urban North, with its different perspectives, and away from the soothing and regenerating woodlands of her Kentucky youth. Diana was not only a mother with a growing child and a husband she didn't like; she was removed from roots and support systems provided by familiar places and people, friends and family. Moreover, there was the stunning discovery that no sooner had they settled down in their new apartment in this new town, Diana was pregnant again. Then Michael got a job transfer to California, working in aerospace-industry marketing.

In September 1967, Michael, Christina, and a pregnant Diana set off on another adventure. This time they were able to rent a three-bedroom house in Sylmar, in the San Fernando Valley. Sylmar was a low-rent, ethnically mixed area with many Latinos. They seemed strange to Michael and Diana, who thought that all people of color were black. Still, it was a place they could afford, and it wasn't as confining as their previous two apartments. Seven months later, Diana was admitted to the Holy Cross Hospital in Granada Hills and gave birth to another baby girl. Ashley Tyler Judd was born on April 19, 1968. Christina was now almost four and immediately fell in love with her baby sister.

For Diana, life in the Valley, as all the residents called it, consisted of changing diapers, playing with Christina, cleaning the house, and having no adult human contact. Every now and then Michael would invite home someone from work, but Diana found all of them interminably boring.

Probably the most horrible aspect of this experience was the fear that her present condition was a preview of the rest of her life: babies, cleaning house, and listening to vapid conversations. She knew she would survive, but she understood that someday soon she would have to escape such an existence.

Then Michael, who was also feeling trapped and wasn't happy with their domestic situation, adopted a lifestyle that made it much easier for Diana to leave him. He started to hang out with a single salesman who liked to party. The two of them would spend many nights out "working," or so they said, but Diana suspected that Michael was engaging in activites that weren't good for the marriage, and she wasn't sure she cared. It gave her the excuse she needed to reclaim a life for herself and her two children.

It was during that time that Michael began experimenting with marijuana and brought some home one night for Diana to try. She flipped out at the suggestion and began yelling at him about being a responsible father, but Michael persisted, suggesting that it wasn't addictive and that it was simply a good way to relax. After all, this was the late sixties, and everyone was doing it. It was expected. Finally, one night, with the children in bed, Michael convinced Diana to try it.

The marijuana provided temporary relief, but in the end Diana knew she would find no solutions at the end of a joint. She therefore began to explore Los Angeles and see what it had to offer. She investigated astrology and attended several meetings of the Theosophical Society. Diana's eyes were opening to a whole new world. The new people she was meeting were strikingly different from those she met growing up in Ashland or even those who lived in her Sylmar neighborhood. "I began making friends," she says. "The conversations I had with these freethinking people nudged open the doors in my narrow life."

Diana soon became involved in politics and was canvassing door-to-door for Eugene McCarthy and marching in peace rallies. Ironically, she also found herself working to support GIs fighting in Vietnam, not in support of the war but because they were Americans and she was appalled by the way American citizens treated returning vets.

In July 1969 the first man set foot on the moon, and Diana's neighbors, Jerry and Sue Heller, came over to watch the landing with Diana on TV. Jerry had a Ph.D. from MIT, and as they watched this momentous event, a lively discussion took place about the historic moon landing. Suddenly, Diana realized that this well-educated man was listening to her, taking her words seriously.

Diana covered her Dodge car with huge peace-flower decals and headed out to see what Hollywood had to offer. The Dodge, which Diana christened "the Getaway Car," led her into West Hollywood, where she found a nice home at 1124 North Larrabee, near the Sunset Strip. The house was one of those fixer-uppers, and

Diana loved it. She had found it herself and made the decision to live there, with or without Michael. A deal was struck with the landlord, and Diana signed a lease for $350 a month.

Diana immediately went to work painting the rooms bright, happy colors. She draped all the lampshades with a delicate fringe and put plants everywhere. Finally, the day came when the family moved in. However, things weren't quite right. She realized that Michael didn't belong in her life anymore, and she finally told him she wanted out of the marriage.

That was the beginning of the end. Soon the arguments began. Michael started sleeping on the couch, and they would pass each other in a hallway or the bathroom without one kind word. The truth was that Diana didn't love Michael. Knowing now that they were never going to be a loving couple, Michael grew resentful. Diana realized that divorce was the only solution, and now her Appalachian toughness would help her through this trying time.

What it came down to was that Diana loved being a mother and hated being a wife, and yet her Baptist background and Michael's Catholic upbringing made them both resist divorce until it was the only viable solution to their situation. Calling her marriage to Michael the darkest years of her life, Diana finally got an interim divorce decree a few weeks before Christmas, 1968. Michael wasn't even in the state at the time; his company had transferred him to another marketing assignment in Chicago. The divorce settlement called for Diana to receive 25 percent of Michael's salary in child support plus college tuition for the girls. The checks did not arrive, and Diana soon realized that she would receive no help from Michael.

When Diana informed the Ciminellas of the divorce, Michael attempted a last-ditch effort to save the marriage, but on September 19, 1971, Michael packed up his belongings and left. He and a friend took both family cars, leaving Diana and the children with nothing. It was a frightening moment because Diana was not sure how she and the girls would survive, but even so, she felt free at last. Diana, with her pioneering family spirit, would find the strength and the courage to forge ahead.

5

A Night of Terror

Now Diana understood the stark reality of her situation. With two kids and not much money, it was time to get a job. Looking through the want ads became a daily routine. She was a quick learner but had no experience. Who would hire her? Then she saw an ad for a receptionist at Mark Gordon Enterprises, just a couple of blocks away. The job offered the additional advantage of not needing to buy a car or spend money on a bus pass.

Diana put on her best interviewing clothes and walked down to Mark Gordon Enterprises, which was one of those vaguely defined show-business operations, convinced she could handle the one requirement: answering the phone. Diana was interviewed by Mark Gordon and even met his wife, Florence LaRue. Everything seemed to go smoothly and Mark promised to get back to Diana in a few days. True to his word, Mark called but told her that he had to hire a black woman. He said his entire staff was white, and some of his black business associates didn't like that.

She was about to panic when Mark offered her a secretarial job with his booking agent. If anybody but Diana and her daughters had been in the room when she hung up the phone, they might have thought she was a touch odd, for she burst into a spasm of happiness, singing "Aquarius" and dancing around the apartment with Christina and Ashley. She was overcome with the joy of having money to support the three of them without having to depend on anyone.

Diana made baby-sitting arrangements with Nancy, who lived across the street. Nancy had been a model and had children of her own. She was now a full-time housewife and didn't mind watching over Chris and Ashley so that Diana could settle into her new position. Whenever she had spare time, Diana would make a few extra dollars doing personal chores for Mark Gordon. He and his family were looking for a bigger house, so he introduced Diana to his real estate agent, and together they looked for a mansion for the Gordon family.

It was 1971, and her new life dazzled Diana. She was in the world of show business, and everybody was so thoughtful and nice to her. That she was a strikingly beautiful young woman didn't hurt, either. While house hunting, she toured one celebrity home after another, but she remembers most vividly inspecting Paul Newman and Joanne Woodward's home. It was on the market because the couple decided to move back to Connecticut, and as Diana casually walked through the mansion, she excused herself to stop in the master bathroom. She slipped in, closed the door and sat down, with the amazing thought: I'm sitting on Cool Hand Luke's throne!

This experience of having a real, grown-up life of her own continued, and she began noticing a change in her two daughters, Ashley, who was two-and-a-half, and Christina, who was six-and-a-half. They were attending West Hollywood Elementary School. Diana began to observe a striking difference in the personalities of her two daughters. It was as if they had sprung from different gene pools. Whereas Ashley was relaxed, thoughtful, and quiet, Christina was rambunctious, quick-tempered, and active. Ashley seemed to possess a peaceful, gregarious nature that allowed her to feel comfortable crawling on strangers' laps and smiling at everyone around her. She had a natural curiosity that led to reading; in fact, Ashley would later become a voracious reader and a serious student.

Even though she was holding down two jobs, as a secretary and model, Diana became a Brownie leader with Christina's troop. The troop members included Mariska Hargitay, daughter of Jayne Mansfield and Mickey Hargitay, and children from other famous families in entertainment and the arts. Christina became best friends with Angelique L'Amour, the daughter of the famous author of western novels Louis L'Amour.

One of the first assignments her new boss gave her was working with the singing group the Fifth Dimension. She had day-to-day contact with up-and-coming stars like Kim Carnes, Paul Williams, and Tony Orlando, but those exciting times were cut short when Diana's boss decided to replace her with his mistress.

Undaunted and now feeling secure about looking for and landing a job, Diana searched again and quickly found another, this time as a secretary working at a huge insurance company. However, there was one glitch. One day her boss called her into his office and suggested they have an affair while skiing down some romantic slopes he had in mind. Diana politely turned him down, worked a few more days, but decided she couldn't take the tension of being around the man and the boredom of being in the insurance business, so she quit.

Now she had to pound the streets again, but jobs come from all sorts of places, and one day while she was playing with Christina and Ashley in a West Hollywood park, near San Vicente Street, she met Ron Wood, a well-known photographer. He taught photography at the Art Center School of Design and offered her a job modeling for his class. The offer sounded good; it wasn't hard work, and she could make use of her good looks without having to sleep with somebody. She accepted immediately.

Posing for the students offered another perk that she hadn't anticipated but would help her out. The booking agent for the school took a liking to Diana and sent modeling jobs her way whenever she could, including a Christmas assignment, as a result of which the whole family got into the act, dressing up in warm flannel and modeling while the students sketched them. One thing led to another, and pretty soon Diana was getting more modeling gigs, including some extra work in a Doors video.

One day she responded to an ad in the paper claiming to need models for a bicycle ad. Since the ad appeared innocuous enough, Diana drove down to Marina del Ray (she had bought a car by this time because it is almost as important as a place to sleep in Los Angeles and sometimes doubles as such) to meet the photographers. She was hired on the spot but immediately sensed that something wasn't right because she and two other models were instructed to wait for the photographers on a large cabin cruiser. As soon as the motor started, Diana knew something was wrong. They were hired for a bicycle ad, so what were they doing on a boat?

Diana stood back and quickly asked herself, Okay, what's wrong with this picture? Here I am with two big guys and two other models in bikinis, no photographic equipment in sight, sailing out to sea, and nobody knows where I am. Diana demanded that they stop the boat and turn around. The other girls were too scared to say anything. When they finally docked, Diana immediately contacted the Better Business Bureau to report her experience and learned that the two men, small-time con artists, were wanted by the police.

Eventually, Diana found a friend in her next-door neighbor, a woman named Roxy Wallace, a singer-songwriter who had signed on with a major label. Diana was intrigued by Roxy's lifestyle and would often go to local clubs to listen to her sing. She took in everything she saw and heard and filed away the information for later reference. At the same time, she discovered she liked the atmosphere and the people. One thing in particular struck Diana. Roxy was doing what she wanted to do and getting paid for it. It wasn't easy, but she was a single woman seeking a music career. She had to overcome many hurdles, but she kept striving and was making some progress. Roxy was a role model for the future except that Diana didn't know it at the time. Then a complication emerged.

Roxy had recently broken up with her live-in boyfriend, James Dean, Jr., and as time passed, James grew interested in Diana and decided to pursue her. One Friday night, Diana and some of her friends went to a bar called the Brass Ring, over the hill from West Hollywood, in Sherman Oaks. James decided to go, too, and followed them in his Corvette. James was an excellent dancer, and Diana was completely taken with his personal charm and natural good looks. Early the next morning, after Diana's children had gone to school, James showed up at the back door. It only took seconds for their eyes to lock and for the two to melt into each other's arms and slip down to the floor to make love. Diana had been alone for eight years, and James reminded her that she was still a passionate woman that morning on the kitchen floor. She was overwhelmed by the romance and ardor of the moment; her heart didn't have a chance.

James and Diana hit it off immediately, and their relationship expanded to the children. He helped around the house, played with the kids, and made their lunches, sticking jokes and riddles in their lunch boxes. When it appeared that James and Diana might be falling in love, for some inexplicable reason they decided to open a video production company. James came home one night with a huge mobile truck and video equipment, but Diana never wondered where he got the money to buy such expensive equipment, and she apparently hadn't asked him what he did for a living, either. Somehow they got Berry Gordy, the founder of Motown Records, to do business with them, and they videotaped Diana Ross when she worked on the film *Lady Sings the Blues*. They also knocked around quite a bit just videotaping Ashley and Christina goofing off. James even taped Ashley's visit to *Romper Room*.

Sometimes James would take Diana and the kids out to a ranch that was owned by an American Indian named Henry Medicine. She and James would relax while the girls rode horses and ran in the fields. The place was no stranger to celebrities and stars. Dean Stockwell used to stop by, as well as a member of the Turtles, and even Dennis Hopper, whom Diana didn't like. The rural setting and the laid-back attitude reminded Diana of Kentucky. People came and went, and there was always food and drink and plenty of conversation.

Everything seemed wonderful. Which of course it wasn't. There was another aspect of James's personality, an unpredictable, violent, and jealous side that Diana hadn't been privy to yet. He would hang out with some hippie types who were into drugs and orgies and high-speed races. At the same time, James became paranoid and suspicious of Diana, which is not uncommon with some men who date stunning women. He would set time limits on how long she should do grocery shopping and would punch some innocent fellow if he looked at Diana sideways.

One night, after berating a man for flirting with Diana, he turned on her with violence. It happened just after the two of them climbed into his Corvette and shut the doors. He whirled around and hit her hard with his open hand across the face and began to yell that she was a whore, just as his mother had been. She wasn't sure which alarmed her more, his blows or his words.

After the initial shock, Diana insisted that he leave her alone and give her some time to think. In an odd way, he did. It seemed as if he were respecting her need for time and space until one night when he called her on the phone. When their conversation ended, he told her to look across the street. She did, and a lump formed in her throat when she saw him standing inside the 7-Eleven, where he had taken a job as a night clerk so that he could keep her home under constant surveillance. The next thing she knew, Diana found a cheap, smashed watch in her driveway, obviously planted by James to keep tabs on her. Her car would break the watch and tell James when she came home. It was creepy. Worse, it was not over.

One night, after Diana asked a male friend to stop by for a visit, James burst through in the front door and attacked the man, throwing punches left and right, and then departed as quickly as he came. He appeared soon afterward at an attorney's office where Diana worked as a secretary. When he came exploding through the door, focusing all his rage on Diana, she buzzed the attorney, who came out and placated James. Her boss later recommended that she get a restraining order.

Diana took his advice and after work one day stopped at her local police station and told her story to an officer named Al. Even though she was fearful of her old boyfriend, she couldn't help noticing how handsome Al was, and soon Al was stopping by her house with his partner, just to check up on things and have a cup of coffee and a little chat, which infuriated James even more. One evening, when Diana returned home, she opened the door and realized that a glass panel of the French door had been broken. She sensed that someone was in the house, but before she could do anything, there was a hand around her neck, and she was being slammed up against the wall as James demanded to know where she had been.

For seven horrible hours he kept Diana and the two girls prisoners in the house as he ranted and raved about how all women—particularly his mother—were nothing but fucking whores only good for one thing. He tore the clothes off Diana and raped her at will as he slapped and punched her, and grabbed at her hair. She lay helpless, afraid he might rape the girls as well as kill her and her daughters. The punching and slapping and raping were horrible, and she prayed that he would not break her arms or legs or incapacitate her. As the night of torture slowly turned into morning, he dragged her into the bathroom while he sat up and shot some heroin.

Finally, at around six in the morning, when James fell asleep, Diana was able to escape, dragging Christina and Ashley to the Holloway Motel, near a Harley-Davidson biker's hangout, Barney's Beanery, at Santa Monica Boulevard and La Cienega Avenue. She had no money, but when the night clerk saw her condition and the two children, he let her have a small room free.

James was still on parole, and when he became conscious again, he knew he would be in very big trouble if Diana told her officer-friend what he had done. He could end up in jail for the rest of his life, and so cruel, maniacal, or jealous as he was, he still did the smart thing and left town immediately, Diana, Christina, and Ashley never saw him again. Diana was grateful that the terror was out of her life but laments that there was no place for her to turn back then.

"I wish," she says, "there had been a shelter for battered women in West Hollywood in 1973. My heart goes out to battered women, especially those with children and poor finances. There's no place scarier than home."

6

Heading Home

WITH BARELY ENOUGH TIME TO RECOVER, Diana felt uncomfortable about what seemed to be another threatening situation. Her boss, the attorney who helped put off James temporarily, had also handled her divorce from Michael, but now he was becoming a problem. What is it with all these males? Diana wondered to herself. They connect with a beautiful woman, and it seems to bring out the worst in them instead of inspiring them to be kind and loving and caring.

In many ways, her attorney-boss, Wade, was a stereotype out of the casting department chosen for the role of a tout around a horse track. He seemed to be the classic Hollywood wheeler-dealer, always with an angle, always with a new idea, always with something happening on the side, and always looking for some vigorish or payoff for himself, all of which was screened behind a wonderful setting that would reassure anyone: a straight-arrow wife who was a college professor, two adopted kids, and the epitome of a happy suburban home life. That was what the public saw, but not Diana, the private secretary. What she observed was a hustler doing cocaine, having affairs, and associating with pimps and hookers.

The experience helped educate Diana about the rough-and-tumble, real world of hustlers and sharks. It toughened her up and made her more street savvy, so that when Wade started paying Diana with bad checks, she grabbed some of his confidential files and held them ransom until he gave her the money he owed her. After reaming him out for taking advantage of a single woman with two children, Wade finally acquiesced and deposited some money into her bank account. Once again, Diana found herself unemployed.

Diana was just twenty-seven and had hit the streets, searching for work, when she received another lesson in men and compassion. Christina was having recurring bladder infections, and when one particularly bad attack hit her, their doctor advised Diana to admit Christina to the hospital. Of course, she had no insurance, so Diana called Michael and told him that she needed some money for Christina's illness. Diana recalls: "There was a moment of silence on the line. 'Well—' he sighed, repeating his now-famous line—'you should have thought about that before you divorced me.' With that, he hung up." He didn't bother to ask how his children were or even what was wrong with Christina.

Diana took Christina to the hospital. A clerk in the admitting office suggested that she call Aid to Families with Dependent Children, which she did immediately, and they were quickly put on emergency medical assistance. That solved the immediate problem; they were on welfare, and it taught Diana more about the world. She would have to badger Michael for years to pay any child support.

Welfare proved a godsend for the moment, but Diana wasn't the welfare-mother type, and she was soon looking for a job. Again, she made a connection and soon had a secretary-assistant position working for an investment consultant, David Chou. He clearly had done well for himself. He lived in a Beverly Hills mansion and drove a Maserati. It was one of those interesting, multiduty Hollywood-type jobs, and Diana's responsibilities included light bookkeeping, managing the housekeeping, and supervising both the gardening and pool services. She also read scripts for the TV series *Kung Fu*, for which Chou was the martial-arts technical adviser. She assisted him whenever he did a martial-arts exhibition.

Diana remembers one particular exhibition that was being sponsored by Mike Stone, a martial arts instructor. When she and Chou showed up for the exhibition and met Stone, Diana was impressed because he was with Priscilla Presley. The two women quickly struck up a conversation and immediately discovered unusual parallels in their lives. They were both fourteen when they met their future husbands, married and lived with their mates' parents, and each had daughters, Ashley and Lisa Marie, the same age. They both had left their husbands, but that is where the similarities ended. Priscilla left Elvis for Mike Stone, and Diana didn't leave Michael for anybody. She left Michael for freedom and a life.

Christina was nine years old and continued at West Hollywood Elementary, and Ashley was six and was just beginning kindergarten. Happily, Christina's medical condition appeared to be getting better, which is more than could be said for Diana's employment. The position with Chou didn't pan out. There may have been a personal factor at work again, since most men who were around Diana seemed to want to do more than just employ her.

Diana, who was getting pretty adept at job hunting, began looking and drifting again, and soon she found another job. This time it couldn't be more conveniently located, and it involved something that she quickly learned to enjoy doing, working at a health-food store, the Golden Carrot, about 150 feet from her front door. The job was fun because the place was patronized by local celebrities and an eclectic Hollywood crowd that soon inspired Diana to start dressing New Age and semihippie, with bell-bottoms, halters, Mexican blouses, and headbands.

As much fun as this lifestyle seemed to be, Diana began to realize that there were other factors involved, too, that all these beautiful people lived their seemingly glamorous lives from paycheck to paycheck, gig to gig, and from one dream to another. Most of them worked as underpaid waiters, chauffeurs, nannies, shop clerks, and "executive assistants." They would be doing exactly the same thing twenty years from now, their hopes blown away in the warm current of Hollywood, showbiz, and the Santa Ana winds. Diana was becoming homesick.

Diana somehow managed to get on *Hollywood Squares* and lasted an entire week, achieving champion status. That was followed by an appearance on *Password*, where she only lasted three days, claiming that the only reason she lost was because Peter Lawford was drunk and more interested in her knee than answering the questions. Diana was thinking about her roots and life where she grew up and where Christina was born and where Ashley had never been.

Of course, life did go on in Ashland among the Judds. Diana's little sister, Margaret, followed family tradition and eloped with a boy that the entire family deemed unsuitable. In keeping with the example Diana had set, Margaret and her new husband lived in his bedroom at his parents' home in Green, Kentucky, and Margaret became pregnant. One thing that was different about the arrangement was that Margaret's husband soon announced that he had no intention of moving out of his parents' home or of getting a job. At least Michael had finished school with a B.A. degree and found work. Margaret responded to her husband's declaration by taking her little girl and heading back home to the comforts of the Judd home at 2237 Montgomery Street in Ashland.

Unfortunately, Glen and Polly barely spoke to each other, and their life together had become intolerable. When she received a letter from Margaret explaining the situation, Diana immediately wrote back suggesting that Margaret move to Los Angeles. They were both single moms, they knew each other well, and their kids would have family around. Diana enjoyed attending the West Hollywood Community Church, and she thought the schools were better in Los Angeles than back in Ashland. That was the sensible side of it.

On the other hand, there was Diana's fading enthusiasm for Los Angeles and coping with its late sixties atmosphere, which was California rock and roll, wild parties, psychedelic drugs, and the youth culture, with women over the hill at eighteen, and everybody fascinated by both the beach and the Beach Boys. Moreover,

Diana was concerned that the girls—particularly ten-year-old Christina—spent too much time watching TV and scarfing down junk food and candy bars. She had taught her girls about their Kentucky roots and even had them learn some old folk songs and hymns from her youth in Ashland and Louisa. However, her girls were growing up Californians, and that wasn't the same as living in Kentucky bluegrass country. Such thoughts did not dampen Margaret's enthusiasm for leaving Ashland for the fascinating life of California, where she would undoubtedly meet and marry a movie star or become one herself. Thus, another Judd was California bound.

Margaret, with the kind of self-reliance and determination that seemed to be in the Judds' blood, loved the idea of heading west. She packed her bags, put her daughter, Erin, in the car, and pointed the hood ornament toward the setting sun. Margaret was smitten with California and quickly found a job manufacturing hand-sewn false eyelashes. Diana was glad to have her sister there for both companionship and support. Every now and then Margaret and Diana would hit the town and dance up a storm at the Topanga Corral. They were both dating and life was looking good.

Sometimes, the sister from Ashland would have friends and dates over to their home, where they would listen to music—Moody Blues, Guess Who, and Cream—and tell funny stories about growing up in a small Kentucky town. In time, Margaret, seeking independence, entered a good job-training program and then found an apartment for herself and Erin. Diana was sad to see Margaret and Erin leave, but she knew that she and her sister had reunited in a meaningful way and that their new bond would last them a lifetime.

Now home was very quiet, and Diana began to reassess her situation. "I began to feel like a John Deere tractor in a half-acre field trying to plow a furrow, where the soil's made of steel." She was getting tired of men groping her rear end and being paid in pennies to be around as a sex object, to be stared at and lusted after while not doing much of anything worthwhile. She felt the need to move on with her life in a more meaningful way.

At the time, she worked for a man named Adams, who

constructed neon signs in Las Vegas. It was not the most exciting job she had ever had, but what made it worse was that Mr. Adams and his wife were so obsessed with material goods that it became too much for Diana. Family, compassion, and living each day to its fullest didn't seem to apply to the Adams household. After a while, Diana quit.

Diana, Chris, and Ashley had been in Hollywood for six years, and maybe it was time to move on. In addition to the string of meaningless jobs, the L.A. smog was wreaking havoc on Christina's asthma, which had periodically flared up since their arrival in Hollywood. Diana felt that the latchkey life was not for her and her two daughters. All uncertainty about her next move melted away one morning in June 1974 when the milkman unexpectedly knocked at the kitchen door and told Diana to be careful because a homeless man was sleeping in her backyard. He accompanied her as she checked it out. The man was asleep by the swing set where her two children played. The idea of someone in a rich country such as America not having a place to sleep stunned Diana, but moments later she realized that she and the girls were really only a paycheck away from the same existence.

Three years before, Diana was seeking out options when she heard from Ginny Vick, a friend in Austin, Texas. Ginny suggested that Diana check out Texas because it was more her kind of place. Ginny said there were lots of opportunities for a good-looking woman in her mid-twenties. With very little to lose, Diana put her two little ones on a plane to Kentucky to live with their father until it was time for school to start. Then the Kentucky nomad loaded up her car and headed south to the Lone Star State. Ginny made arrangements for Diana to stay at the house of her friend David Swann while she scoped out the neighborhoods for a place for herself and the girls.

Diana immediately fell in love with Texas. She and her new roommate, David, got along well, and in exchange for free board, Diana would cook and clean. Soon David was showing Diana around town, taking her to clubs like the Broken Spoke, Soap Creek, and the Armadillo. It was great fun and very relaxed because David and Diana agreed right away to make their friendship platonic. Diana listened to country music for the first time and became a huge fan of the local heroes, the Fabulous Thunderbirds.

Diana was hanging around and having a great time and was even interviewed for a position as the local TV weather girl on the station owned by and named after Lyndon B. Johnson, KLBJ-TV. She was hired, but in the few weeks she was on the staff, she never once got on the air and once again began to wonder what she was doing with herself. She now was becoming more conscious of the fact that she wasn't going to stay a good-looking twenty-five-year-old all her life. She had better get on with marriage, a career, something!

The one thing she didn't like about Austin was the heat. After about six weeks and some serious thought about the future, Diana decided to become a nurse; she had always wanted to do something meaningful with her life. She heard about a position in a hospital in the northern part of Arizona, on the White River Apache Indian Reservation. She decided to check it out, but it didn't take more than a Kentucky minute to turn it down. Too primitive, and the schools weren't good enough for the kids or for Diana to get a nursing degree.

She decided to investigate nursing schools in northern California. She had heard good things about them from somebody—she was not quite sure who—and she was still convinced that schools were better in California than most other places, but she had had all she wanted of Southern California for now—and maybe forever. Diana once more pulled together what belongings she had, packed them into her car, said goodbye to David, Ginny, and Texas, and headed out for Northern California. Then some luck surfaced for her as she traveled the highway, stopping and hanging out in different towns as she drove north to Santa Cruz.

Serendipitously, Diana met an older couple, Dorothy and Henry Wells, who took an instant liking to her and insisted that she be their houseguest on their cattle ranch for a time, until she was ready to move on again. Fortuitously, Dorothy had already reached the goal Diana was now pursuing; she was a retired registered nurse. She could share her experiences and ideas, all of which made

Diana more enthused about pursuing that career. Dorothy, in turn, enjoyed her time with Diana because the older woman, now in her seventies, was lonely for feminine company and some sense of what was going on in other parts of the world. Diana's stay on the cattle ranch came to an end when she realized that the time was approaching for the kids to be back in school.

7

Old Bluegrass and New Guitar

DIANA'S 1974 SUMMER NOMAD DAYS had to come to an end. In later years, in 1993, Ashley would say that her mother was bored to death during this period and that "one day she had an epiphany. She decided to move us to Kentucky, where she's from, and enroll in nursing school." Diana needed to get back to her girls and put them in school, and she herself wanted to attend nursing school. Admittedly, Diana had become a dream chaser without a dream to chase. Perhaps nursing would become her dream. However, first things first; she had to return home to Kentucky and find a place to live.

The children had been staying with their missing-in-action father. Apparently, Michael had been wandering around, too, since they broke up and he was transferred to Chicago. He had left Chicago and moved to Oregon, where he had studied to be a leather craftsman. That was a far cry from his business education and experience, but this was an era when many men found that traditional college programs didn't connect with what they saw was important in life, and they drifted into other channels. Many of them, and some women, too, abandoned establishment careers and suburban lives and traveled westward to freer places in Washington and Oregon, and such Rocky Mountain regions as Colorado.

For Michael it was Oregon, but, more recently he also felt the call to reclaim his roots in to Kentucky. He was renting a summer fishing cabin on the Kentucky River. The locals called this section of the country Camp Wig. Ashley and Christina had been spending a lot of time there lately, and they really enjoyed it, not because it was so un-California but because it was so Kentucky and so family.

Diana saw in the resurfacing of Michael in their three lives and the reconnection with the children as a chance to make things easier for herself and Christina and Ashley. She made a proposal to Michael that she thought would have a positive impact on her kids' lives and perhaps ease any guilt he might be harboring over the many missed child-support payments. She suggested that the past-due child support be forgotten in exchange for letting her and his two daughters live in the fishing house free. That way there wouldn't be any hassle with child welfare regarding a deadbeat dad.

A deal was struck, and Diana was on her way home feeling a bit like a returning runaway child, but her jubilation was tempered when she discovered that the fishing house was really a shack without any indoor plumbing. It was a far cry from the Sunset Strip, but Diana was determined to make the best of this "rustic" situation, and all three of them pitched in to make their stay as comfortable as possible. They grew a lot of their own herbs and vegetables, got fresh butter down the road, and splurged on a $75 Maytag washer—the old-fashioned kind, with the wringer. It actually turned out to be a free form of entertainment on Saturday nights. Diana and the girls would wash clothes and feed them into the wringer, singing and telling stories. Sometimes they would sing along with the radio that played the *Grand Ole Opry*.

Beyond that, Ashley was providing entertainment in her own special way. According to Diana, "Ashley [was] the princess of malapropism. She would inform us that Samuel Morse invented the code of telepathy; she called the Pacific Ocean the 'Specific' Ocean; she complained of humanity [humidity] in the air; and declared after grace one evening that God was a sparerib [spirit]. Ashley also thought that the world revolved around its 'taxes.'"

Diana was happy that the children were developing a relationship with nature and each other. They were becoming resourceful and down-to-earth. The fast-approaching winter of 1974–1975 would test how rugged and resourceful they really were, and as the chill began to set in, and winter threw her bone-chilling blanket over the countryside, Diana understood why the rent was so cheap at Camp Wig. The place had no insulation and was like the inside of an icebox. Most people would have left, but Diana instead purchased a potbellied stove into which everyone would have to shovel coal, including six-and-a-half-year-old Ashley, who was experiencing her first snowbound white Christmas. In the meantime, Diana found a nursing school and registered for classes.

Diana was sharing a classroom at Eastern Kentucky University in Richmond with a bunch of giggling nineteen-year-olds who were just beginning their lives, single and filled with hope. By the time Diana was their age, she was a single mom with two children in a miserable marriage that she longed to escape. Diana didn't have a lot of money, so while the other nursing students were dressed in the latest fashions, Diana came to class looking more like a bag lady than a college student. During the cold winter days, Diana wore a big fur hat and a secondhand wool coat. She said that at a distance people thought she had a dead animal sitting on her head, and while the other women were sporting heels and hose, Diana was stomping around in knee-high rubber boots.

While nobody wanted to be her lab partner in class, everybody wanted to hear about the wild life in Hollywood, kissing Elvis, dancing every night with movie stars and hanging out with the Beach Boys, hopped-up musicians, and their naked girlfriends, as well as why Diana gave up being a high-fashion model. Actually, Diana enjoyed hearing the gossip. It didn't matter what these teenagers thought of her. She was on a journey, and she intended to complete it.

Every night Diana arrived at the shack just as her two daughters were coming home from school. Diana would cook dinner, clean the house, help with the laundry and children's homework, and also make sure she had completed her own homework. Then, at five-thirty the next morning, she'd begin her day over again. Diana and the kids hadn't been to a restaurant in almost a year. However, the one thing that would shine through the life of Diana Judd over the years was that she was a tough woman who worked hard to make life turn out as best as it could for her and her two daughters.

One weekend Diana saw an advertisement for a bluegrass band called J. D. Crowe's New South, which was playing at the local Holiday Inn. Diana knew that if she wanted to remain sane she had to get out of the house. She put on her regular pioneer clothes and went to see the band. She ordered one coke and sat in the corner by herself. It was an exhilarating experience that made Diana feel better than she had for months.

That night did wonders for Diana's spirits, but their existence in the huge freezer-like shack didn't do much for her body or those of her daughters. They could see their breath in the bedrooms and often moved into the kitchen next to the potbellied stove. One freezing night, they all woke up to soaking sheets. Somebody had wet the bed, and they were all wearing the only pajamas they owned. Diana packed everyone up and drove to her parents' home.

Diana may have been proud and unwilling to be a burden on anybody, but she couldn't stand not being able to properly care for her children. The bone-chilling shack wasn't the right place for her kids, and she did what any sensible person would do: get on home to her mother and father. They would stay in the shack on and off for a while, but it was clear that they would have to find something better soon. Meanwhile, Polly took care of her daughter and granddaughters, and Glen gave Diana some money to help. When they left the Judds' home, Diana promised herself that she would be a success, pay them back, and make them proud someday. "Someday" would be ten years later, but at least it was coming.

The year 1975 brought heavy rain and floods to Camp Wig and forced Diana and the girls to evacuate in a rowboat and flee to the home of Diana's brother, Mark. When she returned to salvage what she could from the shack, her heart sank when she saw that everything was covered in mud. They were forced to move into another one-bedroom house in the area. When Michael became a frequent guest, tensions escalated into arguments. It got so unbearable that Diana had to move into another one-room cabin by herself. She left the kids with Michael so that they could finish their last month of school.

Diana trudged through that month, going to the Eastern Kentucky School of Nursing in Richmond, Kentucky, maintaining the best academic record of her class. Meanwhile, she looked for another place to stay. She didn't want to live in the college town of Richmond; she preferred the community of nearby Berea, which was small and more artistic and oriented toward her favorite Appalachian arts and crafts.

One day, while Diana and the girls were driving down the road, they saw an older woman slip on the pavement. Diana immediately turned the car around, pulled up alongside, and jumped out to make sure the lady was okay. They took her to the emergency room, and after she was checked out, they drove her home. They hung out for a while, and during the conversation Diana told the woman, whose name was Caroline Hovery, that she and the kids were looking for a house. The next day, Diana found a letter in her box at school from a woman who said she was a friend of Ms. Hovery's. In the letter the mystery woman said that she would like to show Diana and her daughters a house she was renting, and she enclosed a hand-drawn map indicating its location and with the date and time they were to meet.

Intrigued, Diana and the kids followed the directions and found themselves driving through the rural town of Morrill. As they drove down a long gravel driveway and through the tall trees, Diana and the youngsters couldn't believe the sight before them. High on a hill was the most beautiful house. As they pulled up, an older woman came out and introduced herself as Margaret Allen, a music teacher at Berea College. She was a widow, and her daughter had married Vincent Peale's son. Her own son was the editor of *Reader's Digest*. Margaret Allen taught music at Berea for a dollar a year. Obviously, she was not in need of money and generously offered one of the homes on her large estate, known as Windswept, to Diana and her children. Margaret pointed to a plaque attached to the house that read: Chanticleer. The house was completely furnished with beautiful antiques, quilts, a stone fireplace, and a Steinway grand piano.

It was too good to be true and way beyond anything Diana could manage. Then Ms. Allen said, "Could you afford a hundred dollars per month? It has been empty such a long time. I certainly don't need the money. I just want the right people to have it. Someone who believes in the Golden Rule. I've waited quite long enough for you."

Diana, speechless, was filled with wonderment at the good fortune that had grown out of a simple kind deed. She somehow managed to say thank you and accept the proposition before they settled on final arrangements and left. The timing was excellent, for school would end in two weeks and that would make it easier to move in and get settled, which they did that June. It also fulfilled a plan Diana had to administer a dose of cultural shock to her two girls, who would have to continue their adjustment from a go-go Hollywood lifestyle to a go-slow Kentucky way of life. She was happy that all they had for entertainment was the radio. Diana reflected that from this time on, their lives would be different.

Diana and the girls moved into the house, and soon they were picking fresh apples and making pies. They made bread and yogurt and canned all the fresh vegetables from their garden, and since they didn't own a TV, they would spend their evenings sitting on the front porch telling stories, counting stars, or listening to the sounds of nature.

Then, in this summer of serendipity, it happened. Someone brought a guitar to the house, and eleven-year-old Christina was drawn to it like a magnet, even though she had never shown much of an interest in anything. Something had awakened inside her. She learned quickly and soon figured out three different chords. Christina was learning the guitar, but she didn't have her own instrument until Diana found a used guitar with a pearl inlay. Knowing that the guitar had suddenly become central to her daughter's life, Diane bought it and gave it to Christina, who was ecstatic. She told her mother that it was the most beautiful thing she had ever seen.

As their financial situation improved, Diana was able to buy a few "extravagances" like old albums from the dollar bin. She found one that intrigued her, a bluegrass singing duo called Hazel and Alice. "What a concept!" she said. "A record with two women singing together! I brought it home, and Christina and I listened to it on our record player. As we listened, we became absolutely transfixed."

They were riveted not so much by the songs as by how the two women's voices were themselves musical instruments in their blending, harmony, and intonation. It struck the two women that this music sounded something like the way they did when they would occasionally sing. What began happening then was a kind of chemistry between the two that would, in time, transform them into a single musical entity.

Diana and Christina started to learn the songs on the guitar, and by the end of the summer knew every song on the Hazel and Alice album by heart. On Mother's Day, Diana and Christina presented Polly Judd with a song they learned called "A Mother's Smile." It was a touching moment for them—three generations brought together by music. It was also a defining moment for Diana. She realized the power that music had, how it was a universal language that had the potential to break down barriers and speak directly to the soul. By the end of the summer, Diana was writing her first songs about love, family life, and relationships, such as "Simple, Peaceful, and Good," "Dynamo," "Child of the Light," "Renegade's Song," "Grits," "Soup, Beans and Cornbread," and "Daddy Are You Coming Home Tonight?"

But other things were happening to Diana's growing girls that she didn't fully recognize immediately. When she did, she wasn't entirely happy about it. Christina loved the guitar but hated school, and her mood grew more rebellious and angry. One day Diana learned that eleven-year-old Christina had been skipping school and hanging out at the activity center, hustling pool. Seven-year-old Ashley, on the other hand, loved school and was a straight-A student. She joined the Brownies, took a pottery class, and loved to read. In fact, Ashley's favorite game was playing school; Christina's was pool!

Then there was the nursing school. Diana was bothered by what she was being taught. There didn't seem to be any emphasis on prevention, it was all about cure, drugs, and operations. Diana thought that the business of doctors should be to prevent illness, not charging people who were sick to get well. She admired the Chinese system, where doctors are paid to keep people well, not to cure them when they are ill.

As winter approached, the family looked forward to Christmas, 1976. That they never had much money for presents didn't stop them from having a terrific time. They would go into the woods to find their own Christmas tree and chop it down themselves. Diana remembers the cold winter day with the temperature below freezing, overcast skies, and a briskness in the air when they started out into the forest. Diana always loved the forest but was becoming a little discouraged as the three of them tramped about, unable to find a suitable tree. They were becoming colder and colder until they stopped to rest.

All of a sudden, gentle white snowflakes began softly drifting down upon where they were, adding a delicate filigree to the world around that left the three of them enchanted by the beauty of the moment and the place. A little later, the youngest of the three struck out again and quickly came upon just the right tree for their first Christmas in Chanticleer.

They dragged the tree back to their home, singing Christmas carols and looking forward to trimming the tree. It turned out to be a wonderful Christmas. Homemade gifts were exchanged, and bellies became full. Diana's mom and dad came, and together the family spent the holiday singing, eating, and sitting around the fire reading from the Book of Luke. It was all part of an almost fairyland existence that had become their life at Chanticleer. They made biweekly trips into town for supplies, and when the girls accomplished something, Diana would take them to the skating rink as a reward. Diana would play the piano, and Christina kept learning new songs on the guitar.

By contrast, back in Ashland, things weren't going too well, and it dawned on Diana one day when she and the girls showed up for a visit. Glen Judd said he was going hunting. This would happen repeatedly during their visits home until, finally, Polly told Diana the truth: Glen was going to see his girlfriend. Soon after, he moved out.

Bad luck continued. The girls returned home one day and found find they had been robbed of their record player, some cheap jewelry, and the Smith & Wesson that Diana kept under her pillow. Luckily, the burglar had overlooked Christina's beloved guitar. They learned from the local troopers that the burglar was probably a fellow who lived in a shack down the hill from them. The way they described him, he sounded like one of the characters from the film *Deliverance*. The troopers advised them to stay away from him because he wasn't right in the head.

Despite that advice, the strong-willed Diana, supported by her equally strong-willed daughters, sneaked into the man's shack when he was gone and searched the place but came up empty-handed. This didn't improve things, and Diana felt very uneasy about staying in the house with the girls alone without even a gun to defend herself. Her suspicions turned out to be correct. Early the next morning, when Diana and the girls opened the front door, they found their cat, Hovey, dead, every bone in her body broken. Diana tried to comfort the girls as they cried for their little friend, but this vicious act was enough to frighten Diana into purchasing another gun.

They buried their cat but soon realized that their pet dog, Mule, was missing and that the dog's bed and food were untouched. Diana suspected the worst—that their neighbor down the hill had done something horrible to him—and she spent that evening searching for Mule by the light of the moon. While she was searching, she fell into a snow drift, sprained her ankle, and had to spend the next forty-eight hours in bed. Diana says that they never found Mule and that a local told her that he saw a dog nailed to the shed owned by her creepy neighbor down the hill. It made their stay at Chanticleer from then on a very nervous arrangement and kept them constantly on their guard, although nothing further happened.

When spring came, Diana's sister, Margaret, and her daughter, Erin, came to Chanticleer to vacation, and the young children got to know each other again, as did Margaret and Diana. During this

.time, Margaret had an itch to go to the big city, so she and Diana drove to Lexington, where an odd-looking group of men struck up a conversation with them while they were eating in a downtown restaurant. They introduced themselves to the two women as the Band, a musical group well known to Margaret but not Diana. She proceeded to display her ignorance by asking them whose band they were in and did they know how to play bluegrass.

After all was explained to Diana, the women decided they would have to accept the Band's invitation to hear them perform in concert that night, but that didn't completely dispel Diana's naïveté. She told Margaret that she predicted that the Band might even amount to something in the future. Margaret said she was right because the Band already had superstar status. Diana realized that her obsession with raising the girls and going to nursing school had kept her out of the mainstream.

Glen Judd was now living in his own apartment and openly dating his new girlfriend. While Diana tried to pretend it hadn't happened so she could keep her memories of home and mother and father intact, it was not to be. She felt the bitterness corroding her mother's heart. She visited their family home in Ashland. However, she was not prepared for her mother's desire to seek vengeance against Diana's father. It happens in most divorces, but you just never think it will happen to you or to your family.

Polly could not endure the pain and the humiliation that was consuming her. She filed for divorce. Polly informed Diana that she expected her daughter to testify in open court and condemn her own father. Diana was not willing to do that.

The man who lived down the hill from Diana and the girls was on the rampage again. In the fall of 1976, Diana sent Christina and Ashley to Ashland so that no harm would come to them. She strapped a gun to her waist, pulled the shades, and lived a strange life for the next few weeks. Then it happened. Her prayers were answered. Out of the blue she got two letters on the same day. One was an encouraging letter with a check for five hundred dollars from David Swann, her Austin friend. The other came from her childhood friend Linda Ann McDonald. Linda, who was living in

San Francisco, raved about how fantastic the city was, and invited Diane to come visit her. It didn't take Diana long to make a decision.

She called the children and informed them that she was going on a short trip, packed her car, and drove down the driveway of Chanticleer for the last time.

8

Crossing America
to Find Naomi

IT WAS THE END OF 1976, and thirty-year-old Diana had spent two years back home in Kentucky. She was drawn back to California, this time to San Francisco and her best friend from high school and also to her sister, Margaret. When she had visited San Francisco earlier, she had fallen in love with Marin County. Some think Diana returned to Kentucky so that her girls could be near their father, but even if that were so, now she was leaving Kentucky because that arrangement didn't work out.

Diana was still determined to become a nurse or nurse-midwife. Nurse-midwifery was the latest trend in holistic medicine, which appealed to her, and Marin was more receptive to that concept than the traditional nursing schools in Kentucky. Diana planned to find a place for the three of them to live. Meanwhile, Christina's voice was getting strong, as was her interest in music.

Twelve-year-old Christina would spend her days listening to albums and practicing on her beautiful guitar. She was enthralled by southern rock, country blues, and folk music. She practiced by listening to and imitating singers on discount records. Diana couldn't afford the $9.00 albums and had to buy the $1.99 bargain platters instead, but that was all right. They had the music of the Delmore Brothers, the Boswell Sisters, Hazel and Alice on Rounder Records, and Ralph Stanley.

Diana was learning to play the guitar, too, and was singing harmony to encourage her daughter Christina. She taught both daughters that it was cool to be a hillbilly. Christina had a good voice, but mother and daughter together sounded better. A compulsively neat person, Diana was coming into conflict with Christina, who was a dreamer, junk-food eater, and untidy. Often they used their music to soothe the discord between them. Their conflict over neatness and self-discipline began when Christina was an early teen, and it continues between mother and daughter to this day. The difference now is that they each have learned how to handle it better than they did back in the mid-1970s.

What finally convinced Diana and the girls to leave Kentucky at the end of 1976 was the divorce of her parents, which, predictably, was mean and ugly. Polly was critical of Diana's earlier divorce, and now she wanted her own. In the bargain, she sought revenge for Glen's drinking, his long hours away at work, his lack of affection, and the death their son Brian. The price Polly demanded of her children was that they testify in court against their father and repudiate him. Diana wasn't going to do that—ever. She decided to flee to California before the trial, and she matter-of-factly told Craig Williams, a man with whom she had been hanging around, that it was over in spite of his help with Christina's music and his relationship with Diana. Neither Craig nor Kentucky could satisfy her anymore.

Diana would lose college credits by transferring, but what she could gain was more important to her. When the Judd divorce was settled the first week of December 1976, Diana and the girls had already left for California, dragging a U-Haul behind them with all their belongings. Back in Kentucky, Polly felt betrayed by her daughter, and they wouldn't talk again for several years.

Polly got a job as a cook on one of the many riverboats that moved up and down the Ohio River. She used her cooking skills to make her way, as she had when she was much younger and not yet married. This time she hired a friend of her son's to mow the lawn and take care of the plants around her house in exchange for one meat loaf a month. Being a professional cook again on a riverboat was hard work for Polly. The boats would stay out on the river for ten to twelve days at a time, and she had to cook three meals a day, including in-between snacks for the crew.

The boatmen on those barges particularly favored Polly's yeast rolls and, to the surprise of many, including the men themselves, her special fried liver and onions. She said, "Men who told me they'd never eaten liver before would eat it the way I fixed it. The problem is most people just cook liver to death." Polly's special approach was to fry the liver quickly in very hot bacon fat to make it crisp on the outside but leaving it tender inside. The one boat captain who liked Polly's cooking the most was Wilbert "Wib" Rideout. In 1980 they married, and Polly returned to just cooking for family at home and fixing Wib's favorite dish, her special cucumber-and-onion salad.

Diana's advance-scouting, cross-country tour began on August 4, 1976. It's always scary for a woman to be driving across the country by herself, especially if the car she's driving is an eggbeater. Each morning when Diana would start her trek, she never knew for sure if her car would make it to the next city, but all went well until Ogallala, Nebraska. The car started acting funny, and Diana found herself after midnight in the middle of a Nebraska hailstorm that didn't seem as if it were ever going to stop. She pulled into a gas station and entered the office to wait out the storm, but circumstances took an unexpected turn when the young attendant in greasy overalls told her that he was closing shop and that she had to leave. He also informed her that all the motels were booked up because of the storm and that it would be dangerous for her to wait out the storm in her car. He generously offered her a warm bed at his place.

Diana followed the attendant out into the storm, and through the dark hills until finally he pulled up to a dingy, small trailer. Although Diana suddenly felt apprehensive, she followed the attendant into the trailer. It was terrible—dirty and greasy, with empty beer bottles scattered about—and to get a moment's breather, for she was beginning to freak out, she excused herself and slipped into the bathroom. When she returned, the attendant was casually standing there with his shirt off, holding a beer in his hand.

Diana began to realize how bad the situation was. She was in an isolated trailer with a half-dressed guy drinking a Bud in the middle of Nebraska in a giant storm and nobody knew where she was. In fact, she had told her mother that she was just going on a short trip, and her friends probably thought she was still in Kentucky. It was time to get the hell out of there. Then the gas-station attendant brushed her hair back from her face with his dirty hand and said she was the most beautiful female he had ever seen in his life. He noticed that she wasn't wearing a wedding ring. As she looked furtively around for a way to escape, he mentioned that they were all alone; he didn't even have a telephone. When he moved toward the refrigerator to get them a couple of beers, Diana felt the adrenaline rising and leaped for the door.

She was out the door and plunged into the blustery onslaught of the freezing hailstorm, literally running for her life and fumbling in her purse for the car keys.

My god! Where are the keys? she asked herself in a panic when her fingers couldn't grasp the reassuring cold metal. The wind tore at her clothing, and she began feeling the rain soaking her while her erstwhile lover stood outside on the steps of his trailer yelling at the top of his lungs, the words instantly swallowed by the storm. Was he screaming something about having her keys, or was he venting his rage because she had left him? She hoped it was the latter.

She jammed her hand into her coat pocket and felt surge of relief as her fingers closed around her car keys. She flung herself into the car, jammed the key into the ignition, and sparked the engine into roaring life as she hit the gas pedal and floored it back to civilization. She ended up sitting in the lobby of a local motel until dawn, when the storm had passed and she could call a tow truck to pick up her car and take it to a garage, not the gas station of the night before.

While Diana waited for her car to be fixed, she stayed in a cheap motel and whittled away the hours by writing songs with the help of Christina's guitar, which she had taken with her. One of them was "Stuck in a Motel Blues." The lyrics talk about being surrounded by noisy neighbors, the Gideon Bible in the drawer, and turning on the television to kill time.

Finally, Diana got a call informing her that the engine block had a crack and it would cost $500 to fix. She sensed that she was being hustled by an unscrupulous mechanic, but she wasn't in any position to argue. She sold the car for $125 and bought a plane ticket to San Francisco. However, her ordeal wasn't over, for somebody stole Christina's guitar while Diana was in line buying the airplane ticket!

It was the fall of 1976, and a grateful Diana arrived safely in San Francisco. Her friend was waiting for her at the airport. After catching up on old times, Diana toured Marin County, located on the north side of San Francisco Bay. She was looking for an apartment she could afford for herself and the girls. The only place under $500 was a one-bedroom apartment over a real-estate office. The rent was $295 a month. She took it. Next, she went to the local school and enrolled Ashley and Christina for the next semester. Then she headed back to Kentucky.

Her father questioned her about wandering around and living in different parts of the country, but she was a grown women with children and a strong will, so all he could do was help her. That meant getting out the biggest U-Haul he could find among those trucks his gas station rented and letting her use it. Then brother Mark helped Diana and the girls load all their belongings into the truck and watched them pull out, headed for a strange home three thousand miles away. Diana still remembers her father's parting words. "I don't know about your common sense, but you sure got more guts than anybody I know!" Her mother's reaction was different. She felt that her daughter was deserting her just at the time when she needed her most, to help her get through the divorce.

It was a long trip, but they made it without any notable trouble, arriving in late 1976. The Judds settled into a one-bedroom apartment in a very small village named Lagunitas. Christina slept in the bedroom, and Ashley and Diana slept on a mattress in the other room. Diana enrolled in night school at the College of Marin in Kentfield. Christina got the only bedroom because she had a tendency to talk in her sleep or sleepwalk, and neither Ashley nor Diana wanted to deal with that. It was enough that Diana had to find work, apply for nursing-school grants and student loans, and sign up for welfare to get medical coverage.

Diana was lucky to find a waitressing job in the nearby upscale town of Sausalito, but it didn't work out. The restaurant was too popular, too busy, and too much for Diana. They fired her, but it didn't bother her. She admitted to being the world's worst waitress and was working at it because it was the only job she could get and she needed work to pay the bills. She always regarded work as the rent each of us pays for the space we occupy on earth, but it was hard for her because she was supporting herself and two girls, paying for school, and stuck in a minimum-wage job. In spite of it all, she tried to be cheerful and look ahead to what she hoped the future would bring after she finished nursing school and became a licensed nurse. Then, finally, she would have a respectable career and earn a decent wage.

Her new employer, Sally, grew up in a section of America that is part of our romantic heritage, just as Diana grew up in the Kentucky bluegrass heritage country. Sally was raised in the California Gold Rush country and became involved with a man who "done her wrong" to the point that she did hard time in prison protecting him. Then he left her. She learned an important lesson about men and life, just as Diana had. Sally moved to San Francisco and became a collector of sought-after rarities. Her collection of fine art and antiques in time became one of the most famous in San Francisco. The same was true of her array of beautiful and accommodating women, who, in turn, gave Sally a client list of the richest and most powerful men in San Francisco, who enjoyed patronizing her chic, upscale whorehouse.

Along the way, Sally adopted a new name, taken from one of the four most powerful men in California. He became a multimillionaire swindling the American taxpayer in building the Central Pacific Railroad and later founded a great university on his farm when Harvard snubbed his offer of an endowment in the name of his dead son, Leland Stanford Jr. A new woman was born, with a new life and a new name, Sally Stanford.

Periodically, politicians, police captains, and wealthy men who were regular customers of local whorehouses were required to maintain appearances by expressing public outrage that such establishments existed! These protests would lead to newspaper interviews, righteous letters to the editor, and indignant editorials leavened with the appropriate police raids when all of Sally's clients were dining at home with their boring wives. Sally understood the game, but she wasn't going to have men, with their intrinsic hypocrisy, take advantage of her again, and after one raid too many, Sally did what the police, politicians and Pooh Bahs of San Francisco couldn't and didn't want to do. She closed down Sally Stanford's whorehouse for good.

She continued to live in her sumptuous, antique-filled Nob Hill mansion but took a short ride over the Golden Gate bridge to a quaint waterfront town called Sausalito, located in liberal-minded Marin County. There, on the waterfront, with a spectacular view of Baghdad by the Bay—San Francisco—she did three things that were important to her. First, she opened a fine restaurant she named the Valhalla; second, she moved the famous barber chair in which she always sat during business hours from her closed San Francisco whorehouse and installed it at the end of the bar, where she could observe the bar and the dining room; and third, she ran for the Sausalito City Council and was elected.

Sally was different from Diana. She was a tough-looking, heavy-set broad with a wild demeanor. She was also very careful with her money and checked all the provisions bought for the kitchen and measured the amount of whiskey in the bottles behind the bar every night after closing to make sure her bartenders were pouring a fair but not overly generous drink. She knew exactly how many shots should come out of a fifth of whiskey and therefore how much money each bottle should gross for the house. If it didn't work out that way, some bartender would catch hell.

The talk among the male patrons of the Valhalla was that Sally wouldn't tolerate any of her "girls" going out with customers or being treated as if they were whores. That was then—on the other side of the bay—and this was now, and Sally wasn't having any of it.

She also hung provocative female paintings over the urinals. One showed a gorgeous naked woman staring down toward the urinal with her lips pursed together and her eyes wide open in appreciative surprise at what she was seeing displayed down there. Some men were known to be unable to use the urinal under the gaze of the women in the paintings there because they would get an erection and be unable to pass water. Sally would eventually become the mayor of Sausalito and write her autobiography, *The Lady of the House*, which was later made into a TV movie.

9

The Music That Echoes
America's Heartbeat

In addition to the adventures experienced by Diana when working at the Valhalla and the two girls adjusting to a different culture in northern California, Diana and Christina found a mutual bond that held them together: music. They had already been fussing with each other for several years as Christina grew older and found new ways to mess up her space and Diana learned to further dislike Christina's lack of neatness. They could always put aside their irritation with each other through music. They saved their money, bought albums, and were always interested in the current rage in the world of music. They began to focus on some of their favorites, such as Bonnie Raitt, who became an inspiration to them, especially Christina. Christina bought every one of her albums, and the three would crank up the volume and dance around the apartment to Bonnie singing one of her country songs.

Deep inside the psyche of Diana and her girls lay a legacy of Kentucky bluegrass and country music with which Diana grew up in Ashland and to which Christina and Ashley were exposed. Diana was raised in the environment of Kentucky bluegrass and country or hillbilly or down-home music for the first twenty years of her life; that was the tradition of her people.

Kentucky is a particularly rich region musically, with songs and music dating back to the first pioneers to venture through the Cumberland Gap and settle in the hardwood forests and along the many rivers of this virgin territory. Ashland is situated on the Ohio River, not far from Cincinnati, at the corner of bluegrass country where Ohio, West Virginia, and Kentucky meet. Kentucky became a meeting ground for traditional music from the South and popular songs from the North. Ironically, years later, the melding of that music that would become known as the Nashville sound and would be Naomi and Wynonna's signature style. However, given the importance of radio broadcasting in making country, folk, bluegrass, and other music popular, Kentucky was deficient in stations that broadcast and promoted Kentucky's musical treasures.

Other places, however, such as Atlanta, Dallas, and Nashville, offered such programs as the *National Barn Dance* and the *Grand Ole Opry* broadcast over their radio stations. As a result, Kentucky talent such as Bradley Kincaid, Merle Travis, Bill Monroe, and Cliff Gross had to leave Kentucky to establish careers and make a living. That same situation appeared to hold true of the Judds. Leaving their native Kentucky affected the way they performed their music, and making it more universally acceptable to wider audiences.

Country music is the essence of the American experience. It tells stories of American men and women in powerful lyrics that reveal hidden parts of our national identity and, very often, painful aspects people are inclined to mask. Its stories and its poetry appear to be simple and are presented in narrative form by the performer that relates to a listener's experience. Its power is in its easy communication with the audience and its apparent simplicity, but most country artists will confess that it is done with great care, timing, and intonation so that the artistry seems artless.

A major theme common to much country music is home and those things related to it, such as loving relationships, loyalty, and the threat of betrayal or abandonment. The songs represent the nation's preoccupation with the values of home, from the rural idealism of agrarian America, to home and hearth as a haven in a heartless nineteenth-century world, to the twentieth-century affection for that "Little House on the Prairie." The home includes the dwelling as well as the people in it and those who live nearby. Since the country-music version of home is a constructed ideal, it usually does not include hard work or sickness or crop failure.

Visions of an ideal rural home continue today, even in the time of an industrialized America, and are the levee holding back the evils of the city, with its depravity and alienation. Country music reflects the American cultural anxiety about urbanization and technology supplanting human values and riches. Despite suspicions and fears, many Americans leave their homes in the country to experience city life, but once there, they feel lost and out of place and long to return to their birthplaces. In country music, the lure of the city gives in to a greater desire to return to "the authentic center of American life."

A paradox exists in American culture, and it is one that is given voice in country music. We see ourselves on the move, restless, mobile, as were the young Judds in their early years. Still, the idealized home maintains its strong embrace. The paradox comes alive in two songs found in Travis Tritt's *Country Club* album, beginning with "The Road Home," which tells the story of a man who cannot wait to get to the city. Once there, he forgets why he wanted so badly to be there and longs to go home. Then there is "Dixie Flyer," the name of a train, which is a song about a man who is restless and wants only to move ahead at high speed, to learn of the wider world, until he no longer is able to do so. All the while he is experiencing his adventures, the folks at home sit and watch the train go by.

These two songs offer contradictory images of home. The folks of the idealized version of home are not of the real world; they are mythical and exist only in the minds of those who tell their stories. The home folks, as seen from the road, however, are of the real world and live in the present. These two versions must remain separate, with the road symbolizing our culture and home symbolizing nature and the way God meant us to be, the first always changing and the second ever constant.

Since the "home" in country-music lyrics is something that most of us experience only in our imaginations, our yearning for the serenity and safety of home cannot ever be realized. The road represents the course we have chosen to pursue, having left home behind in a place—our minds—to which we can never return. This accounts for much of the melancholy in country music—it is almost a forlorn wail for something we have left behind and to which we can never return.

Country music was originated in the South and Southeast at the founding of the thirteen original colonies and the new, independent America by people who were poor or mavericks seeking opportunities, first in the new colonies and later, beyond the Appalachians, where land was either free or cheap. Land was the magnet that drew settlers through the Cumberland Gap, following Daniel Boone from Virginia into what would become Kentucky and Tennessee. Of course, what is now the state of Georgia was originally founded by the British crown as a penal colony to which debtors were transported.

It was these early, mostly English settlers who brought with them their music, their ballads, and their musical instruments from the British Isles as they settled in the South. Even at the beginning of this century—a hundred or more years after these settlers had moved west into the Appalachians—researchers found that traditional Anglo-Celtic ballads were being sung, just as they had been in seventeenth- and eighteenth-century Britain. These British ballads mixed with the songs and experiences of other kinds of American music, such as the German and Spanish folk music of the American Southwest, and the jazz and blues from the black slave communities in the South, particularly New Orleans and along the Mississippi River. The musical instruments of country music evolved from the same sources: The fiddle and mandolin were typically Anglo-Celtic, the guitar was from Spanish Mexico, and the banjo stemmed from African-American sources.

Slave music had strong religious overtones, since the church was the central point of black life then. The Christian church was the only institution slave owners permitted their slaves, and the church was, and remains, central to the fabric of black life, the black community, and black music. Certainly the emotional quality of black music and spirituals had an effect on how country music emerged and is sung.

Most historians say that country music began mostly among the rural poor whites, who brought folk music from Elizabethan England, Scotland, and Ireland. It came to the isolated hills and villages of southeastern America, where it remained for a couple of centuries while it became Americanized and began to reflect the New World, new work, and new circumstances. One researcher, Cecil Sharp, was astonished to discover in 1917 that in the hills of Tennessee and Virginia, around the town of Bristol (notable for its Main Street being the boundary line between those two states), mountain folk were accurately singing English folk ballads from seventeenth- and eighteenth-century England.

Of course, some things did change. For example, references to sex were acceptable in the original English lyrics of some folk songs but were not when they crossed the ocean and moved into America's hill country. Other changes included shortening the old ballads and making them more personal and emotional once they arrived in America. Ballads that in the original English version might run thirty to forty stanzas or more were reduced to three or four, and tales of death, desertion, and destruction were given more circumspect lyrics, often with a reference to God's role in our lives, as befitted the Puritan ethics of the New World.

Another influence on country music came from nineteenth-century popular entertainment. Minstrel shows and later vaudeville helped to popularize songs, performance techniques, and arrangements that were incorporated into country music. In a minstrel show the music was performed by white entertainers in blackface, telling jokes, singing songs, and performing longer, dramatic pieces—a major form of entertainment throughout the country in the nineteenth century and early twentieth century. It was gradually replaced by the vaudeville show in the 1880s, which was different in that it was a collection of unrelated musicians, jugglers, acrobats, comedians, and dancers.

Vaudeville had all kinds of singers, for example, and the music presented was a mixture of popular songs from the North and country folk songs of the South. Vaudeville theater circuits spread throughout the country, and the fiddle was the main instrument for playing country and folk for much of the time. The banjo was common among black musical groups and thus not considered proper for upper-class white entertainment. Another instrument, the guitar, was imported from Spain and considered more appropriate for much of the 1800s until 1902, when the Gibson Company began popularizing its highly regarded guitars and mandolins in order to increase its sales.

Breakthroughs in new technology led to the first mechanical recordings of country music. Originally, Edison cylinders, then the flat 78 rpm discs, or records, and finally, and most significantly, radio, which brought it to millions of people starting in 1922.

The problem facing early radio was the same one that radio and TV broadcasting has faced from its invention to this day: programming. Where does one find enough interesting programs to fill all the airtime? An early solution for the young, burgeoning radio industry was music. The first station began, as we noted, in 1922, and within two years there were hundreds of radio stations; today there are over ten thousand in the United States. At about the same time, Thomas Edison was developing the commercial phonograph, but country music didn't appeal to the early recording companies because they figured country meant just that—namely, that the people who liked country music were just hillbillies who were living in the sticks and the hills and too poor to own a phonograph or buy records. The first major country-music program that was broadcast regularly with a live audience in the studio was a radio barn-dance program aired on Saturday nights over WBAP in Fort Worth, Texas, beginning on January 4, 1923.

To the surprise of the budding recording industry, a modest record by a country musician, Fiddlin' John Carson, did remarkably well, and programmers suddenly decided that perhaps there was money in country music, at least some of it. Thus, music scouts began touring places like Tennessee and Kentucky looking for country talent, or as they were called then, either folk or hillbilly singers. The first real country-music superstar was Marion Try Slaughter, who came out of East Texas to New York City in 1912, changed his name to Vernon Dalhart, and pursued a career as a popular stage and opera singer. He was only moderately successful and was looking for a way to energize his waning career through expanding his repertoire of song styles, moving first into black-dialect songs and then, almost by accident, into what would become his breakthrough country-music record.

Some historians believe Dalhart was the first of a long line of American pop singers who would undergo what would later be called "the Nashville Treatment," which involved a pop singer pumping up his waning career by switching to country music. The next country star and a musician who was country from the start was Riley Puckett, who had been blinded as a child and grew up singing country songs on street corners and at parties so he could earn a living. By 1922 he had a radio show on Atlanta's WSB that ultimately established him nationally as a country singer. However, it was Dalhart's success with two country songs that woke up Tin Pan Alley music promoters in New York. Dalhart cut a record for a skeptical Victor Records of "The Wreck of the Old 97" on one side and "The Prisoner's Song" on the other. Victor executives were stunned when Dalhart's recording sold 6 million copies.

After discovering that millions of people enjoyed, and would pay money for, country-music records, the Victor Company went looking for more of this kind of music and in July 1927 sent Ralph Peer to Bristol with his wife, two engineers, and a load of recording equipment. Peer had been in the recording business a couple of years before with a company called Okeh but quit to start an apple-pie-baking company that failed, and now he had the idea to do field recordings of country or hillbilly songs. They weren't going to wait until country folk artists wandered up to New York's Tin Pan Alley. They would bring Tin Pan Alley to country music. Coincidentally, it was the successor to the old Victor Company, RCA Victor, that would give the Judds their first commercial contract.

Meanwhile, Peer rented an old hat factory in downtown Bristol, draped it with blankets to muffle sound, and set up recording equipment. Then he planted a story in the Sunday paper that he planned to record hillbilly music. He already had lined up some talent from an earlier scouting trip, including Earnest "Pop"

Stoneman and his family. The story resulted in a flood of phone calls to Bristol and scores of mountain musicals submitted to "the record man." During the beginning stage of modern country music's development, it was never referred to by that title, but, rather, by a variety of other names, such as Old-Time Tunes, Familiar Tunes—Old and New; Songs for Dixie; Old Southern Tunes; Old Familiar Tunes and Novelties; Southern Fiddling and Song Records; Mountain Ballads; and Old-Time Southern Songs. Northern journalists and the record-buying public persisted in calling it hillbilly music, and a story in a 1926 issue of *Variety* associated the music with North Carolina, Tennessee, and adjacent mountain areas and stated that it was "played by illiterate whites obsessed with the Bible."

A. P. Carter and his family lived in the mountains of Virginia, where he made a living as a combination farmer, carpenter, and fruit-tree salesman. He, his wife, and his sister-in-law had been singing at mountain get-togethers for about ten years when he heard about Peer and his recording session in nearby Bristol. So he loaded up his family in his model A, and they headed through the twenty-five muddy miles for Bristol and country-music history. Peer and his wife and engineers were a little taken aback when A. P.'s wife, Sara, and very pregnant sister-in-law Maybelle showed up, along with three children.

Peer's wife took the youngsters and entertained them with talk and ice cream while A. P., Sara, and Maybelle cut an astonishing six records, with Sara singing lead on five of them. Peer knew the minute she opened her mouth that he had a winner. The sides recorded that day included "Bury Me Under the Weeping Willow," "Little Log Cabin by the Sea," and "Single Girl, Married Girl."

The Carters' easy-flowing church-harmony style made them the first successful country vocal group, even though they didn't achieve great financial success for several years. In time, however, they became a legendary group responsible for "Wabash Cannonball," "I Am Thinking Tonight of My Blue Eyes," and "Worried Man Blues." Although by the end of the 1930s they had approximately 270 records in circulation and were famous worldwide, they never became rich. The Carter family, as a group, finally broke up in 1943, with Maybelle performing with her daughters into the 1960s and A. P. singing with his children until he died in 1960. Daughter June Carter became a long time regular on the *Grand Ole Opry* and wound up marrying Johnny Cash.

Astonishingly, during the same recording sessions Ralph Peer held in Bristol with the Carter family, he also discovered, two days later, one of the mythical talents in twentieth-century country-music history. His name was Jimmie Rodgers, and he became the first country-music star, in the modern meaning of that phrase. Rodgers distinguished himself by melding several different elements of rural southern music into a distinctly identifiable style, adding, curiously, an imitation of the Swiss yodel that he dubbed "the blue yodel" and which became his trademark.

Other performers, such as Fiddlin' John Carson and Vernon Dalhart, had been early big sellers, but Rodgers was consistently the biggest of this era and—the mark of a star—could sell records solely on the basis of his name. His music was noted for the strong influence of the blues. His recording stardom began with that Peer session in Bristol in 1927 and lasted for the next six years, during which he sold an unprecedented 20 million records. He wrote most of the songs himself and had an impact on many of the country-and-western stars who followed him during the next ten or 15 years, including Ernest Tubb, Jimmie Davis, and Gene Autry.

When the Great Depression hit America, it sharply cut into the record business for some years, with sales nosediving from 107 million records sold in 1927 to only 6 million in 1932. As America began to recover, so did the country-music business, first with stars performing the same rural country melodies, such as the Monroe Brothers, the Blue Sky Boys, and J. E. Mainer; then cowboy tunes from the West and Southwest began edging into the repertoires, ushering in such acts as the Cowboy Ramblers as well as musical themes of the polka, jazz, and blues, with improvisation—common already with jazz—becoming significant. What was emerging toward the end of the 1930s was a new form of country-and-western music, along with big bands playing dance music that was called western swing.

WSB radio in Atlanta is a good example of the spectacular

marriage between radio and country music that is still vital even today. The first popularization of country music came from the recording industry during the 1920s, but with its explosion in America during the late 1920s and the 1930s, radio became the most important medium for promoting country music. The first commercial radio station was KDKA in Pittsburgh, which began broadcasting in 1922. By the end of that year, there were 510 radio stations on the air, with 89 of them located in the South. WSB in Atlanta was one of the very first commercial stations.

Country music, however, first became a major element of programming at WBAP in Fort Worth, Texas, starting in January 1923, and was beamed by a powerful signal that could be heard from Hawaii to New York and from Mexico to Canada. Soon two big barn-dance programs featuring country music hit the airwaves from different parts of the country. One was the *National Barn Dance* out of WLS in Chicago, starting on April 12, 1924, a station owned by Sears, Roebuck whose call letters stood for "World's Largest Store."

The main announcer for the *National Barn Dance* was an ex-Memphis newspaper man, George D. Hays; he quit to move to Nashville to work for WSM, which called itself "the Air Castle of the South." The station was owned by the National Life and Accident Insurance Company (WSM stood for "We Shield Millions"), and it was one of the most powerful stations in America, with 100,000 watts broadcasting on a clear-channel wavelength.

In late 1925, Hays experimented with putting a seventy-seven-year-old country fiddler on the air for an hour, Uncle Jimmy Thompson. The response was electrifying and stunned the executives at WSM. One month later, three days after Christmas, 1925, and a few weeks after the station went on the air for the first time, Hays broadcast an imitation of the *National Barn Dance*, playing country music every Saturday night to an enthusiastic radio audience that didn't, however, include some of Nashville's city fathers. These civic leaders could not countenance a hillbilly image for their city when they had been fostering the idea of an academic, intellectual Nashville as the "Athens of the South."

The rest is country history except for one more footnote about how Hays made an off-hand remark during a performance in December 1927, two years after its inception, when his show followed a grand-opera broadcast. He said that his show was "Grand Ole Opry," and the name stuck for the next seventy-one years. The *Grand Old Opry* went on to strike a chord with radio listeners throughout the country, especially with those whose musical tastes weren't being met by radio stations in mass markets.

The *Grand Ole Opry*, and Nashville because of it, became the emotional center of America's country-music business long before that became a fact in Nashville itself. The *Opry's* huge following led it to move several times in its first two decades in search of a larger space for its performers and growing audience. From a small parlor initially, it moved to two other locations within National Insurance's own building and even tried out some local theaters and, once, a revival tent in East Nashville. In 1941 the *Opry* finally came to its best-known location, on Lower Broadway, at the 3,500-seat Ryman Auditorium. It remained there for thirty-three years, then it was moved again to the Opryland country-theme amusement park in 1974.

In spite of the success of some early performers and radio shows, it wasn't easy being a country musician in those earlier years when even on the *Grand Ole Opry* performers got paid only five dollars a week. They had to hang in there through the birth of the recording and radio industries, the Great Depression, the postwar boom, and up until today.

In the early days of radio broadcasting, during the 1920s, the federal government immediately saw that radio could reach and influence millions of Americans. It immediately regulated radio, claiming that the airwaves belonged to the people of the United States and therefore Congress must control them. One of the laws passed, which was designed to prevent the spread of alien propaganda, forbade a foreigner from owning a broadcasting property. For most of the other regulations, Congress quickly borrowed the interstate commerce laws that regulated trucking and applied them to broadcasting, and also assigned different levels of power permitted to various stations.

Out of the hundreds of licenses granted by the newly created

Federal Communications Commission (FCC) in those early years, fifty of the most powerful signals, 50,000 watts, were set aside for certain stations in various parts of the country, with no other station permitted to broadcast on that particular wavelength. Known as "50,000-watt, clear-channel stations," they could be heard for thousands of miles, particularly at night. At first, many of the country-music, barn-dance programs were aired on these clear-channel stations, such as WLS in Chicago, WSM in Nashville, and WWVA in Wheeling, West Virginia, and spread the sound of country music over the North American continent.

The dissemination of country music by records and then radio received an unexpected boost from the Great Depression by an odd strike that began in 1940 and disrupted the entire American music business. Songwriters, unlike book authors, newsmen, and magazine-article writers, had been organized into a union so that they could be paid every time one of their compositions was played on the radio or a jukebox or by a musical group. This union was called the American Society of Composers, Authors and Publishers (ASCAP), and whenever one of its members' works was played, ASCAP collected a fee, which was later paid (in part at least) to the artist. In connection with this system, ASCAP had a contract with the major radio networks and radio stations—which were banded together in the National Association of Broadcasters (NAB)—which expired in 1940.

There were many musical artists that ASCAP didn't bother with because of its generally elitist attitude in those days and its disinclination to deal with modern symphonic composers and many country-and-western composers. In addition, the broadcasters were annoyed with ASCAP because it tended to be heavy-handed and difficult in its licensing dealings with broadcasters. Therefore, before the ASCAP contract expired, the broadcasters formed their own music-licensing organization called Broadcast Music Inc. (BMI) and hired the radio-station manager from KFI in Los Angeles, Carl Haverlin, as its first president. He held the job for the next twenty or thirty years until he retired.

BMI rushed in to sign up a lot of artists neglected by ASCAP, ranging from Bela Bartok to many country-and-western composers and performers. When the ASCAP contract expired in 1940, the broadcasters sat tight to see what would happen. That's what they would do for the next nine months, during which ASCAP forbade the playing of any of the show tunes and popular songs it licensed. Broadcasters played either songs no longer under copyright or songs that were BMI songs. The result was that most of 1940 was known as the era of "Jeanie With the Light Brown Hair." That was one of many Stephen Foster songs not in copyright, and there were lots of country-and-western songs played and often sung by the popular singers of the day. The year before the ASCAP strike, NBC started broadcasting a half-hour segment of the *Grand Ole Opry* to millions of listeners, with the result that Roy Acuff, with his rural country songs, was soon a nationally acclaimed performer and star. By the time World War II ended, country music could be heard throughout the nation, with some six hundred radio stations devoting at least part of their play list to country songs. "Official" recognition of country-and-western music began to appear in such journals as *Billboard*.

There was more than one style of country music. There was the newer western swing style, and there was the older rural style that was Roy Acuff's specialty. In addition, there was a more popular type favored by artists Eddy Arnold and Red Foley and a bluegrass kind of country music from the Kentucky region where the Judds lived that was popularized by Bill Monroe. In the early 1940s, Ernest Tubb began to play and sing like the late Jimmie Rodgers, that is, a rougher presentation of tough emotional stories about drinking too much, chasing around too much, and the despair of infidelity and divorce. This music got to be known as "honky-tonk" after the bars where the songs were performed.

Another disciple of Jimmie Rodgers was the man who became a very popular movie cowboy, businessman, radio station, and baseball-team owner, Gene Autry. In the 1930s this former telegrapher for the St. Louis and Frisco Railroad Company of Oklahoma recorded "I Left My Gal in the Mountains." Autry's rendition went on to become one of the top recordings of the year, and Autry eventually became a movie star.

Through subsequent Hollywood western movies, singing

cowboys like Gene Autry and Roy Rogers would unite country music and western movies, thereby unwittingly creating what would become known as the country-western music genre. The two forms of music, country and western, were historically distinct, but through the magic of Hollywood, they became one in the minds of millions of people. At the end of the war, no particular part of the nation could claim to be the center of country music. Hollywood, Chicago, New York, the Appalachian Mountain states, and Texas all had significant connections to it. All that would change in just five years, from 1945 to 1950, when Nashville was transformed into the mecca of country music, even if that's not what the city fathers had in mind. What did it can be summarized in three words: *Grand Ole Opry*.

The *Grand Ole Opry* and George Hay, "the Solemn Old Judge," had been competing for radio supremacy with the *National Barn Dance* in Chicago for some years, and in time the *Opry* began drawing and holding the audiences better. Later, Ryman Hall in Nashville, where the *Opry* was based, became the place to be on Saturday night. One can never be quite sure just what was the magical moment or the magical act. For example, did major country stars want to appear on the *Grand Ole Opry* instead of the *National Barn Dance* because it was the better of the two, or was it the *Opry* the better of the two because major country stars were appearing on it? The answer to both questions is probably yes. Some say it was George Hay's smart management, and others say it was the *Opry* leading the way with new trends in country-music programming.

For example, in the 1920s and 1930s the emphasis in radio barn dances was on instrumentals, with songs and singing taking a backseat until the arrival of Roy Acuff, who got into country music because of a sunstroke. He was an old Tennessee boy who grew up playing baseball and was on the verge of signing a professional contract with the New York Giants when he was felled by too much sun. During his long recovery, he learned to play and love the fiddle, and by the time he recovered from sunstroke, he decided he would rather play music than baseball.

After knocking around a bit with various acts and in various towns, he ended up as a regular on the *Grand Ole Opry* and lead the shift of emphasis from instrumental-dominated programs to vocals. By 1943, Roy was the highest-paid country-music entertainer in America, having sold 30 million records and pulling down $200,000 a year for singing his old standards, such as "Wabash Cannonball," "Wreck on the Highway," "Night Train to Memphis," "The Precious Jewel," "Unloved and Unclaimed," and "The Great Speckled Bird."

Following in Acuff's footsteps was Bill Monroe, the king of bluegrass, and Hank Snow. Of course, WSM, which broadcast the *Opry*, had a signal that reached Hawaii and Canada. That is where a young man in Nova Scotia first heard it and became determined to star on the *Grand Ole Opry* someday. That's just what Hank Snow did. He wasn't the only listener to travel a great distance to be in Nashville and witness a live performance of the *Opry*. Almost a million people do it every year.

With the *Grand Ole Opry* as a magnet in Nashville, country stars began moving their homes and their business to the Tennessee community. Such performers as Eddy Arnold, Roy Acuff, Red Foley, Ernest Tubb, Bill Monroe, Hank Williams, Webb Pierce, and Marty Robbins became a common sight in town. Following the trend, the two oldest Judd women would set up housekeeping in nearby Franklin. In a relatively short time, the whole business infrastructure of the country recording business moved to Nashville—publishers, record companies, tour bookers, and all the other people that made up the country-music industry, starting with Roy Acuff and the Smokey Mountain Boys, from Knoxville, Tennessee, who came to Nashville in 1938 and by 1939 found themselves in the lead spot on the *Opry*. Acuff's recordings of "The Great Speckled Bird" and "Steel Guitar Blues" in 1937 rocketed him to the Top Five in country sales for that year, and these songs were recorded on the American Record Corporation label, which was soon bought out by Columbia Records.

Soon many other large, New York–based record labels established their presence in the South by buying small regional labels. In a short time, Nashville became the center of country music in America, independently of the *Grand Ole Opry*, which would ultimately move out of the old Ryman Auditorium to a bigger and better place in a *Grand Ole Opry* theme park in another part of Nashville. At about this time all the various names for country music, such as hillbilly, folk, and the rest, were consolidated and called country and western. It can also be noted that the early American view of folk musicians coming from the Southern Bible belt may have had some validity, since Nashville is also the religious and Bible-publishing center of America.

During World War II people migrated to different parts of the country to help in the war effort; millions of others joined the armed forces. As a result, country music spread to sections of America and to enormous groups of Americans who hadn't heard it before, with the result that it became vastly more popular than before. So popular, in fact, that television producers, always sensitive to public taste, started booking country stars, such as Hank Williams, Eddy Arnold and Roy Acuff, on national television programs. Country performers became successful by keeping track of what the public liked. As a result, melodies such as "Cold, Cold Heart," "Your Cheatin' Heart," and "I Can't Help It," by Hank Williams, became so-called crossover hits when they were recorded by such popular stars as Tony Bennett, Guy Mitchell, and Frankie Laine. Before long, Hank Williams was touring all around the country, becoming a star, with many city fans in addition to his cadre of country followers. His rocketlike career of six years of stardom was cut short by his untimely death in 1952.

There were other landmark occasions to measure the sweep of country music into the popular domain. Ernest Tubb brought a *Grand Ole Opry* show to New York City, performing in Carnegie Hall in 1947. Tubb and Eddy Arnold were setting sales records and were now on the same level as the better-known pop-music artists, with Ernest earning $50,000 in the first half of 1947 and Eddy Arnold pulling in an astonishing $2,700,000 for that year. Part of their success may have been due to lyrics becoming racier, for they were now singing about drunkenness and cheating in love with such songs as "There Stands the Glass" and "Slippin Around" as well as "I'm Movin On," "If You've Got the Money, I've Got the Time," and "The Wild Side of Life."

While country music could be heard throughout the country, another form of popular music suddenly came out of the country format and would sweep the nation and edge out country music. A young truck driver and country-music singer named Elvis Presley sang country music from about 1954 to 1956. Soon he would be in the forefront of a pop-music revolution that contained touches of country and black-rhythm songs. The new music would be labeled rock and roll and would push country music off the charts and radio as stations shifted formats to made room for it. Country, however, wasn't going to stand still in the face of the rock challenge. By the mid-1950s, it was a big music industry, and a lot of people had a great deal at stake. It responded in basically two ways and with one objective, namely, to change the country sound into something else that people liked more.

One group of performers—Marty Robbins, Sonny James, and the Everly Brothers—decided to meld a rock sound with country so that it would be more appealing to a younger audience. Doing so made sense to them because they were among the younger country entertainers of this era. The second decision involved taking the hard banjo-and-fiddle sound out of the music and giving it a more popular, fuller cascade. Thus, the fiddles, banjos, and steel guitars were packed away, and out came the piano, the violins, and a backup chorus for a lusher sound. This change put the new country-music approach between classic country and easy-listening pop music, and it was dubbed "the Nashville sound." More important than the new name, it worked with Jim Reeve's classic "Four Walls." Created in 1957 for RCA, "Four Walls" became the forerunner of this new approach. It was produced by Chet Atkins, who has been a powerful figure in the country-music business for a long time in addition to being a major artist himself.

The new Nashville sound clicked and was quickly imitated by other country artists. By the early 1960s, country artists were crossing over and over again into the popular-music market with what turned out to be big sellers and hits. Some of the hits were Johnny Horton's "Battle of New Orleans," Hank Locklin's "Please Help Me, I'm Falling," the legendary Patsy Cline's "Crazy," and Jimmy Dean's "Big Bad John." Predictably, this Nashville sound

Smiling Wynonna at the 1995 Fan Fair, Tennessee State Fairgrounds, Nashville
(Tammie Arroyo)

Wynonna in front of the huge Wynonna billboard at the 1994 Fan Fair, Tennessee State Fairgrounds, Nashville (Tammie Arroyo)

(*Above*) Naomi Judd with husband Larry Strickland, all dressed up (Darlene Hammond)

(*Right*) The littlest Judd, Ashley, with romantic interest Michael Bolton (Darlene Hammond)

(*Right*) Wynonna along with Vince Gill at the Country Star restaurant in Las Vegas (Tammie Arroyo)

(*Below*) All-star country music threesome: Wynonna and Naomi Judd along with Garth Brooks (Darlene Hammond)

(*Above*) The three Judds together: Wynonna, Ashley, and Naomi (Gregg Deguire)

(*Left*) Wynonna on her Harley-Davidson motorcycle at the City of Hope softball game, June 6, 1993 at Greer Stadium, Tennessee (Tammie Arroyo/Celebrity Photo)

(*Above*) Wynonna and
Naomi Judd with Bob
and Delores Hope at
taping of the Bob Hope
Christmas TV Special
(Tammie Arroyo)

(*Right*) The Judds
(Ashley, Wynonna and
Naomi) at the twenty-
eighth annual Country
Music Association
Awards in the Grand
Ole Opry Theater,
Nashville (Tammie
Arroyo)

Wynonna Judd at her induction in the Country Music Walk of Fame, Nashville (Tammie Arroyo)

A study in white elegance: the singing Judds, Naomi and Wynonna (Darlene Hammond)

Wynonna on stage at Mesa Marin Raceway, Bakersfield, California, October 7, 1993
(Tammie Arroyo)

(*Above*) The Judds with their awards from the Academy of Country Music at a ceremony at the Knott's Berry Farm in Buena Park, California (Tammie Arroyo)

(*Left*) Wynonna in front of the Country Star Restaurant, Las Vegas (Tammie Arroyo)

helped the music business boom in, of all places, Nashville, which, along with New York and Los Angeles, had become one of the three largest centers for recording albums in the country.

Country-music loyalists continued to play what in the mid-1960s was called "hard country," meaning that it was the classic country sound still loved by the old-time country fans, even though it may not have had the widespread following it enjoyed after World War II. This hard-country rebellion against the Nashville sound would continue for years and even in 1998 was spearheaded by such notable artists as Willie Nelson and Johnny Cash. It was that honky-tonk sound, and it was being played, ironically, by a core of California country artists whose loyal fans were Southerners. These musicians had moved to the Golden State during the hard times of the Great Depression or to find war work during World War II. This California crowd included Buck Owens, Merle Haggard, and Wynn Stewart. They employed the fiddle and steel guitar in their music as part of their sound mix, which gave it that distinctive old-time flavor. They also eschewed the lush choruses and other pop instruments and rarely did crossover songs. They were oldtime country-music purists who dismissed the Nashville sound as phony and gimmicky.

Indeed, some younger artists such as Ray Price and Faron Young agreed, and instead of playing the new country sounds went back to the genuine older versions. Of course, everybody was looking for a niche that would distinguish them from the competition, whether it meant moving in a new direction or standing still.

Some of the country artists adopted the concept of the Nashville sound in that they left behind classic country music, but performers like Johnny Cash added some elements of folk music into his characteristic style. Others also blended in some bluegrass to create a variation of the Nashville sound. They included such writers-singers as Willy Nelson, with his "Blue Eyes Cryin' in the Rain" and "Funny How Time Slips Away." This group of innovators included Tom T. Hall doing "Harper Valley PTA," Roger Miller and his "King of the Road," and by the time the 1970s came along, Kris Kristofferson. There were also attempts to merge country and rock into something called country rock, featuring the Flying Burrito Brothers and Poco.

None of these variations seemed to catch on or match the popularity of the Nashville sound, which was decidedly easier on the ear for most people and became the style of other artists, such as Glen Campbell and Charley Pride. Even Ray Price decided to abandon his experiment into honky-tonk and go back to the Nashville sound, but some refused and stuck to their own musical styles.

This later group became known for a time as the Outlaws and included Waylon Jennings, Willie Nelson, and several others. They performed in T-shirts and jeans and thought the fancy clothes and hairdos of the Nashville crowd were phony. This outlaw contingent appealed to a strong segment of the listening audience and was particularly successful from the end of the 1970s to the middle of the 1980s, but the Nashville sound didn't go away. It still had many fans, and the easygoing crowd made many of the Nashville artists very popular, including Ronnie Milsap, Anne Murray, Kenny Rogers, Conway Twitty, Alabama, Loretta Lynn, Crystal Gayle, and Dolly Parton.

The Outlaws were just one of many independent groups that did what they liked and showed that country music was flexible enough to allow them to do that. The core of country music— honky-tonk, blue grass, traditional—was always there, and artists drifted in and out of the adaptations and variations that suited them and that sold their records. George Strait made a name for himself in the early 1980s with a derivation of western swing music. John Anderson going back to hillbilly and Ricky Skaggs, to blue-grass, so the focus kept changing, but the Nashville sound continued to be popular.

A major influence came on the air and into millions of homes in 1984 with the launching of the CMT-TV channel, which early on featured back-to-tradition country music with Randy Travis and Dwight Yoakam. Then came a country-music phenomenon, Garth Brooks, with a style he called new country. He attracted millions of new fans. An example of his popularity was *No Fences*, his second album, which sold some 10 million copies within the first year. His third album, *Ropin' the Wind*, did equally well.

Naomi and Wynonna came along with the right distinctive sound. When they entered the mainstream country-music business in the mid-1980s, the sound had become completely urbanized and moved far from its rural-only roots. It dominated American radio, with twenty-five hundred stations devoted to country music, 43 million fans, and record sales around $1.5 billion. The singing Judds were boarding the country-music express at the right time.

10

The Birth of a Woman
Named Naomi

DIANA HAD ARRIVED AT A PLACE in her life where she needed to make a personal commitment to herself or perhaps reinvent an image of herself that was more appropriate to the life she intended to lead. She left her husband, her parents' broken home, and dead brother, Brian, behind while she psychically pioneered a new life for herself and her two daughters. A key to crossing such a Rubicon was change, and that's what she wanted now. It came to her that a name had always been important, that it meant nothing until you gave it meaning. There is, indeed, an ancient and mystical belief that things don't actually exist until you give them a name.

Although Diana was a name that was given to her, she felt she had changed, that a lot of water had flowed down the river since her Ashland days and that she had grown into a woman who actually didn't know that little small-town country girl named Diana. She decided to change her name and wanted one that would symbolize who she was and what she was striving to be. But to what?

A name and a mystical connection echoed from the past, and for a moment Diana was back in the basement of Crabbe Grade School, looking at that pretty but bewildered, mentally challenged girl with the name that stuck in Diana's head until years later: Naomi. She loved the story in the Bible her mother had told her. The biblical Naomi followed her husband to a strange land where she was widowed with two daughters-in-law. She roamed in search of a home and eventually found one in her former homeland but left one daughter-in-law behind and found her reward with the help of the one remaining. It was symbolic of what was happening among the three Judd women.

Naomi was a woman who symbolized courage and fidelity in the face of loss and adversity and decided to return to her own people so as not to be a burden on her two daughters-in-law, Orpah and Ruth. But Ruth and Naomi were so devoted and loyal to each other that Ruth insisted on staying with Naomi and spoke to her words of devotion that have captured the human spirit for thousands of years afterward: "For whither thou goest, I will go; and where thou lodgest, I will lodge: thy people shall be my people, and thy God my God: Where thou diest, I will die, and there will I be buried."

Thus it was in Sausalito, California, that 32-year-old Diana Judd Ciminella, empathizing with the struggles of a biblical character with two children, became Naomi Judd.

The strange part was still to come. When Naomi petitioned the courts for an official name change, she learned that she had never signed the final dissolution papers with her husband and was therefore still married to him. Even so, Naomi registered at the College of Marin, and for the first time she was introducing herself as Naomi Judd. Naomi preferred this nursing college, which focused more attention on prevention and patient awareness. She also acquired valuable practical experience at Kaiser Hospital in Oakland, where she would help deliver babies and talk drug addicts into cooperating with their program. She really took a liking to nursing and seemed to be a natural.

She began to learn about the connection between mind and body and how stress can directly affect one physically. This knowledge put Naomi into a philosophical and spiritual frame of mind. Often when Naomi would take the girls for walks they would discuss such weighty topics as the meaning of life and who is God and does He or She exist. Naomi tried to be a part of her girls' everyday existence and attempted to meet all of their friends and their friends' parents. Before allowing thirteen-year-old Christina to baby-sit, Naomi insisted on meeting the parents of the children she was to watch. Soon after, Christina wanted to change her name, too. She said, "When I discovered music, I felt like I took on a whole new identity." She became Wynonna, which she picked from the song "Route 66." Nine-year-old Ashley agreed to go back to Judd but didn't want a new first name.

Naomi was now working days as a waitress and attending nursing school evenings, getting no more than three or four hours sleep a night. Even so, Naomi did complete her nurse's training, obtained a license in the state of California, and began to earn money as a nurse. One of the first things she did was to give Wynonna professional music lessons. Soon they began hanging around local musicians and occasionally singing, including making a record together at Tres Virgos studios. The Marin County area was like an upscale Morrill, Kentucky. Wynonna had become wrapped up in her music to the detriment of her schoolwork and house chores. Wynonna wanted to quit school and study music full-time, but Naomi refused.

The holidays arrived again, and Thanksgiving, 1977, turned out to be rather depressing because Wynonna and Ashley missed Grandpa and Grandma, who were on the verge of divorce. The three finished their meal in thirty minutes and then had nothing to do. When Christmas arrived, Naomi sent the girls to visit their friends in Los Angeles, where they were able to stay with Nancy, their old neighbor. Naomi was alone and set out to see somebody she knew in a town north of Sausalito called Petaluma, but as she drove the mountainous roads, she hit something wet or slick on the road, the car fishtailed, and before she knew what was going on, she realized that her vehicle was facing oncoming traffic. She was slammed up against the door and must have become unconscious, for she couldn't remember anything until she heard some workers prying open the car door.

Naomi was rushed to the hospital, and the doctor informed her that she had a compressed fracture to her lumbar vertebrae. She wasn't able to either feel or move her legs and wondered if the condition would be permanent. While still on the gurney, Naomi called her friend Nancy in Los Angeles to tell her what happened and sent her love to Wynonna and Ashley. Naomi stayed in the hospital for a week and was then placed in a full back brace. She spent a month recovering at her apartment with the two girls. Three months later, Naomi was up and about, hitting the dance floor with her new friend Asia Lee, who was in the hospital at the same time as Naomi.

There was no money coming from Polly or her paternal grandparents, and Michael Junior had moved to Ocala, Florida, working in marketing and advertising thoroughbred horses. Naomi continued to wait tables and earned extra money doing freelance photo shoots around San Francisco. When she got a little ahead, she bought herself a flashy red-and-white vintage 1957 Chevy for eighteen hundred dollars, and even though she had to be careful with the money, she sprang for another twenty-five dollars to get vanity plates that said "Red-Hot." It was typical Naomi. Her looks, her car, and her license plates made people stare everywhere she went, which was something Naomi always enjoyed.

In any event, she was now saving a little money, which gave her both the incentive and the inclination to look around for other opportunities. The nursing would be a means by which to support herself and her little family, but she had grander ideas and was always reaching for the brass ring, which was symptomatic of her personality. Most single mothers would be satisfied to have a steady job and to keep a low, conservative profile, staying out of trouble. That was not the way with Naomi. She had dreams, and they would not be fulfilled emptying bedpans or staying home baking cookies.

11

Hillbilly Women

AT ABOUT THIS TIME Naomi began to think about forming a band, with Ashley, Wynonna, and herself as the singers and guitar players. She would call the band Hillbilly Women. She enrolled Wynonna for guitar lessons and bought herself an Ibáñez guitar and Ashley a fiddle. Naomi had a secret agenda—most mothers do. She thought that Ashley felt like an outsider whenever she and Wynonna would sing and play music. Starting a band might be a way to include Ashley and help the family bond. She and Wynonna could play, and Naomi was sure her very bright daughter Ashley could quickly master an instrument. The first song the threesome learned was "Old Joe Clark."

Ashley gave the fiddle a chance, but her interests were focused elsewhere. She preferred horseback riding with her girlfriends Juli Gensley and Elesha Wright, not playing in a band with her mother and sister. A musical inclination got lost along the way with Ashley.

There was a marked personality difference with Ashley, too. She had a free and easy style that made it easy for her to mix with and communicate with people. She was very much like Naomi part of the time but not like Wynonna any of the time. Wynonna was much more withdrawn and introspective. Ashley could and would speak her mind without offending anyone. Whereas she was able to listen without appearing bored, Naomi and Wynonna would fluctuate in their ability to communicate well.

The relationship between Wynonna and her mother was volatile and somewhat unpredictable. Tempers could be short, and emotional rockets would often explode. Mother and daughter would get into some real shouting matches. It characterized their lifelong relationship and began to surface when Wynonna was an early teen and has continued to this day. The music made an enormous difference in that it broke down barriers between mother and daughter and magically created a separate kingdom to which they could retreat and merge in a battle-free zone of harmony and sheer pleasure. It was a place both of them enjoyed. They would invite friends over for dinner and perform or simply roll out a blanket during the afternoon and play into nightfall.

In time, Wynonna improved her guitar playing, inspiring Pete Adams, her teacher, to bring her, Naomi, and Ashley to his Tres Virgos studio for a recording session. Pete had built the modest studio over a garage in the Marin Country community of Mill Valley with some of his friends, including a guitar player, Mike Stevens, who was also the founder of a regional music magazine, *BAM* (Bay Area Music). The three women rehearsed at the studio and did some practice recording. Naomi and Mike also started dating.

Even though Ashley wasn't into the music like her mother and sister, the three were learning and improving their singing together, particularly Naomi and Wynonna. These two women were so immersed in the music scene that Naomi added a course in engineering to the curriculum she was taking at the College of Marin so that she could learn the technical side of the recording business. She audited the course, which meant that she received no credit. The reward at the end of the semester was that somebody would get to do a class demonstration tape. An added benefit of the engineering class was meeting and befriending Susie McKee, who was taking the class for the same reason, except Susie was a step further along the music road than the Judds. She was already in a band of her own: Susie and the Cowpokes.

Naomi offered to sing backup for Susie, and Susie invited Naomi and Wynonna to visit her where she recorded to audition. While they all fiddled and fooled around for a while, Wynonna's thoughts focused on the fact that Susie was making a living playing and singing at local clubs and bars, which strongly appealed to Wynonna. Then out came Susie's electric guitar, and she began to intrigue Wynonna and Naomi with her crossover style of music that was western and pop at the same time.

That session, Naomi's growing friendship with Susie, and mother and daughter becoming more deeply involved in music began to focus the Judds and drive them even more toward a life devoted to music. Their musical career was helped by Naomi's nerve and personality. She had not been a dedicated student in the engineering class, attending only three sessions, but she was able to convince the instructor to let her and Wynonna do the class demonstration tape. In some ways that may have made sense, since most of the other students were interested in the engineering and not the musical aspect of the course. Even so, it did seem odd to some people that she was chosen. That Naomi was such an attractive woman also probably helped.

Naomi and Wynonna sang the Delmore Brothers' song "Hillbilly Boogie" and ended up with their first demonstration tape. A demonstration tape is basic to getting attention, auditions, work, and recognition. It's a musical resumé demanded by record producers, club owners, and music publishers. Now the Judds—at least two of them—had their own demo.

Naomi was exhilarated by having the tape and began mixing more and more with musicians and performing in public with Wynonna every chance they got. One thing that surprised those who watched and listened to them perform was that the greater was not the older partner. People would watch them start to perform expecting the mother, who looked like an older sister, to play the lead. That's not what happened. Wynonna had the big voice, and Naomi sang the harmony.

On October 15, 1977, Naomi and the girls were finally able to move out of the cramped one-bedroom apartment where they had been living since arriving in the Bay Area. They were about to move into a duplex house at 6840 Sir Francis Drake Boulevard. To make things easier, soon after, Naomi's sister, Margaret, and her daughter, Erin, moved to a house nearby, in Forest Knolls, which was convenient for the sisters and good for the children, who went to school together.

Finally, on December 15, 1977, Naomi graduated with her nursing degree from the College of Marin, which was a very important milestone, even though she still had to devote the next three months to prepare for her state boards and then wait until summer to find out whether she had passed. It had been a long road, but now Naomi Judd was officially a registered nurse. It was the summer of 1978.

During this time, Naomi had stopped waiting tables at the Valhalla and had begun to work at Rancho Nicasio, a western-theme restaurant in Lucas Valley. Free of the burden of school studies, she liked working there. The customers were polite and friendly, and there was live music. Meanwhile, Wynonna got a job at a nearby Arabian horse farm, which she also enjoyed, for she had grown loving animals, as had her sister. She found pleasure working in the open with the magnificent Arabians and listening to country music all day while cleaning the tack. She even took the initiative to save up her money from that job to buy tickets to a Merle Haggard concert.

One day, while Naomi and Ashley were driving down Fourth Street in San Rafael, two men who claimed they worked for George Lucas said they wanted to use her 1957 Chevy in a movie they were going to shoot called *More American Graffiti*. At first Naomi was skeptical—she thought it was a come-on line—but when they gave her a business card with the name *Industrial Light and Magic Company*, she reconsidered. Naomi ended up renting her Chevy for four hundred dollars a day and was quickly utilized as an extra in the movie and later hired as a production secretary to Tom and Steven Lofaro of the film's staff. A perk from working on the movie was meeting Harrison Ford, who offered to take her for a motorcycle ride, but Naomi turned him down, thinking it wasn't the right thing to do under the circumstances. To her, it didn't seem professional.

Always looking for the big break, Naomi was able to wangle a part in a country-and-western nightclub scene for Wynonna, while she got a nonspeaking bit part sitting in a prison bus across from Cindy Williams. In her autobiography, which recounted these days, Naomi says that the role enabled her to get a membership card in the Screen Actors Guild (SAG), a claim we can't confirm. It seems inconsistent because usually one has to have a speaking role in a film to get a SAG card. You do not need one to perform onstage in clubs and bars, and that's what she and Wynonna, under the guidance of Susie and their other musician friends, started doing.

Meanwhile, Mike and Naomi were still dating from time to time, but the relationship was beginning to sour. Naomi was a pretty, vivacious woman whom males noticed. After she had finished her state boards and was waiting for the results, she and Wynonna were playing gigs at various places around the Bay Area. One night in May 1978, Mike was watching them perform at the Shadowbox in San Francisco. He obviously couldn't abide the kind of attention men were showing Naomi and decided to end the relationship.

At this point in her life and with all she had already been through, Naomi wasn't going to put down her guitar and pick up an apron or negligee for the exclusive pleasure of any man. She had things to do, places to go, and people to see, and besides, Pete Adams continued to take her around and keep her plugged into the local music scene. Naomi and Wynonna kept playing whenever and wherever they could. The other fellows at Tres Virgos studio let Naomi and Wynonna hang out and even make some more demos. On one occasion, they got three musicians from Susie's band and laid down the tracks to three songs; "Kentucky," "Oatmeal Cookies," and "Let Me Be Your Baby."

On another occasion, Pete, Naomi, and Wynonna went up to Point Reyes Station, and Naomi and Wynonna performed in a place called the Dance Hall, doing several numbers, including an original called "Lazy Country Evening." Then they got a chance to do backup vocals for the house band, the Moonlighters, at the place were Naomi waited tables, Rancho Nicasio. She was even able to return some favors by getting the boss to book Susie's band. As always with musicians, actors, and other performers, everyone was helping each other.

Naomi and Wynonna felt they were making strides in the music world they enjoyed so much, even if it barely paid. Naomi loved the joy and freedom they were finding now, and so did Wynonna. Ashley, four years younger than Wynonna, didn't feel a part of their musical adventure, but she was pleased that her mother was happy.

Money continued to be tight. The main source of the family's livelihood came from Naomi's waiting tables, and in one unhappy evening it all ended. One night Naomi needed a baby-sitter for Ashley because Wynonna was not available. Nor were any of Naomi's regulars. Against her better judgment as a mother, she left Ashley, who was now ten, alone at home while she went off to work; they needed the money and Naomi thought Ashley would probably be all right.

She fretted through the first few hours of work, telephoning home every fifteen minutes until about 11:00 P.M., when she called and there was no answer. Worried, she asked her boss if she could just run home and check up on Ashley. The boss, for some reason that she never clearly understood, refused and said if she left, she shouldn't return because she would not have a job. Naomi left, anyway, only to find Ashley quietly sleeping when she got home.

Morning came and with it the realization that Naomi had no job, no boyfriend, and precious little money. She felt frustrated and immediately began to think about her situation, concluding that she didn't have to remain in Marin County anymore because she was just waiting for the results of her nurse certification exam. On top of that, Naomi and Wynonna were feuding again because Wynonna was inattentive in class and not doing well in her studies. The Christmas holidays were approaching, and Naomi got enough money together to send Ashley to her father back in Kentucky. With Christmas came an odd arrangement. Naomi and Wynonna spent it with Glen and his new wife, in Flatwoods, Kentucky.

Because Naomi and Polly were angry with each other, they did not visit her. Naomi did leave a gift on Polly's doorstep. Afterward, Naomi and Wynonna returned to Marin County to pack so that they could leave northern California. They left Ashley with her father in Kentucky. A curious living arrangement was developing among the three women. Naomi and Wynonna stayed together, while Ashley lived far away in another place. Nevertheless, it would become the Judds' standard living arrangement.

From the Bay Area they drove south to Southern California, where her friend, Nancy, allowed them to crash at her house for a while. When they arrived in Los Angeles, Naomi immediately took the first job she was offered as a waitress at Beverly Garland's Howard Johnson's on Vineland and the Ventura Freeway in the San Fernando Valley. At the same time she looked for a manager or an agent who could help her and Wynonna with their singing careers, even though she could now work as a nurse. She even bought some inexpensive jackets and had "Hillbilly Women" embroidered on them.

Unfortunately, every waiter, waitress, ribbon clerk, and cabdriver in Los Angeles is looking for an agent or manager or has an original song or wonderful movie script in his or her pocket, and while some of them ultimately make it into show business, the vast majority do not. So, in time, Naomi began to realize the obvious: She was spinning her wheels at approximately the same rpm as she had done up north. She also missed Ashley and wondered if she was doing the right thing. As she had before in her life, she turned to the Bible and found a particular passage that gave her strength.

Mathew 7:7-8: "Ask, and it shall be given unto you; seek, and ye shall find; knock, and it shall be opened unto you: For every one that asketh receiveth; and he that seeketh findeth; and to him that knocketh it shall be opened."

12

Enter the Love of Her Life

BEVERLY GARLAND'S IS A MULTISTORY Howard Johnson's hotel next to the Ventura freeway in North Hollywood–Studio City with conference rooms and a large restaurant and bar. Garland built it with the money she earned acting in the movies, and because it's a show-business-connected place, show people on tour come there to meet, eat, drink, and sleep. It was a good place for Naomi to work while looking for a manager, an agent, and the key to the stairway leading to stardom. Thus, it was not unusual that she should encounter country singer and promoter Mickey Gilley at Beverly Garland's restaurant and it was even less surprising that as soon as she knew who he was, she began flirting with him and talking about her singing career. It was an accidental but prophetic meeting, because Mickey Gilley and his two cousins are a country song in themselves.

The oldest of the three cousins, who were all born in Ferriday, Louisiana, summed up their relationship when they were neighbors growing up. He said they fought a lot and still couldn't be separated. "There was constant rivalry, but we loved each other very much." That comment came from cousin Jimmy Swaggart, the controversial TV evangelist. Jerry Lee Lewis, the second oldest of the three cousins, is the controversial, renegade country singer. The youngest is Mickey Gilley, a country and western performer who for years owned the most famous honky-tonk bar and bull ride in the state of Texas, Gilley's, in the town of Pasadena.

All three cousins have seen hard times and trouble. Jimmy was preaching morality on TV and pulling in $150 million a year to support his ministry on a 250-acre complex that has a seven thousand seat church, a four hundred-student Bible college, and a TV studio outside Baton Rouge. Unfortunately, Jimmy was caught with a hooker, which temporarily destroyed his career until he appeared on TV with a sobbing apology to his flock and a plea for understanding and forgiveness. That performance apparently worked until he got caught again both drunk in public and with another prostitute, who was willing to talk on TV.

Jerry Lee was a flashy rock star whose two 1957 hits, "Great Balls of Fire" and "A Whole Lotta Shakin' Goin' On," made a fortune. In 1958 he married his thirteen-year-old cousin. His fans were appalled, and Jerry Lee was shunned, which led to his overindulgence in booze and drugs. It finally got so bad that Jerry's wife telephoned his cousin Jimmy for help. Swaggart arrived in Ohio, where he found Lewis drunk and disorderly onstage, trying to perform. Swaggart walked out onstage, grabbed Jerry's microphone, and said to the audience, "I'm Jimmy Swaggart, and Jerry Lee is my cousin. I love him, and I think you know that I love him, and I've come to take him home."

Mickey sports a gigantic pendant around his neck with diamond initials. He ultimately lost his honky-tonk to bankruptcy and now owns a theater in Branson, Missouri. At the time Mickey met Naomi in Beverly Garland's, he was flying high, traveling around the country for seven months a year, performing, promoting his line of western clothing through retail stores, and running his huge Texas nightclub, which was featured in the movie *Urban Cowboy*.

Soon after, Naomi began telling Mickey about herself and Wynonna, who was drinking a milk shake at the counter and waiting for her mother to finish work. Mickey, who was with a large group of people, including his press agent, Sandy Brokaw, said he would like to met the younger Judd. Naomi didn't see any problem, and introductions were made, and Wynonna joined the Gilley table. As soon as Naomi finished her shift, she and Wynonna were off to join Mickey for a taping on *The Merv Griffith Show*.

After the taping, they went out for Chinese food and then to the Palomino on Lankershim Boulevard, in a tacky, semi-industrial section of North Hollywood, to watch some live music, which included J. D. Sumner and the Stamps Quartet. The Palomino was probably the hottest country-western club for miles around, and despite (or perhaps because of) its location, it was usually jammed with big-name country stars and fans. In the years after Naomi and Wynonna first went there, however, it had modified that policy and featured a broader range of musicians, including Elvis Costello and the Red Hot Chili Peppers. That policy apparently flopped despite its good intentions. The Palomino closed down in mid-1995.

However, the night that Mickey brought his group there to hear the Stamps Quartet was different. Mickey loved the Stamps. In fact, they had backed Elvis for the last seven years of his life. Later that night, Naomi met the bass singer, Larry Strickland, from Raleigh, North Carolina, and they talked. Larry told her that he and his group had just moved to Nashville to make it in country music. Naomi was attracted to him but thought that he was too much of a playboy type. During the evening, the Palomino announced that they had amateur night when singers could perform with the house band. Naomi and Wynonna knew they had to return. They did, the next night with some friends, and sang "Kentucky."

Both Jeff Norton, a TV producer from Nashville, and Naomi were a part of this Hollywood country-music crowd. Inevitably, they met and talked about her and Wynonna's plan to move on to Nashville and become country stars. Jeff was supportive and said that he had an idea that could work out for all three of them. He was putting together the ingredients for a *Hee Haw* TV show in Las Vegas and needed help, which Naomi could give him by going to work as his executive assistant or secretary in the office. In return, he would help them get settled in Nashville.

Naomi agreed, and she and Wynonna were on the move again. They did check in with Ashley back in Kentucky, however, and told her she would have to stay there a little longer, until Naomi found a place to live in Nashville. It was a tearful occasion, but just another one in an endless stream of telephone calls between Naomi and Ashley during those years when Naomi and Wynonna were chasing their dream without thinking about Ashley's.

In Ashland, the Ciminellas and the Judds were troubled because Ashley was not included in Naomi and Wynonna's travels around the country. The Ciminellas contemplated some kind of legal action, but the elder Judds, who were divorced, were too preoccupied to do more than think and talk at that moment. Glen had to endure the fear of a kidney transplant, and Polly had gone to work as a cook on one of the scores of riverboats that plied the Ohio River.

In spite of everybody's disapproval, March 1979 found Naomi and Wynonna "on the road again," as Willie Nelson would sing, headed toward Nashville, even though it meant that fifteen-year-old Wynonna would miss a semester of school. Wynonna didn't much like school and would just as soon drop out permanently except that Naomi was adamant that she obtain a high school diploma. As they drove across the mostly arid deserts of the West from California to Nevada and, later, through Arizona, New Mexico, and Texas, Naomi realized that living in Nashville would be been the biggest gamble of her life—if one overlooked her unfortunate marriage to Michael Ciminella—and she wondered what would happen to her and her children. She would let Wynonna take the wheel on those long, deserted chunks of highway, sit in the passenger's seat, and gaze with concern at the unpredictable, talented creature who was her daughter.

Wynonna wasn't worrying. She was blowing bubble gum, steering the car, and amazingly, singing, at the top of her lungs, songs of freedom and joy. In recent months, Wynonna had been growing more independent, more willful, and disturbingly rebellious, and Naomi wondered to herself what Nashville would do and mean for them. She was convinced that music was now an important part of both their lives but feared that a rebellious Wynonna might embrace music and reject her mother, ending up by running off with some good-for-nothing country musician. Naomi finally decided that the music they both loved would make them either succeed or fail.

Before Nashville, they had to go to Las Vegas and work for Jeff Norton (in return for free room and board), and when they pulled into the Aladdin Hotel, they found that Jeff and his crew occupied an entire floor. Soon Naomi and Wynonna were sharing a room, and while Naomi worked during business hours in the production office, Wynonna would help out or set time aside to practice her guitar and singing. Sometimes in the evening a crew member from Jeff's show would offer advice to the Judds on their music and style. At night, Naomi and Wynonna would venture downstairs in the Aladdin and check out the music headliners. They got lucky one night when they saw Loretta Lynn perform. Naomi says she watched her act very carefully, studying her moves, her clothes, the lighting, everything and anything that might help Naomi and Wynonna when they went on the road with their act, as she was sure they would someday.

Back home in Kentucky, the family grew impatient with Naomi's behavior. They believed that she should return home, find herself a husband, and settle down to be what God intended her to be: a good wife and mother. What was Wynonna doing out of school, what were they doing in Las Vegas—not exactly the place for a teenage girl to be hanging out—and why didn't they return to Ashland? The family seemed to be constantly on the phone calling Naomi, asking her to stop her nonsense, but Naomi had her heart set on music and was determined to move to Nashville and become a big star. If she could, it would be the salvation of her life and that of her daughters.

After three weeks at the Aladdin, the *Hee Haw* crew had to leave. Jeff hadn't shot one foot of film. Moreover, the bills were staggering, and apparently Jeff was unable to pay them. The solution was that everybody would leave town that night, with Naomi and Wynonna heading back to Marin Country and Jeff skipping out without paying the hotel or the crew. Naomi was willing to play along if it would get her to Nashville, and in the end it did. Jeff got her two one-way tickets from San Francisco to

Nashville and said he would help her when she got there. It seems naive, but Naomi believed that Jeff would keep his promise. So she arranged to have a mover take what furniture they had along with her red-hot car and ship it all to Nashville while she and Wynonna took off and headed for their new home there.

Naomi and Wynonna arrived in the country-music mecca on May 1, 1979, and were disappointed to see that it looked like every other city they had seen. It was like arriving in the Emerald City of Oz and finding out they had 7-Elevens and McDonald's restaurants just like every other place on earth. A man from Jeff's office picked them up at the airport and gave them an old Impala to use until her car arrived. He drove them to a cheap motel and told Naomi to report to work at nine the next morning, and while the motel was very depressing, at least they were closer to Ashley, who was only a five-hour drive away. The next morning, Naomi went to work and brought Wynonna with her, since she couldn't leave her in the motel room by herself. Jeff's office was located on famous Music Row, where all the big recording and publishing companies were located. Jeff rented space in the Fender building, not too far away from RCA.

As soon as Naomi and Wynonna walked into Jeff's office, it became obvious that he was a small-time businessman. The office had a tattered air and a small staff consisting of a bookkeeper and a fellow who booked small-time, unknown acts—just the kind of place every secretary who doesn't want to be one fears working in because she knows she may never escape. Naomi had no choice. She sat at the old desk, gave Wynonna something to read, and started to work.

Mother and daughter lived in a dumpy motel, and Naomi was paid $150 a week to work for somebody whose dreams were clearly bigger than his abilities or connections. The Judds survived on bologna and crackers and fruit, and when Wynonna had her fifteenth birthday on May 30, Naomi couldn't even bake her a cake. The only present she could afford to give her was a drive in the country.

Now Naomi decided it was time to fetch Ashley. It had been five months since they said goodbye to her in Kentucky, and they couldn't wait to take her back to Nashville with them. They went to Ashland and collected Ashley from doubting in-laws, who apparently were more concerned with not having her on their hands than insisting she be brought up in a proper home and not on the road like a Gypsy girl.

How would they get into show business now that they were in the country-music mecca? One idea Naomi had was to create a radio program, and so at night, while the girls were watching TV, Naomi would retreat to the bathroom and work on her scripts which were musical versions of A&E's *Biography*. The the idea was to take an old song that had been written about a true event, then tell the story behind the song. Naomi would write the scripts for the half-hour program and incorporate Judd music in each dramatization. She did her own research at the Country Music Foundation Library during her lunch hour and recruited help wherever she could find it.

She was charming and persuasive enough so that she was finally able to get the use of the Baptist Communications recording studio and the help of some unemployed actors to work with her on her project. Naomi and Wynonna played the main characters in these little musical biographies, but nothing ever came of the project, except that Naomi collected more contacts and more experience. The project inspired hope and expanded the musical horizons of the Judds, which would help enrich their style later.

The place where they were forced to live didn't provide them comfort. The four walls of the motel seemed to be closing in on them. Again, Naomi didn't sit still hoping something would happen. She got in touch with a friend who knew someone in Nashville who might be able to help them find an inexpensive place to live. It turned into a new beginning with a friend of a friend, Charles Bidderman, who asked the Judds to house-sit for a month. The Judds jumped at the offer. He lived in Franklin County, outside Nashville, and it was a place that reminded Naomi of Ashland. They were so taken with the down-home feel of the town that they decided to look for a house of their own. Their living conditions had improved, but at work bill collectors were constantly calling, and a few were even showing up in person. Jeff would always sneak out the back door, leaving Naomi to deal with irate creditors demanding their money. It had turned into an unpleasant place to work. With the exception of one day.

Naomi was sitting at her desk when Jeff walked in with some new clients, a couple of fellows from the band J. D. Sumner and the Stamps. There was Ed Enoch, the lead singer of the band, and dark-haired Larry Strickland. Seeing Larry again made Naomi's heart skip a beat, and she apparently had a similar effect on him. Within a week Larry was calling Naomi for a date. She agreed, they set a time, and Larry pulled up Charles Bidderman's dirt driveway in his Corvette. They immediately decided that they didn't want to go to a club, bar, or movie.

Instead, they took a drive to the countryside to look at a house for Naomi to rent. A while back, an old farmer had told Naomi about an abandoned house that he thought might be available. Naomi and Larry drove around listening to the radio until they found the road, Del Rio Pike. The abandoned house was on that road. Getting out of the car, they walked around the place while sharing stories from their past and sealed the moment with a kiss. Then they drove into town, bought ice cream cones, and walked around the quaint town of Franklin.

Naomi decided that the old farmhouse had some possibilities and that Larry did, too. Naturally, she didn't know there would be problems in renovating both the house and Larry. Their relationship started off well, and after their down-home, get-acquainted casual date, Larry kept in touch with Naomi, but something wasn't right. It soon dawned on her that their brief acquaintance and that kiss didn't mean she had exclusive spooning rights. She found out that their relationship was not exclusive. That was underscored when Naomi called his hotel after he had told her that he was rooming with Ed, and a woman answered.

It was not a happy time. In her personal life, she felt devastated, for she realized that she had already fallen in love with Larry and now he had broken her heart after just one date. On the financial side she wondered if she and her little brood would ever have real financial security, for they had to scratch for every penny and she had a job that barely paid them enough to eat.

It wasn't long before Larry began to seriously court Naomi, starting with a true confession. He told her he wanted to be completely honest, that he was married but separated. His wife was a stewardess named Birgit, and they lived in Raleigh, North Carolina, but when he began touring with Elvis, he was gone for 285 days a year, and his absence took its toll on their marriage. They were now separated but on good terms. Naomi agreed to go out on more dates with Larry, and on the third one Larry confessed that he was head over heels in love with her.

Meanwhile, back at the office, a stream of bizarre characters—generally divided between bill collectors and struggling musicians—came through the front doors looking for a break. There was one character by the name of George Black who made quite an impression. Something about him touched Naomi. He was on lithium, a medication for manic depression, and was trying to pull himself out of a deep melancholy that had started when his wife deserted him.

George told Naomi that he was a songwriter who had written hits for Elvis Presley and Ricky Nelson and was in Nashville to write and sell songs. Unfortunately, he suffered from another disorder called agoraphobia, the fear of public places. Naomi told him that he could call her at home at night if he was lonely. He did, and it seemed to help him. Most of their contact was over the phone, but occasionally he would stop by the office and play her a song he was working on, and she noticed he always had on the same outfit. She took him under her wing and brought him to the local Sears to buy some new clothes.

While George talked with Naomi on the phone that evening, he heard Larry in the background and immediately cross-examined her about the male voice. She explained it belonged to her boyfriend. George went ballistic on the phone. How dare she tell him Larry was her boyfriend when he—George—was her boyfriend! Fulminating with rage, he yelled into the phone, "I'm going to have to kill him," and then all she heard was a click.

True to his word, George showed up later at Naomi's house with a gun shoved in his belt, blood in his eyes, and looking for Larry, the impostor as boyfriend. The situation became tense because

Larry was there with a friend, Richard. Naomi had already called 911 and was trying to calm George down until the police arrived.

Instead of violence there was sadness as George broke down and began tearfully telling his story of having been in a sanitarium in Alabama, constantly pumped up with drugs. Then one day, George said, he was watching *The Merv Griffith Show*. Mickey Gilley was singing one of the songs that he, George, had written and for which he won a Grammy. After seeing that show, George plotted to make a new life for himself, which is what he came to Nashville to do. The astonishing part of the story for Naomi is that *The Merv Griffith Show* was the very same one that she visited with Mickey and that she was the one who convinced Mickey to sing that song. She said that George was so dumbstruck by this story that "he could only gaze at me through the screen door as if I were an angel of God sent to guide him." After that night, she never heard from George again.

After Wynonna and Ashley made their annual visit to Ashland, Naomi decided to rent the abandoned house in Franklin. The three of them then packed up their belongings and moved into the 120-year-old house on Del Rio Pike Road, for which Naomi would pay $350 a month rent. Together they all turned out to fix the place up, replacing bad windows, rebuilding stairs, scrubbing the floors, and planting flowers. Naomi bought three used mattresses from the Goodwill, and within a short time they had a place they could call home.

Then Naomi enrolled both girls in school. She made sure she was home from work to greet them when the school bus dropped them off. A week later, the van arrived with all their furniture from Marin County—the Chevy hadn't yet arrived. It was nice to have some additional pieces of familiar furniture to help make the place more homey. Finally, the Judds were settling into a family routine, with Wynonna going to Franklin High School and Larry coming around regularly to help out with the chores and the kids.

Naomi and Larry still had stars in their eyes for each other, and happily the girls liked him. Larry could see that the girls and their mother didn't have any money—not even enough for a phone—so he told Naomi that he wanted to talk to her on a regular basis, even though he would be on the road playing performances around the country, so he paid to have a phone installed and underwrote the phone bills. Things were getting better, and one evening, after the foursome finished their supper inside the house, they moved out to the front porch. Naomi felt at peace and made the announcement: "Our U-Haul days are over, my children. We're finally home. We've found the Promised Land."

13

Naomi Perseveres

NOW EVERYBODY WAS SOMEWHERE: Larry was on the road performing; the children were in school in Franklin; and Naomi realized that she was nowhere in the employment aspect of her life and really needed to do something about her dismal little job. If nothing was to come of the job itself, then she needed to start meeting people and making contacts on Music Row for the benefit of herself and the girls. Naturally, some of the first people with whom Naomi would socialize would be other secretaries. A good friendship developed between Naomi and one of those secretaries, who had the same name as Naomi's mother, Polly. Naomi, Polly, and her pals would meet at the very popular Music Row hangout Maude's Courtyard and gossip over a glass or two or wine as Naomi sought out ideas and contacts so that she could bring the Judds closer to their dream. One of the most valuable aspects of this kind of secretarial socializing was that Naomi was learning who was who and what was what on Nashville's Music Row. For example, one friend, Bonnie Rasmussen, would give her free promotional records and inside information as to which producers had a good reputation and which didn't. Naomi wanted to learn about this sort of thing as soon as she could because her job with Jeff wasn't paying enough to support her and the girls. Her nursing certification from the state of Tennessee had arrived, and it was time to shift from the world of tape cassettes to the world of IVs—to go from fending off Jeff's creditors to emptying bedpans.

Naomi wasn't sorry to leave, but she did feel sympathy for Jeff. His wife had left him and had taken the children, and he could never be in the office before five for fear he would bump into a creditor. When she told Jeff that she was going to start nursing, he did not react well, for Naomi was probably the only person holding him and his business together. Because he believed Naomi's departure meant that the end was near for him and his company, he started to yell and pound his fist and even grabbed a walking stick, waving it in the air and threatening to kill her. She was so startled that all she could do was turn and run. She never saw Jeff again, but the following week she spotted a For Rent sign outside his office.

Meanwhile, Larry had returned from a road tour and traded in his Corvette for a Lincoln town car. On Thanksgiving he put the three Judd women in the elegant vehicle and they drove east to Raleigh, North Carolina, to visit his family. Naomi became excited when he said he wanted them to meet his family—it's the mark of a man with serious intentions on his mind—and even better, she took an instant liking to his parents, the Stricklands, even though she immediately sensed that they didn't like the fact that Larry was in show business. Naomi was introduced as a respectable, stable registered nurse, not a woman who wanted desperately to get into show business herself. The wonderful holiday spirit left Naomi vulnerable and totally unprepared for what happened next.

The Stamps were playing a gig in Kernersville, North Carolina after Christmas, so Naomi, in a surprise visit, went to see them and Larry perform. After leaving the kids in a motel, Naomi drove to the concert hall. Just as she was pulling up to the Stamps tour bus, she saw a young blond woman throwing her arms around Larry, kissing him and telling him that she missed him. Larry didn't notice Naomi at first, and when he did, he was obviously trapped. Naomi was devastated again, for she had loved and trusted a man too quickly without anticipating that old male perfidy that is the subject of so many country songs. She was hurt, angry, and did what she had always done before, which was to pull herself together and focus on something else important in her life. This time it was to find a nursing position. She wanted one that would allow her to pursue music and take care of the girls. She found it as a night-shift nurse at nearby Williamson County Hospital in Franklin.

Fortunately, winter had arrived, and it gave her something else to focus on and worry about besides Larry. It was the coldest time she ever remembered, even colder than when she lived in that fishing shack near Ashland. She recalled coming home one night from work when it was freezing cold and snowing. They were so still so poor that she held her shoes together with dental floss. That was bad enough for her, but the mother in her panicked when she walked through the back porch's screen door of their little house. The place was as cold inside as it was outside. The only heat they had came from one of those cast-iron, potbellied stoves, but the fire was dead because they had run out of wood. Quickly she checked the girls' bedrooms. They were empty, so she instinctively rushed into her own bedroom. There she found her two daughters, huddled together with towels and rugs and anything else they could find to keep them warm.

She had a job, but she hadn't made it through to her first paycheck, and it seemed as if fate, the weather, indeed the world itself, were conspiring was against her. She was at her lowest point, but for the sake of her children she would stoop lower if she had to, and she did. She called Larry to borrow money for food and firewood, but he wasn't home. His roommate told her that Larry was out with another woman. Naomi says she was numb with despair at that moment. So she broke up some of the pieces of furniture and fed them into the stove, which soon radiated some of the precious warmth the three of them needed. Then she made another call, to the head nurse where she had just started working, and explained she was temporarily in a tough situation with two girls to care for at home, and asked for an advance on her salary. She got it, and now the world was looking better. Soon it would look even better.

Larry began calling and saying he was sorry for the hurt he

caused her and he was trying to be better and what could he do to help. He came over and began doing the shopping, washed dishes, mowed the lawn, fixed things that were broken, and gave Naomi money. He was not a man who splurged on himself. He spent his money on the three Judd women, buying them a portable TV, which they put on top of the stove one night. The TV melted. Then, Larry's car was destroyed by fire and water, in reverse order, when it became submerged in a flash flood that almost trapped the three Judds. It was salvaged, but something had gone wrong with the wiring, and the whole thing was incinerated. Naomi arranged to buy another car through friends.

Then, unexpectedly, February 11, 1980, proved to be a milestone day. Naomi had succeeded in talking and singing their way onto Elmer Alley's early-morning show on WSM-TV, and she and Wynonna were so excited that they got up at 3:00 A.M. and showed up at the station before anybody else. When Jerry Whitehurst, the bandleader, and his group, the Waking Crew, arrived, Naomi introduced herself and told him they were the guest singers for that morning.

"That's fine," he said, "but where are your charts?" Naomi had no knowledge of the technical side of music production and didn't have a clue what he was talking about. Even if she had, they didn't have any "charts." She explained to the bemused Whitehurst that she wrote their songs in her head and hoped that if she and Wynonna played their number through once for the band before they went on the air, they could all follow along when the show went live. That's what they did, and it worked. Naomi was pleased. She was also surprised and delighted when she later found out that they were getting paid twenty-five dollars each.

A more important pleasure would develop over time because there was a positive audience reaction that resulted in their getting invited back repeatedly, which had the wonderful effect of giving them their first on-air professional experience, some extra money, and some local audience exposure. It also gave them a temporary nickname, the Soap Sisters, which grew out of their impoverished existence and Naomi's idea that she would make soap at home instead of buying gifts for family and friends. The three women set up a production line. Naomi would supervise the making of the soap, and the girls would shape the bars. Wynonna would then wrap each one in a piece of brown paper Ashley cut from old grocery bags.

Because of their unusual and outgoing personalities, the Judds were becoming well known in and around Franklin and Nashville. Children at school were even beginning to recognize Wynonna from her early-morning TV appearances. Naomi wanted to capitalize on people recognizing them. All they needed was a little bit of luck. The best exposure she thought she had was their appearances on *The Ralph Emery Show*. Actually, her nursing work would prove an important door opener in time, which was hard to predict then.

Meanwhile, everyone was hustling. Larry was away on tour in Europe, opening for Jerry Lee Lewis, Mickey Gilley's cousin. Naomi called on one of the owners of the South Shop in Nashville, Craig Deitschmann. She hoped he could find somebody who would produce her radio program or give the Judds a chance to record. In the self-assured, almost brazen style for which Naomi is famous, she walked into Deitschmann's office and began conning the receptionist. She pretended that she had already spoken with Deitschmann and used the name of a man she didn't know to arrange a meeting with one of the in-house record producers. Suddenly she found herself in another office talking with producer Jon Schulenberger. Even though he turned down the radio-show idea, he did accept Naomi's invitation to come for dinner at her house with his daughter so he could audition Naomi and Wynonna.

After hearing Naomi and Wynonna sing at supper, he seemed enthused and impressed. Suddenly, Schulenberger changed his mind. He decided that he didn't really want Naomi and Wynonna. He wanted to record Wynonna alone. That didn't sit well with Wynonna, for they had appeared as a duo at celebrity golf tournaments, church services, Baptist conventions, United Way luncheons, and on a small radio station, WIZO. They made so many appearances in so many places around the community that the Franklin newspaper, the *Review Appeal*, printed a big feature story on them.

Despite Wynonna's reluctance, Naomi and Jon Schulenberger convinced her to record a four-song demo. Jon shopped it around Nashville's Music Row and got the usual rejections—except for one. Jimmy Brown was one of the producers to whom Jon sent the tape, and although he passed on it, he agreed to meet with the Judds. He told them that together they had a very unusual act but were still a little raw. He suggested they work on their music. When they got their act down, he would be happy to consider them together as a mother-and-daughter duo.

The breakout year for the Judds would be 1981. Schulenberger wasn't able to get them a recording contract, but Naomi would persevere, giving demo tapes to anybody who would take them. She was casting tapes everywhere in the hope that somebody who understood their music would do something about making the Judds stars.

Meanwhile, she was picking up extra cash any way she could, whether through additional nursing assignments or odd modeling jobs. Patsy Bruce was in charge of one of the modeling agencies on Music Row that got her assignments. She arranged for Naomi to appear in a TV movie called *Living Proof*, starring Hank Williams. Naomi didn't like the role too much when she found out she was to play a groupie, but she did like the money—$630—she made for uttering one line. Naomi was also on a country game show called *Fandango*, hosted by Bill Anderson.

As it so often happens, the big break would come through luck. Besides all the odd jobs, Naomi was an RN at Meharry Hospital, where she was the only white nurse. It was here that destiny would take her hand and lead her into Dianna Maher's room. Dianna, seventeen, had been critically injured in a car accident. Her distraught parents were at her side during her entire stay in the hospital. She was attended to by Naomi.

Coincidentally, Dianna even had a little brother named Mark, and one day, as Naomi was commenting on how she also had a brother named Mark, Dianna finally recognized her from *The Ralph Emery Show*. Dianna told her that she and her mother had watched the show and had often tried to get her father to catch the Judds' act, which was promoted on the show as the Soap Sisters. It turned out that Dianna's father was part owner of Creative Recording Studio and in the music business. Instantly, Naomi knew that this chance meeting might be the opportunity she had been hoping for all along.

Naomi, with her usual brass, showed up at Brent Maher's studio, where they talked a little about Dianna, and then they did what Naomi refers to as "the Music Row handshake," in which you pass a cassette to the other person as you shake hands. She asked Brent Maher to listen to her homemade tape (made on a K mart recorder) and said goodbye. For the next couple of days, Naomi waited by the phone, hoping it might be Brent. He never called.

As a winter freeze struck, the pipes froze again, and the outhouse that they used at the time was itself falling apart. They were sometimes forced to go in the area behind it. They had to stay indoors much of the time during these bitter cold weeks. They ate sparingly because it was difficult to go shopping or, just as important, to temporarily separate from each other. It was a time when Wynonna and Naomi had one of their horrendous fights, which would become more common as Wynonna grew older. Wynonna locked herself in her room, and Naomi stayed in hers, as did Ashley, until the next morning.

A few days later, Larry returned from touring. They went over to his place for hot baths and hot food until the pipes in their home were repaired. After the repairs, they all returned to Del Rio Pike Road, and suddenly the phone rang.

Naomi Judd with husband Larry Strickland (Gregg Deguire)

(*Left*) The Judds with legendary Grand Ole Opry star Minnie Pearl, at the Academy of Country Music Awards, Knott's Berry Farm, Buena Park, California (Tammie Arroyo)

(*Below*) Ashley Judd with nephew, Elijah, and Elijah's mother, Wynonna, at the Kids Choice Awards, April 1997 (Gregg Deguire)

(*Above*) Wynonna Judd with her mother, Naomi, at the Fan Club softball game, Hermitage Landing, Nashville (Tammie Arroyo)

(*Right*) Naomi Judd with music giant Quincy Jones. (Gregg Deguire)

Wynonna in concert at Caesars Palace in Las Vegas (Tammie Arroyo)

(*Left*) Wynonna signs autographs at the 1994 Fan Fair, Tennessee State Fairgrounds, Nashville. (Tammie Arroyo)

(*Below right*) Ashley Judd at the "Tribute to Style" Vogue Italia party, Rodeo Drive, Beverly Hills, California, September 9, 1996 (Gregg Deguire)

(*Below left*) Naomi sizes up a picture of daughter Ashley at the thirtieth annual Academy of Country Music Awards in the Universal Studios Amphitheater where she and daughter Wynonna made their first appearance as a headline act. (Tammie Arroyo)

(*Above*) Ashley and Naomi Judd with Troy Aikman at the thirty-second annual Country Music Awards, April 23, 1997 (Gregg Deguire)

(*Left*) Naomi at a book signing of her autobiography, *Love Can Build a Bridge*, in Brentano's bookstore, Beverly Hills, California (Tammie Arroyo)

(*Above*) A lineup of stars, including Natalie Cole, Wynonna, Ashley, Naomi, and Lyle Lovett (Tammie Arroyo/Celebrity Photo)

(*Left*) Wynonna and Naomi with their awards at the twenty-sixth annual Academy of Country Music Awards in the Universal Studios Amphitheater, Studio City, California (Gregg Deguire)

Ashley Judd in her University of Kentucky sweatshirt at the Independent Spirit Awards, March 25, 1995 (Gregg Deguire)

14

The Phone Call to Stardom

NAOMI HAD ALL BUT FORGOTTEN about Brent, so when he did telephone, she was taken off guard. He told her that he had finally gotten around to listening to her tape and really liked it. His initial reaction was that the tape was wacky and different, but he wanted to talk. Those words were magic to Naomi's ears.

Eddie Bayers was the drummer in the singing Judds' band and has been part of the Nashville music scene for some time. He describes what happened: "One thing in my industry—you're always looking for something which would be different, that will follow through and have crossover potential and things like that. Actually, I had known their [the Judds'] producer, Brent Maher, before, and I was working with him on some other projects. I think he was doing some commercials or something, and he was an engineer at the time as well as producing. Ken [Stilts] wasn't their manager at the time [he became their manager later], and he and Wayne Bowles were working together when I first started working on what was just a engineering assignment for me. Brent said, 'Listen, I'm going to be doing some demos on the mother-daughter team...' And of course I knew nothing about them.

"Anyway, Brent was telling me what happened. His daughter,

Dianna, had a severe accident, and Naomi was actually her nurse. Now, all of us in the industry always get demo tapes, with people always coming up and saying, 'Listen to this! Listen to this!' He said that at the time, when she was a nurse, Naomi said, 'Hey, I got a tape of me and my daughter!' He said at the time, 'Oh, yeah, sure you do.' So he takes the tape and thought, Oh, what the heck, I'll put this thing on, as he was driving along. He said he almost drove off the road because it was just that good. Well, he obviously followed through and called her up and said, 'Okay, let's make some demos.' And actually, when we went in and did some of those first few demos, they ended up being some of their first big hits."

Later, when Bayers went out on other jobs, he would ask if anyone had heard of the Judds, and when they usually said no, he told them they would be hearing about them soon.

Brent met with the Judds to discuss in what direction the Judds were heading. The three got along well, and it appeared that they would spend a lot of time together in the future. Brent Maher was a dream come true, or as Naomi puts it, "like water after a drought." It looked as if Naomi had finally broken through the wall surrounding the world of country music. Next, Maher brought Don Potter into the picture to help direct Naomi and Wynonna. Potter was an inspired choice. He used to play lead guitar for Chuck Mangione, and Brent thought that he might add some color and experience to the twosome.

As it worked out, Naomi and Wynonna loved Potter. He was both a master musician and a decent human being who wasn't into game playing—so different from many men Naomi had known—and he proved to be even more valuable one night when Naomi was expecting a call from Larry. Naomi wanted to make Larry jealous, so she asked Don to answer the phone, but he refused to do so and took her outside for a walk in the evening instead.

It was a very valuable walk, Naomi remembered. "Don began talking to me about jealousy and guilt." He told her that she should realize that guilt often motivates us to do something that we shouldn't do, while love has the opposite effect. He told her to be honest with herself over how she felt about Larry and stop contemplating revenge. Naomi felt she had begun a special personal and professional relationship that would help her as an entertainer and enrich her as a woman.

One day—May 25, 1982—Naomi picked up fourteen-year-old Ashley from cheerleading and drove to Wal-Mart to shop. One minute the two were walking down the aisle together having a good time, and then Ashley went to the back of the store to get something. Then Naomi heard Ashley screaming. As a man shot past Naomi, Ashley came running toward her mother, tears streaming down her face. Naomi screamed out for someone to stop the man, and several store clerks chased and caught him in the parking lot. He was identified as Thomas Gary Beard. Arrested, he ultimately pled guilty to aggravated sexual battery for molesting Ashley in the store. On September 29, 1983, he was sentenced to sixty days of hard labor in the Williamson County jail.

It was a moment of stress the two shared together, but Naomi didn't spend as much time with Ashley as she did with Wynonna. Naomi and Wynonna have a love-hate relationship, sometimes soothed by love and longing expressed in their music. Ashley, the youngest, has never expressed passions similar to those of her mother and sister. She seemed excluded in many ways. Naomi and Wynonna would often leave her to tour for months or ship her off to relatives while they tended to their careers. Ashley was an afterthought, a mild encumbrance, someone who had to be recognized but not a major focus of love and attention. Ashley would say she grew up thinking her mother was a phone booth on Route 66 from which she would get disembodied voice messages when there was no one to tuck her in at night.

That she would push herself through school and search out a career in movies without the support or encouragement of either her mother or sister is extraordinary. Moreover, that she would succeed as well as she did and still feel strong love for her mother and sister is even more amazing. Indeed, her demeanor and personality were markedly different from the other two Judd women. She is consistently well mannered, intelligent, and without anger or bitterness. Jeri Trimmer, the mother of one of Ashley's classmates, Paige, told Naomi that she was glad Paige had someone like Ashley as a friend.

Ashley was a sweet girl, but her mother was constantly on the move, sometimes forcing Ashley to wait for hours to be picked up after cheer leading practice. One time she was so late that the school was deserted and Ashley was quietly waiting on the curb in the dark. Ashley was a very self-reliant girl. At fifteen she entered a modeling competition and won. As a result, a top-notch New York modeling agency flew Ashley to Tokyo for the summer to model.

When Ashley returned, she invested her money in a money-market fund, which was a savvy thing for a fifteen-year-old to do. She was also a runner-up in the Williamson County Junior Miss Pageant. In addition to being self-motivated away from school, she was strong academically. At the time, Wynonna was weak; in fact, she would have preferred to drop out of school just to sing professionally, but Naomi wouldn't permit it. In contrast, Ashley's teachers loved her. One even suggested that she could become the first female president of the United States.

One other telling difference that divided the Judd women involved their reactions to Larry. Naomi was a one-man woman who loved Larry and put up with his excuses and explanations because she wanted him as the man in her life. She figured that accepting his faults was part of the price she had to pay. Wynonna felt the same way and was growing up to be a younger Naomi in many ways—certainly when it came to relationships, even though she would ultimately have a harder edge to her professionally than her mother had.

Ashley and Larry, however, were a different story. Everyone was impressed with Ashley, and so was Larry, who thought she was a fine girl with a lot of talent. However, that feeling was not reciprocated. Ashley was not impressed with Larry for a very simple reason. From Ashley's vantage point, he failed miserably the acid test of male-female relationships. He was unfaithful to her mom.

Larry and his band would arrive in a town, and by the end of their set on a Saturday night, they would have their pick of a bedmate from among a hundred women willing to sleep with them. There was a group of Elvis fans left over from the days when Larry sang backup that followed the band on the road. They could be found at every gig, waiting to be chosen as a late-night diversion by the men who had been providing entertainment earlier. Larry faced a great deal of temptation and apparently didn't try hard to resist. Ashley didn't like the fact that her mom was very much like those other women, ready to give Larry the great gift of her body just as soon as he drove up the driveway.

Naomi would respond violently when she was reminded of what she knew was true, such as the one night Larry had returned from the road and Naomi found a fancy gold watch on the nightstand. A closer look revealed an inscription inside that read, "I love you." Naomi grabbed a hammer, woke Larry up, and as she was smashing the watch, warned him that his head would replace the smashed watch if she found another love gift from one of his women. Naomi suddenly found herself turning paranoid. The love trap into which she willingly put herself transformed her into an irrational, jealous, bitchy nonwife.

There were times, when she would secretly drive at night to a place Larry was playing and sneak around to see who he was with and where he was going. Often she didn't like what she saw, but she still wouldn't give him up. She would search through all his clothes, his mail and his phone book, and she admitted that her jealousy was verging on the pathological. Apparently that didn't bother Larry, because the next thing he did was to present her with a diamond ring and ask her to marry him. It would have been easy to say yes, but she waited. Shortly afterward, Larry had a gig in North Dakota, and when Naomi phoned his room in the middle of the night, she learned he was bedding down elsewhere. Overcome with rage and jealousy, Naomi was waiting for him with a .38 revolver. As he walked into the house, Naomi shot the gun, breaking the window in the dining room. Once again she told him to leave.

A few days later, Larry would come crawling back and she would forgive him. It was hardly a good example to set for her daughters, who were learning that this was the way it was with men: You love them, they love you, and then they cheat on you, and you take them back again. Of course, men aren't as stupid as women think. They learn that they can cheat and still return home.

They discover there is hardly anything you can do to a woman that twenty minutes of abject begging won't heal. It's the essence of every third country song.

Naomi wasn't oblivious to what she and her children saw; the children were involved whether they wanted to be or not. Naomi would ask Wynonna to take Larry's begging calls of apology when she didn't have the emotional strength, and even worse, Wynonna would. She would call up some of Larry's other female bed partners and tell them to leave her family alone, which had to be traumatic for her, a joke to the other women, and a puzzlement to Larry. She finally accepted the grotesque irony of her relationships with her daughters and her man, for she realized that she insisted that her daughters respect her when it was obvious that she had abandoned respect for herself and had traded it for a good time in bed and groceries on the table.

The reaction of the two girls was different from what Naomi perceived. Ashley was repulsed by a man dishonest with and exploitative of her mother. Wynonna thought of it in simpler terms: Whenever Larry was around, the menu at home changed from beans and corn bread to chicken and vegetables. She also was keenly aware of Larry's musical connections and respected him as a talent in his own right.

Unfortunately, Larry's band, Memphis, didn't seem to be going anywhere. They went from gig to gig, but nothing ever came of it. Naomi wanted more, and Larry's experience was instructive. She could see that it just wasn't a matter of talent in show business. You needed something else to get you through the door, and Naomi understood she couldn't do it by herself. She needed a manager or an agent to help her. The opportunity came on June 24, 1982, when Naomi drove to Opryland to catch up with some people she had met in Las Vegas who worked on *Hee Haw*. As it turned out, Ricky Skaggs was performing. They started to talk about music, how they had met at an Emmylou Harris concert, their kids, and all the usual subjects one covers about when renewing an acquaintanceship.

While they were talking, Naomi became aware of a man behind Ricky who was eavesdropping, but she didn't give it much thought, since men looked at her often in public and she was used to it. This time it was significantly different because after Ricky excused himself to tape his show, the fellow approached Naomi and introduced himself as Woody Bowles, a public-relations man. He wanted to know more about this mother-daughter singing duo because he promoted musical groups and he might be able to help her. An appointment was made for Naomi and Wynonna to audition for Woody.

Wynonna and Naomi arrived on time, and several people who had been invited to hear the audition were with Woody. After the introductions and the tune-up, the Judds gave the group a miniconcert. As always, they sang their hearts out. When they finished, they looked to the group for some reaction, and everyone was quiet, especially Woody, who just sat there with a blank expression on his face. Finally, when Naomi asked what he thought, he said, "Gold mine." Elated, the Judds returned home, and Woody immediately began trying to hustle their demo tape, but with no success.

Then he decided to try a connection he had outside Nashville. He flew to Los Angeles to play the Judds' tape for Dick Whitehouse, vice president of Curb Records. Impressed with what he heard, Whitehouse flew to Nashville so that Naomi and Wynonna could audition live for him. He told them he wanted them to audition for a wealthy man who produced albums on a small record label called Dimension. He already had some notable artists, such as Ray Price, Sonny James, and Eddy Raven. Whitehouse and Mike Curb of Curb records worked with him.

The man with the money was Ken Stilts Sr., a businessman who made a fortune manufacturing hot-water-heater blankets that wrapped around the tank and kept the water hot. During the energy crisis, he made a fortune selling them and had used his newfound wealth to enter the music business.

Wynonna and Naomi packed their guitars one more time and headed out for yet another audition. When they arrived, Ken Stilts and his secretary, Martha Taylor, were the only ones present. Once again, the Judds sang their hearts out. As they played, the girls would look for a reaction from Stilts—a smile, a groan, something, anything—but he remained inscrutable. Feeling rejected,

Wynonna and Naomi stopped at McDonald's and wolfed down a couple of Big Macs. Even though they felt depressed, Naomi knew that this was only the beginning and told Wynonna they were going to persist until they found somebody who would "discover" them.

The next day, Ken Stilts called to say he wanted to be their manager. They got off to a rocky start when Naomi refused to give Stilts power of attorney to sign checks for them. She had learned that she had to be in control of their destiny and not leave her money to some man who would pretend to look out for the "little women" while robbing them blind. Not that she didn't trust Stilts; she didn't trust anybody when it came to business.

She wasn't going to answer to any man for her livelihood and kept returning Stilts's contracts unsigned until he understood her position. After hours of negotiating, Naomi finally agreed to the contract that Ken had drawn up.

The first company the new Judd team approached was RCA. At that time, RCA was the dominant recording company. The time had come for RCA to hear the music. Brent, Ken, and Woody decided that the Judds would make a stronger impression if they auditioned live instead of just sending a tape. Ken set up an audition time, but unfortunately, the night before the audition, he suffered a heart attack and was rushed to the hospital. Nevertheless, he insisted from his hospital bed that Naomi and Wynonna audition as planned.

Brent picked up Wynonna and Naomi and drove them to their audition at five-thirty in the afternoon. He parked, and they walked past the Fender Building and Naomi's old workplace toward the RCA building. They continued through the long hallways and into a room filled with men who might hold their destiny in their hands. Everyone felt nervous as they filed past the walls lined with gold and platinum record albums. When they arrived in the room, Naomi reached out and took Wynonna's hand and smiled. Nervously, Wynonna returned the smile and squeezed her mother's hand.

The two Judds were grateful that the RCA vice presidents, Joe

Galante (whom everybody knew as a rising star in the recording business) and Randy Goodman, along with producers Tony Brown and Norro Wilson, were casually dressed. Suits and ties would have been intimidating. Eddie Bayers was present and described the circumstances:

"At that time they were basically very outgoing. Even Wynonna was outgoing; so was Naomi. They were very excited to be in this position and to see that something might happen out of this moment. So there they were, pretty much a live act, with Don Potter playing the guitar and Wynonna singing and Naomi doing harmony. They were just sitting there singing, which was pretty inspirational, but it was their raw talent that stood out. Most of the time, when we cut an artist, the artist doesn't even sing the song. You're listening to a demo tape of the song, and then you go into the studio and record. In a lot of cases the song being played is not being sung by the artists, but, rather, a demo singer who sang the song when they pitched it to the artists. So it was unusual for the artists to actually be in the room with you and sing a song they have written."

Everyone settled down. The Judds sat across from each other and began with "A Mother's Smile." They sang a few more songs before they stopped to observe the reaction. The room was still and quiet when suddenly Wynonna mentioned that her mother had just written a new song. Although Naomi mildly protested, saying the song wasn't finished, they sang it, anyway. When they had finished, Norro Wilson was the first to speak. "Man, if that ain't a number-one song, I'll quit this business!"

The RCA group wanted to talk in private, and they asked the Judds to wait at a nearby restaurant, O'Charley's, for a few minutes. They said they would join them shortly. Wynonna, Brent, and Naomi ordered something to eat. When the record men came in, they announced, "Congratulations, you're now RCA recording artists."

Naomi was so excited, the first person she wanted to call was her dad, so she borrowed a couple of quarters from Brent and called home. When she told her father the good news, the only thing he was concerned about was that she might quit her job as a nurse.

When they told Larry the good news, he was happy but confused. He wanted to know how this could happen so quickly to Naomi and Wynonna when he had not yet had similar luck. The big day of their success and the two most important men in Naomi's life didn't understand it!

15

Putting Your Heart on Vinyl

IT WAS 1983. Naomi's dream was coming true, and unlike most artists who struggle for years working on their craft, polishing it, auditioning, getting rejected, Naomi had never felt rebuffed. Naomi, Wynonna, and Ashley were ecstatic, and Naomi couldn't wait to tell her nursing and Music Row pals. She decided she would tell everyone that weekend and made plans to meet them. Meanwhile, Wynonna got together with her friend, Mindy Gentry.

Fifteen-year-old Ashley said she wanted to stay home alone. She asked Naomi to call before she returned. Why would Ashley want her mom to do that? Naomi had barely made it out of the Del Rio section where they lived when she decided to turn back. Her instincts proved to be correct, because there were two high school boys drinking beer on the back porch. Always the dramatic queen, Naomi grabbed a butcher knife and started waving it around in front of the boys, moving just inches from one boy's face. She told them she was crazy and that they should leave and tell their other friends to stay away, too.

Predictably, Ashley and Naomi got into a screaming match, and Naomi later recalled that the whole business of bringing up teenage

girls—particularly pretty ones who are strong-willed and willing—
with all those hormones raging around inside them, can be a scary
experience for a woman in her position. Still, it was what she felt
she had to do to protect her little family.

Pretending to be crazy was something that came natural to
Naomi given what happened when she heard that eighteen-year-
old Wynonna had a crush on a gas-station attendant in his thirties.
Naomi drove to the station holding a .38 revolver in clear view and
warned the man to stay away. However, this crazy, emotionally
charged behavior was not the exclusive property of Naomi.

Naomi once uncovered photos of the girls having a drinking
party in the backyard and taking things that weren't theirs, and on
another occasion Wynonna ate some casserole that she wasn't
supposed to touch. Naomi was so angry that she charged into
Wynonna's room "like a mad bull" and chased her out of the house
with only a slip on. Wynonna wasn't cowed. Instead, she took the
car, stole some money, and ran away for three weeks—a lot of hot
blood there. Such behavior would surface throughout the years and
continues even to this day.

Wynonna did possess some common sense. She may have a hair-
trigger temper like her mother and be naive about the ways of the
world, but Wynonna was enough of her mother's child that she
would not do anything stupid. She didn't run off to shack up with
the gas-station attendant or some kid she found on the road.
Instead, she headed that car east and turned up in Florida, at a club
where Larry—Naomi's erstwhile boyfriend—was playing. He
showed her understanding, gave her shelter, and eventually
convinced her to return home, which is exactly what she wanted
him to do.

Naomi was glad she was safe and welcomed her daughter home,
thinking that Wynonna was struggling with the frustration of not
being allowed the total independence she desperately wanted but
knowing deep down that she wasn't quite prepared to handle it and
that she still had to depend on Mom for a while longer.

After Wynonna returned home, she and her mother signed a
recording contract with RCA that made Wynonna, at age eighteen,
the youngest female performer RCA had ever signed. The only

other artist signed at that young age was Elvis Presley. The result was immediately apparent and surprising to the singing Judds.

As Eddie Bayers, longtime musician and professional colleague of the Judds, noted, "it actually happened too quickly for the Judds in some ways, and it was all an incredible surprise. Things started taking place, especially for Wynonna, like one can't just go into a store or restaurant anymore without people noticing you. All of a sudden you start to realize that you're not so-called normal anymore, and it's not always as comfortable as people think it is. It was very hard for Wynonna at first because she would say, 'What is going on. I thought we just went in there and sang.' And, of course, that's what they do, but it's just that there are a lot of aspects about it that people don't realize at first, and it can become very stressful."

The producers' initial strategy was to assemble a minialbum with six songs on it, using a good band for the Judds, and then send them out on tour. The objective of the quality minialbum was to promote it with disk jockeys all around the country in the hope that they would play it and build a popular audience for the Judds nationally. Then, when they started booking them into clubs, they could get better venues and not a lot of honky-tonk beer parlors with rowdy cowpokes. The last consideration was very important to Naomi because she wasn't going to put her teenage daughter in a situation where she would be surrounded by a bunch of drunks every night, nor, for that matter, did she want to be in that kind of environment herself. At the same time, BMI became the publisher of songs the Judds wrote.

Having settled on the strategy, they then turned to the specifics of what songs would be included in the minialbum, an important decision because it had to be high-octane material. They were competing with other artists—many if them proven successes—for the attention of disk jockeys and radio-station program directors, and the album had to showcase the Judds in the most effective way. Not everyone understands the delicate balance between program material and a radio station's success, for it is a two-way arrangement.

On the one side, record producers and their artists are in competition with many other artists who want radio stations to play their songs. It is free exposure, and it's what the producers think will make the artist popular and sell lots of records and concert tickets. On the other side, the radio station is also in competition with many other radio stations. There are, as we noted, some ten thousand radio stations in the country and probably fifty to a hundred stations in each market area competing for listeners. The number of people listening to each station is measured by various rating services, and that information is used to sell advertising to merchants in the community. Television stations and newspapers are rated for the same reason.

In the advertising business, fees charged for advertising are often based on a simple formula, namely, the cost per thousand people reached with the advertisement. As an example, the standard at one time was seven dollars per thousand, which means that for every thousand people who read a certain newspaper, watched a certain TV channel, or listened to a particular radio station, the advertiser would pay seven dollars. This is how newspapers, TV, and radio stations make a living. A radio station doesn't want to air programs or, in the case of the music business, play songs that people don't like. Radio stations want people—certain kinds of people—to tune to their station, and more than newspapers and TV, which are general in what they offer the public, radio stations are specialized: all news, talk, rock music, golden oldies, urban (a code word for black), classical, and country music, just to name a few of the categories.

It came down to this: The Judds and RCA had to figure out what songs would appeal to disk jockeys and, much more important, program directors. Disk jockeys and program directors, in turn, had to figure out what they thought would appeal to their listening public. There are many factors that affect these judgments, and in the end it is often a giant crapshoot because it is difficult to predict public taste with certainty, since it is so fickle. Also, particularly in the radio business, a great temptation exists to tip the scales of judgment with some under-the-table inducements. The bribery of program directors, disc jockeys, or both with money, drugs, women, and other goodies is something that is a constant factor and is not always uncovered. It even has a name, "payola."

(Because the Judds are an integral part of what is called by recording-business insiders the vinyl trade, we'll take a look at promotion and payola in the next chapter. You can't understand how recording stars like the Judds succeed and become rich and powerful unless you understand the vinyl trade.)

The Judds and their team were putting together their minialbum and picking six songs for it. Right away they chose "Change of Heart" and "John Deere Tractor." Next, Brent suggested "Had a Dream for the Heart," and although Naomi and Wynonna didn't know the song, Larry said it was familiar to him. Brent said it was the B side (secondary side) of Elvis Presley's hit "Burning Love." The Judds listened to it and after working the song around a bit until it fit their own style, decided, finally, that it was a keeper. This is the way the play list in an album comes together: the artist's favorites, suggestions from other people, and songs of other artists that fit the tempo and the mood of the album that the artist can adapt.

It is an unpredictable and uncertain creative process, and the most important aspect is how the artist herself "feels" about the music when it is finally recorded, because if it doesn't feel right, the artist usually doesn't communicate with the audience. For example, "Killing Me Softly" has become a signature song for Roberta Flack even though she wasn't the first one to record it. (She actually heard it on her headset in an airplane flying across country and fell in love with it.) It is so associated with her that almost no other artist would dare to use it on an album.

Brent arranged for the Judds to meet with songwriter Harland Howard at their home to see if he had any material the women could use. Naomi was nervous about Harland's visiting their modest home. She thought he might think that they were trailer trash. She knew Harland's work, that he was skilled and highly respected. She loved one of the songs he wrote for the legendary Patsy Cline, "I Fall To Pieces," which became a big hit. Naomi also prowled around Nashville's famous Music Row, checking out available songwriters. At a place called the House of Gold, she was introduced to songwriter Kenny O'Dell. It happened that he had just finished writing a song about a teenage girl who tells her mother about her first love entitled "Mama He's Crazy." In some ways that song connected with Naomi's own life and her relationship with Wynonna, but she tried to judge it independently. It would definitely be in the new album and would become an important song for the Judds.

Ken Stilts was finally released from the hospital after his heart attack and was back working for the Judds. But they couldn't expect any money for at least a year. It would take that long to cut the minialbum, distribute it, and arrange for the tour.

Eddie Bayer saw this happen with numerous artists. "Other people have illusions. They think your act is out there, and you start getting all this instant fame, but as far as any money being available immediately, that's not the case. People have to wait sometimes a year to receive their residuals. So people think you're millionaires, and you're not."

When Naomi explained their situation to Ken, he was appalled to learn she was trying to get by on her nurse's salary and that her ex-husband had never given her alimony and rarely sent a child-support payment. He gave Naomi one thousand dollars to see her through, and the first thing she did was buy the two items she and the girls had dreamed about having, a washer and a dryer.

Ken had not told them they would also have to spend their own money in putting together the album. The next step was to obtain a photograph of the two singers for the album cover. That meant they would need new clothes.

The Judds' unpretentious home had no closets for clothes, so they hung one season's wardrobe on a rack and kept the other at Larry's place. With springtime approaching, it was time to switch wardrobes. Naomi packed up the winter clothes, stuffed them into universal storage containers, plastic garbage bags, and put the bags in her Chevy. Unfortunately, she had also emptied trash in the garbage bags. The Judds didn't have a trash-collection service, and would drop their trash bags into various dumpsters they spotted around the community. Wynonna took the Chevy and, seeing the garbage bags, dumped them off in various trash bins along the way. That was the end of their winter wardrobe.

Joe Galante at RCA came to the rescue and offered to buy the Judds clothes for their album cover, even though he was surprised at the outfits Naomi and Wynonna selected. Naomi purchased a fuchsia and purple sweater and rose-colored slacks, and Wynonna followed in her mother's footsteps with a purple outfit as well. Norman Seef, a well-known rock-and-roll photographer, did the shoot but confessed that he didn't understand what the Judds were up to with those outfits. For a time, Galante and RCA considered getting different outfits and ordering a reshoot of the cover photo, but Naomi insisted on leaving the photography the way it was.

It was the spring of 1983, and Wynonna was about to graduate from high school and devote herself to music. She had been at best an average student in contrast to Ashley, who was exceptional. Now the magic moment of graduation had arrived, but the two Judd women had several arguments and shouting matches just before, and Naomi decided to punish Wynonna by not showing up at her graduation. To this day, Naomi regrets her decision. Meanwhile, the Judds had to support themselves until they became stars, so Naomi continued working as a nurse, and Wynonna signed on with a temporary help agency, Jane Jones, which sent her out on low-level receptionist and clerk jobs. Neither of those jobs would last much longer for the Judd women.

Finally, it was time for the talking to stop and the singing to start on their album. They gathered a band together that included Eddie Bayers on drums; Mark Casstevens, guitar; Jack Williams, bass; Sonny Garrish, pedal steel; Bobby Ogdin, keyboards; and Gene Sisk on piano. In producing recordings, the different elements are called "tracks" and are frequently recorded, or "laid down," at different times and then edited together electronically with a computer—to create each song and, finally, the album. This was the process that Naomi and Wynonna followed with the band. They laid down the music tracks over three days of stops and starts until they finally had what they wanted, and then the Judds laid down the various vocal tracks. According to Naomi's analysis, their style was spontaneous, emanating from somewhere deep down inside each of them emotionally. The album cost some thirty-six thousand dollars to produce, and now it had to be promoted with radio stations around the country in order to earn that money back and, hopefully, a lot more.

Meanwhile, Naomi's father, Glen, came to visit with his new wife. They played their tape for him, which they thought would please him, since it was dedicated to him, but he seemed distant and unresponsive. He took them all to the theme park Opryland, and everybody had a good time, even though they did not understand what was troubling Glen. Actually, his kidney transplant was failing, and he was on massive doses of medication.

Naomi's mother, Polly, still lived in Ashland with her new husband, Wib Rideout, across the street from the old house in which Naomi had been raised. Even though Naomi and Polly had a bitter parting years before, they were now able to conduct long conversations on the phone that ultimately led to an invitation to visit. When Naomi and the girls did visit Polly in Ashland, they relived the old days in Ashland, and all of the Judd women seemed to like Wib. After the three of them returned to Franklin, Wynonna decided it was time to leave. She initially moved in with Woody Bowles, one of the Judds whom Ken Stilts later bought out, and his wife but ultimately got her own apartment and, maybe as important to teenage Wynonna, a puppy. She named her Loretta Lynn.

By this time, the album was complete. It was time, at RCA's expense, to tour America's largest radio stations to promote their maiden musical effort. Details were coordinated through the RCA offices in five different promotional areas into which the company had divided the country. Each area boasted a representative to handle touring artists. The strategy was to introduce the singing Judd women to key disc jockeys and program directors along with one song from the album, *Had a Dream*. RCA hoped the song would build interest in the Judds and create a demand for their record and, subsequently, their album. Naomi and Wynonna readied themselves for the tour by purchasing new luggage, which seemed sensible, since they would be living out of it. Their first RCA guide, Jack Weston, had worked with a number of performers, but rarely with such a combination: a shy performer like Wynonna and a born extrovert and show-business talker like Naomi. That they both had long red hair and were strikingly attractive, particularly Naomi, did not hurt, either.

Both Judd women were nervous when they arrived at the first radio station, but for Naomi this only lasted a few seconds. She stunned the disc jockey with her appearance, and he told his audience, "Too bad this is radio, folks, 'cause you gotta see this mother-daughter duo to believe it. They look like sisters and have red hair." From that moment, Naomi had the disc jockey in the palm of her hand as they joked around. The Judds kidded the DJ while giving screwball traffic and weather reports—it would be cloudy with a chance of meatballs, and all yellow cars should take the next exit.

As in all radio stations, employees throughout the building work with the radio dialed to their own station so they can hear what's going on. It's part of the fun and glamour of being in broadcasting. The staff quickly knew that the singing Judds were no ordinary guests, and soon they were clustered around the windows of the studio, watching the fun. The listeners were having a good time, too, and voted affirmatively with their phone calls. The DJ was happy that all his telephone lines were lit up—a very auspicious beginning for the Judd women's first professional promotion tour. Their record was played, and they were talked about, which was the object of the whole exercise.

Naomi and Wynonna were swept up in a promotional whirlwind as Jack Weston's other RCA colleagues shepherded them across the country. Naomi called it a restaurant tour of America, since that's where the two of them and radio DJs spent much of their time. While it was important that they also spend as much time as possible on the air, repeating the Judd name and playing *Had a Dream*, the off-the-air schmoozing would prove just as meaningful, because there would be other tours and other albums and the Judds wanted to romance the radio people.

They finally ended the tour in Los Angeles, where they also were interviewed by Lon Helton from *Radio and Records* magazine and Bob Kingsley of *American Country Countdown*. It was crucial that the Judds cultivate such individuals in order to create what show-business people call "the Buzz," or word of mouth, which gives birth to reputations, myths, images, and all the ephemeral elements of success. The tour proved a commercial and

professional triumph. It was also clear that the personal
relationship between mother and teenage daughter had grown more
intense.

On this tour, the Judds stayed in nice hotels, in contrast to the
tacky truckers' motels they lived in when traveling in years past.
Although they could have gotten separate rooms, the two decided
to share one because they liked being together—sometimes. They
had not yet accepted the fact that they would soon belong to their
fans, all those people who would adore them and make them rich
and famous. Being in the public eye and their need to present the
best image possible made Naomi less tolerant of mistakes by her
teenage daughter. If Naomi saw Wynonna do or say something
inappropriate, she was instantly all over her, which immediately
triggered an angry response. The very thing Naomi wanted to
avoid would often occur: a public scene. As Naomi herself said,
"Things could get pretty explosive at any time and anyplace."

With the tour over in Los Angeles, the Judds flew back to
Nashville and Franklin to await the results and the next step in
RCA's plan for their professional development. While they were
gone, Ashley stayed with a school friend, Lisa Cicatellis, but when
the singing Judds returned, they followed the same routine they
were used to before the album and the tour. Wynonna went back to
work at the temporary-help agency, Ashley continued to go to
school, and Naomi once more worked as a nurse, cleaned house,
and shuttled Ashley back and forth to school.

While they awaited feedback from the tour, Naomi and
Wynonna did experience a quick moment of excitement on their
way to do a radio interview at the Opryland Hotel. As they were
driving along, all of a sudden on came *Had a Dream*. It was the first
time they had heard it played over the radio from the average
listener's vantage point, and it was exhilarating. The DJ said some
nice things about it, and that pleased them, as did some other
reviews that were now coming in from the tour. The prestigious
Rolling Stone characterized the singing Judds as having "more soul
than a moccasin factory." *Billboard*, one of the major voices of show
business, summarized the phenomenon of the new singing Judds

thusly: "They are a publicist's dream. Not only does the new RCA vocal act look good and harmonize superbly, it has a family history that reads like a Judith Krantz novel." For country-music artists, it doesn't get any better than that. The singing Judds had become the new rage of Nashville's Music Row.

16

The Dark Side
of the Disc Business

THE RECORD INDUSTRY, despite its pretensions otherwise, is very much like the cornflakes industry or the car industry or the clothing business or the book business. It consists of a system to create a product, boost a demand for that product, and distribute it to places where consumers can buy it. It's all that simple, or it would be if it didn't involve a lot of people and their egos who make it complicated.

Simply put, performers like the Judds create a music recording. This involves somebody writing a song; someone else organizing backup musicians, recording technicians, and studios; recruiting a performing artist; someone to rewrite or "arrange" the original composition to fit the mood and style of the performer; and finally, a director to pull it all together and actually record the song. All of this costs money, which the record producer puts up in exchange for a percentage of the income, in the hope that it will sell millions of copies at a huge profit.

Music math is fairly simple. Today it costs about $400,000 (not the puny $36,000 the first Judd album cost) to produce a record that sells for about eight dollars wholesale, meaning you need to sell fifty thousand to break even. Music producers look to sell several million records, after which the cost per record drops to pennies each. If a record sells a million copies at eight dollars, less a million for the artist and production costs, the producer makes $7 million profit before taxes. Thus, major record producers, such as Joe Galante of RCA in Nashville, Ahmet Ertegun of Atlantic Records, and the man who became the richest one of all, David Geffen, are motivated to constantly search for new talent they can record and promote.

In his early days, for example, Geffen began hanging around Los Angeles nightspots, like the Troubadour, where little-known singers were doing one-night stands, hoping to entice some record promoter to sponsor them. One of the first ones to catch Geffen's attention had been touring such spots all around the country. Her name was Joni Mitchell. Before long, Mitchell and Geffen were living together, platonically, while he promoted her to new levels of success. He shaped Mitchell's first four albums, which are acknowledged as her best, and began directing her career and that of other artists.

Then Geffen connected with an unknown singer living in an Echo Park rooming house, Jackson Browne. Browne introduced him to a nowhere group living in the same place that called itself the Longbranch Penny Whistle. Geffen bought their contract for five thousand dollars and renamed them the Eagles. They went on to become one of the top recording musical groups in the country. Geffen would become Hollywood's first billionaire and, after the record business, form the most exciting new movie-studio and entertainment company in a long time when he, Steven Spielberg, and Jeffrey Katzenberg joined forces in the new DreamWorks company.

The second phase of producing a blockbuster record album is to create a market demand for it. That's the same thing Procter & Gamble does with a new soap; Kellogg's, with a new breakfast food; and Ford, with a new car. In those industries and others, the approach is similar: get the customer to want what you're selling by advertising it, and by convincing the customer that it is emotionally important to him or her and that their life will be better for buying it.

Most products are rarely sold on the basis of pragmatic results. Soap, for example, is not marketed as a product to make you clean, but something that gives you a softer, more luminous skin and makes you look pretty. Sex appeal is being sold, not cleaning power. Laundry soap promises cleansing power so that your husband and child won't have to wear dirty clothes, which reflects on you as a wife and mother. Again, pride and ego are being sold, not cleanliness. With cereals it is health and vigor that is being promoted, not food. With cars it is sex, the macho appeal, the sophisticated-woman appeal. With records it is emotion that's being sold.

As with many other products, the recording business depends mostly on people sampling the artists. They hear a song on the radio; that is the key medium, although occasionally movie sound tracks such as *Titanic* provide a showcase. As singer Bette Midler notes, "Radio is very fickle. If you can't get your records played, you can't sell those records. The stations change formats frequently, and the formats are narrow. You can take six months out to do a movie and when you come back you find all the formats have changed. So you're working with musicians, browbeating yourself to make a record you're not sure anyone's going to hear."

As a result, the objective of record companies is to get their recordings played on the radio, where millions of listeners can sample the song and, if they hear it often enough, convince themselves that they can't live without their own personal copy. In the case of popular music, you must get your song on the Top Forty popular stations or country-music stations around the country if your record is going to be a success This is an absolute rule, with no exceptions.

One way to do this is to send your artists on the road, to call on stations and plug their songs as Galante and RCA did with the singing Judds. However, the artist may be too shy to do this. Wynonna, at the time of their first minialbum, probably couldn't have done the promotion tour on her own. The artist may be socially inept and incapable of sucking up to DJs and program directors, or he or she may have too big an ego and think that plugging his or her record around the country involves too much shlepping. There may be a dozen other reasons why you can't or don't want to send the artist on the road to promote the record.

Frequently, independent promoters are then called in to do the job. They are freelance operators who are also called record pluggers, or more commonly, "indies." These indies have enormous skill in convincing radio-station program directors to play the songs they are pushing. They do not work for any specific recording producer as a rule; that is too limiting. They preview new recordings first, decide which are going to be promotable hits, and try to represent the producer to the radio-station program directors whom they know. While they are usually not on salary with a specific record producer, many are on retainers and are given generous bonuses for placing records with important radio stations in such big radio markets as Los Angeles, New York, Philadelphia, Chicago, and Boston.

Indies became increasingly important in the 1970s because the business was changing. For a long time after World War II, the record industry was regarded as recession-proof; it was impossible for a producer to make a mistake that would not be offset by a new growth in sales. Later in the 1970s, however, record sales began to slump. In desperation, record companies did what other manufacturers have done and still do. They forced their distributors to take a lot more records in bulk through the back door than were moving out the front door in sales. The strategy was to make their retail distributors pay for the slump by taking on larger quantities of records than the market demanded on the theory that those distributors would ultimately sell them over the years; it became their problem to move them. To make their own books look good, record producers shipped tons of records to retail stores and marked these shipments as sales.

However, retail stores were not powerless and did not depend on only one record company to supply them. Beyond that, they were banding together into chains, giving them stronger bargaining power, and so the surplus of unsalable records was being shipped back to the producers that had already posted them as sold on their books. The producers knew they has to build a demand for their product, and the only way to do that was to get their records played over and over again on popular radio stations. The indies were the specialists who did that. In the 1970s and early 1980s, as the singing Judds were beginning to record, the fees paid to one independent promoter to push one song skyrocketed from a few hundred dollars to $100,000 or more per song!

The work of the independent record plugger was complicated by several problems and many human factors. There are independent record promoters who specialize in C & W music (country and western), albums and "urban" radio (which means stations catering to black audiences) and stations catering to Latin music, which, by the 1990s, would become the dominant sound in some communities.

Probably the most sought after were the Top Forty promoters. They appealed to the most affluent record-buying market: the children of middle- and upper-class suburban whites. For these promoters the ideal spot was to be on a Top Forty station's play list, but the problem with that was twofold. These stations, in theory, were only supposedly playing the forty records that were already hits, so how did one introduce a new record? Beyond that, there weren't forty slots to fill at a Top Forty station because songs carried over from week to week and there were only a few openings each week as records ran the course of their popularity and dropped out of the Top Forty.

This situation added to the strength of the indies. Program directors often preferred working with them rather than record promoters, who worked for the record companies. Representatives of record companies came into the radio station with only a stack of their own company's records, and their loyalty was to that company. In contrast, the indies were loyal to the radio stations' program directors and were looking out for them because of the symbiotic relationship they had with each other

The indies became even more powerful in the business in 1978 (shortly before the Judds would break in with their first album) with the birth of a loose-knit organization that called itself "the Network." The Network consisted of a bunch of independent record promoters who met in New York and agreed to informally work together. There was Dennis Lavinthal and Joe Isgro, both out of Los Angeles; Fred DiSipio, whose home turf was Cherry Hill, New Jersey, near Philadelphia; Gary Bird, from Cleveland; Jerry Meyers, from Buffalo; and Jerry Brenner, from Boston. The Network worked the Top Forty stations in their markets, and whenever one of them was hired by a recording company to push a record, he would pass it off to his colleagues to handle in their respective territories.

If you were to meet some independent record promoters, you would think you had accidentally wandered on to the set of *The Godfather*. They projected symbols of conspicuous consumption. They were men who thought of themselves as rich, tough, and savvy street guys—probably because they were. Joe Isgro was probably the stereotype, with his pencil mustache, shifty eyes, and unshaved face, tooling around Los Angeles in his Rolls-Royce with two animals who passed as bodyguards.

In any event, the independent record promoters were, and are, key to getting records on the air, which is what makes them sell in the record stores. How do they get them on the air? Why does a program director put one company's record or album on and freeze out a competing recording? There are various answers; some are honest, and some are not. Sometimes the program director wants to play the best recordings because doing so attracts the biggest audience and thus his station can charge more for commercials. As the program director makes his station more profitable, he feels pride in doing a good job. He may even enjoy some financial reward at Christmastime in the form of a bonus from his grateful employer.

On the dark side, the promoters do things to make the program director or disc jockey happy. In the old days, happiness for program directors was supplied by promoters in the form of booze, bribes, broads, and drugs. This was called, informally, "payola," and when it was discovered that disc jockey Alan Freed in New York, on station WINS (then a music station but now Westinghouse's all-news outlet in Manhattan), was taking payola, he took the fall and never recovered. In fact, some friends say that the reason he died prematurely in 1965 was that he drank himself into oblivion as a result of the shame of the payola scandal.

Who can say what the real story is about program directors' decisions? The buzz these days is that payola is still rampant throughout the industry but that it is more sophisticated and more carefully done. The indies play some role and perhaps they insulate the major record companies from the payola payment; they may even launder it. The record companies employ the indies to place records; how they do it is not the responsibility of the company. During the heyday of indie promoters, record companies were paying around $70–$80 million—much of it to the Network—to promote their records, and with that much money moving around, it is almost certain that a lot of it slips into receptive pockets. The payola syndrome indirectly affected the success or failure of every artist's albums and would continue to resurface well into the 1980s and 1990s.

In the mid-1980s (by which time the Judds were being promoted as RCA country stars), another payola scandal erupted after an NBC news story reported that two members of the Network apparently had mob connections, based on DiSipio and Isgro meeting with organized-crime figures in 1986. Both men denied any mob connection and rejected further allegations by NBC News that the old routine of trading money, drugs, and women for air play of records was continuing.

The report spurred federal grand juries in Newark, Los Angeles, and New York to probe the allegations, caused twelve record companies to cut connections with all indies instantly (at least for a while), and forced DiSipio to leave the business after a heart attack in 1987. DiSipio claimed it was all a lie. "There was absolutely zero truth to what they said about me. It was just a very unfortunate situation. One shot in a million. I mean, there I was, on my way to the rock awards. I was Italian, I was in New York, and I was in a hotel lobby where some people were. That's all there was to it. Those reporters should be crucified for what they did to me with no facts whatever."

Nevertheless, the U.S. Justice Department launched an investigation of payola, once again establishing one of those committees to which government officials love to give military-sounding names, as if to strike fear into the enemy. It was called the Organized Crime Strike Force, and was headed by prosecutor Marvin Rudnick, who focused on MCA and its record company, among others. Suddenly, one day Rudnick was relieved of his assignment and replaced by prosecutor William S. Lynch. Rudnick retired to private practice, claiming he had been pushed out because his investigations were getting too close to people in high places with connections in the White House. There was talk about collusion between the head of MCA, Lou Wasserman, and Ronald Reagan just because Wasserman had once been Reagan's agent. Anyhow, Rudnick said that the Justice Department would go after someone else to shift attention away from these powerful people.

The strike force didn't go after Fred DiSipio, but it did investigate the leading independent record promoter in the country, a man who made $10 million a year of the $50–60 million that the Network indies earned annually. On November 30, 1989, Joe Isgro, forty-one, was indicted by a federal grand jury for payola, mail fraud, filing false tax returns, conspiracy to defraud Columbia Records, and conspiracy to distribute coke. This indictment was, in turn, connected to a federal investigation of a Sal Pisello and of mob connections with the Music Corporation of America—owner of Universal Studios, MCA records, and then Putnam Book Publishing. *60 Minutes* reported on the MCA investigation and how it was quietly dropped for reasons not clear to the public but perhaps owing to the fact that MCA had strong connections in Washington. Indicted along with Isgro was former CBS Records executive Ray Anderson and a colleague of Isgro's, Jeffrey Monka, a convicted cocaine dealer.

Isgro and the other top men in the indies group had been already alerted that trouble was brewing when one of Isgro's former bodyguards, David Michael Smith, surfaced in Los Angeles. He had been hiding in England to dodge a grand-jury subpoena for his testimony about Isgro and others in the independent record-promotion business. Smith had been literally next to Isgro much of the time and privy to conversations and activities that might be embarrassing to him. What lured Smith out of hiding and back to

Los Angeles is not clear except that he had dreams of big bucks from a book or a movie deal about his life story and is quoted as saying, "The evidence I've got is going to dramatically change the music industry."

That struck a lot of people in the industry as the statement of a man who was no rocket scientist. If the industry did have the mob connections Smith implied it did, his was not a public comment designed to ensure a long and happy life. As Jay Leno said about another, similar situation when actor James Farentino was stalking Tina Sinatra, "Wouldn't it have been simpler to just make an appointment with Dr. Kevorkian?" In fact, when time came to set bail for Isgro after he was indicted in November 1989, the government's attorney at the hearing, Drew Pitt, asked the judge for the highest bail possible. He claimed that Isgro "was threatening to harm David Michael Smith."

While that was going on, Larry Tisch, the investor and hotel man, gained control of CBS when the top executives of that venerable network panicked about losing their jobs in the face of a threatened takeover by Ted Turner. Once he took over, Tisch dumped all those executives, who had sought him out as someone who would rescue them. Then, like the good investor he was, Tisch started selling off pieces of CBS so he could maintain control but get his money back. One of the biggest chunks he sold off was CBS Records, run by those grungy-dressed people on the ninth through eleventh floor of CBS headquarters in Manhattan and often the biggest single generator of CBS profits. The music division went to Sony as part of the Japanese penchant for buying American entertainment properties. That was about the time that David Michael Smith came back to town and testified about deals with CBS Records and others that would lead to indictments involving Isgro, several of his colleagues, and Ray Anderson, formerly of CBS Records.

On February 26, 1988, the grand jury indicted Ralph Tashjian, his wife, Valerie, and William Craig as key players on the Isgro promotion team. They were charged with supplying radio-station employees in Los Angeles, Fresno, El Paso, Cincinnati, Kansas

City, Jacksonville, and Atlanta with $230,000 in bribes and ample quantities of cocaine—usually delivered by Federal Express. This largesse was to promote records by Bruce Springsteen, Cyndi Lauper, Prince, Hall and Oates, Phil Collins, and Paul McCartney. Late in May, the charges against Valerie Tashjian were dismissed, and Ralph pled guilty to payola, which is only a misdemeanor, and two felonies: filing a false tax return and obstruction of justice. He was sentenced to sixty days in rehabilitation at a halfway house, three years' probation, plus a $100,000 fine and five hundred hours of community service.

Meanwhile, the Isgro case ended in a bizarre way when Assistant Attorney General Jo Ann Harris, who headed the criminal division of the U.S. Attorney General's Office, publicly reprimanded the department's own staff, including William S. Lynch, the lead prosecutor against Isgro, for mishandling the case. Apparently, Lynch was sent to Los Angeles from Washington to take over the case and deliberately hid important evidence, prompting the U.S. district judge in the case, James M. Ideman, to dismiss it and then roar from the judicial bench, "This is a case where the government's misconduct was as outrageous and egregious as anything that I have seen!"

What was hidden by the prosecution was conflicting testimony by Dennis DiRicco, who was Isgro's former tax attorney. Apparently, when he testified at a trial in San Francisco, DiRicco said one thing under oath; later, before the Los Angeles grand jury, he contradicted his earlier sworn testimony. It was this last testimony before the grand jury that triggered the indictment against Isgro, and DiRicco was clearly lying either in his San Francisco or his Los Angeles testimony. Beyond that, Lynch told both the judge in the case, Ideman, and the defendant's lawyer, Donald M. Re, that there was nothing in DiRicco's testimony of significance to the case. Lynch apparently actively covered up the truth to help his case, causing U.S. District Judge Ideman to observe, "The misconduct was extremely premeditated; it was repeated over and over again over a period of weeks and even months. The government, having been caught with a smoking gun in its hand, denied that—first denied that it had a gun, and then they denied that is smoking."

The issue here is a doctrine laid down by the U.S. Supreme Court in a 1963 ruling, *Brady v. Maryland*, that applies to both the conduct of attorneys and police. John L. Brady was convicted of murder in a trial in which evidence that could have helped his case and which was known to the authorities was kept from defense lawyers. The Supreme Court ruled that public authorities, in essence, are not sworn to prosecute defendants; they are sworn to discover the truth and prosecute the guilty while defending the innocent. To do that, they must hand over to the defense all the evidence that they uncover, and in the Brady case they didn't. Brady's death sentence was overturned, although his conviction stood. What also stood is now called by lawyers the Brady doctrine, and it was this doctrine that the prosecutors violated in the Isgro case.

Retired prosecutor Rudnick commented from his Pasadena offices: "I'm very disappointed that an experienced prosecutor could have blundered so badly. There is clearly payola going on in the record industry. I wish the U.S. attorney general would make the same effort to find out what went wrong with these prosecutors as when they moved me out." Irving Azoff, formerly with MCA and one of the big power brokers of the recording industry, along with Ahmet Ertegun of Atlantic Records and Walter Yetnikoff of CBS, also attacked the investigation. Azoff said, "While at MCA, we were constantly criticized by the press for claiming government misconduct; maybe now those protests will be better understood."

MCA was the initial target of prosecutor Marvin Rudnick and the Organized Crime Strike Force. The government got one conviction, that of Salvatore Pisello, on tax evasion related to money paid to him by MCA Records. Pisello is now out of prison, living in Los Angeles and trying to sell two movie scripts about the Mafia. One is a comedy; the other, a drama. After the Pisello conviction, the investigation stalled.

The fact remains that the music industry operated with widespread payola for years. It occasionally surfaces again, creating a major scandal from time to time. The industry got stung with those major scandals and upheavals in the late 1950s and early 1960s, and in the 1980s they erupted again.

In 1990 the court dismissed the case against Isgro, but in September 1992 it got a federal appeals court to reinstate the case, returning it to Judge Ideman's court while also criticizing Lynch's behavior. While he had to hear the Isgro case again, Ideman ruled that he would ban any testimony by the discredited DiRicco or the introduction of new witnesses who would cover the same ground as DiRicco might have if he were allowed to testify. At the same time, Judge Ideman criticized the Justice Department for failing to acknowledge that what Lynch did was wrong and for taking thirty-nine months to investigate the ethics of the attorneys involved. This brought an immediate response from Attorney General Janet Reno, who said the judge was right and that the ethical-review procedures of the department would be overhauled immediately to speed them up.

As a mark of how things change while remaining the same, Fred DiSipio, after dropping out of the record-promotion business and saving himself from prosecution, quietly was back in the record-promotion consulting business. He went to work behind the scenes in 1991 for Charles Koppelman, the chairman and CEO of EMI Records in North America. His association with EMI became known two years later, and it startled many in the record business that such a reconnection would be acknowledged publicly. Fredric Dannen, author of a book about the record industry, *Hit Men*, observed, "The hiring of DiSipio by EMI is just another illustration that the record industry has no memory and no shame. Independent promotion never went away."

DiSipio responded, "If I was a nefarious character, why would presidents of companies, chairmen of the board, vice presidents, artists and artists' managers, continue to call me?" DiSipio, at sixty-six, is a decorated war hero who has denied any connection with the mob. "I'm not like that. I never became successful or could have earned the trust of so many individuals in this industry from being a wise guy [a mob member]. My reputation has always been one of a gentleman."

Joe Isgro is back in business but has broadened his activities to include motion pictures. Most recently, Isgro was the executive producer of the 20th Century–Fox movie *Hoffa*, which starred Jack Nicholson and was directed by Danny DeVito.

Obviously, the Judd women are not directly involved with all the activities that are described here, but it is the nature of the business they are in and the people they may have to deal with in the music business.

17

Back on the Road Again

THE JUDDS HAD LEARNED THEIR CRAFT, had come to Nashville and penetrated Music Row, had made a minialbum, and had gone on the required promotional tour. Now it was time for them to hit the road and perform. The only problem was that nobody asked them to.

Then, out of the blue, they received a telephone call from Marshall Grant of the well-established group the Statler Brothers. He had heard the Judds on one of their radio interviews during their promotion tour and was so impressed that he called RCA in Nashville and arranged for them to open for the Statler Brothers at their next appearance in Omaha, Nebraska. The women were ecstatic and pulled together a band of studio musicians. They all headed north to Omaha, where they opened on the night of March 20, 1984—their first official, professional, live performance. It was a night they had been waiting for.

Naomi and Wynonna were anxious and nervous. They discovered that the concert was a complete sellout—standing room only. For them, the concert was the Rubicon they had to cross. As they were standing by to go on, Naomi said she felt sheer panic. She told herself that there were thousands of people out there and that the Judds weren't ready—they needed more time, we're going to be humiliated—but her fears were interrupted by a booming voice from the loudspeakers announcing, "Ladies and gentlemen, the Judds!" and the curtain went up. All of a sudden, their band shifted into drive, and the Judds were singing as they had never sung before.

A little later, Naomi and Wynonna would say that neither remembered anything that happened while they were on stage. It was all one giant blur. One of the band members did say that Naomi was so nervous, she forget to thank the band afterward, but thought they did a helluva a job. That seemed to be the opinion of Roger Caitlin, writing the next day in the *Omaha World Herald*. He called the Judds a surprising opening act, a female duo owing as much to country roots as to the Andrews Sisters. He compared them to the famous Bonnie Raitt and predicted "almost certain stardom for the Judds." Caitlin continued: "The audience seemed to enjoy the fine music from the two...but they were absolutely astonished when Naomi introduced herself as the mother and Wynonna as the daughter." This audience was not the first to be surprised at how young Naomi looked.

When the Judds returned to Nashville, they learned that they had been rediscovered—by the same people! When they found out how professionally the Judds performed in Omaha, the executives at RCA realized that everything they had been telling themselves about the talented duo was actually true. They wisely decided to capitalize on the Judds' success by booking them to do more concerts. The first one would be in Cleveland, Ohio, but they dismissed the studio band and only kept Don Potter, the Judds' faithful standby, on acoustic guitar. Omaha had boosted the singing Judds' poise and self-confidence, but when they showed up at Cleveland's Front Row Theater for their next performance, they found that it was a different setup than was Omaha.

The Front Row was a theater-in-the-round with two thousand seats—which is a little scary for inexperienced performers. The traditional theater, with the proscenium arch and elevated stage set back from the audience, gives the performer, psychologically, a sense of security. The audience literally can't get at them. There are physical barriers between the performer and the audience, and the crowd is on only one side of the performer. In theater-in-the-round, the audience surrounds the performer, and the stage is elevated only slightly above the audience level. Performers reach the stage by walking down an aisle and simply stepping onto the stage.

The designers of theater-in-the-round would have you believe that such a familiar setting produces a feeling of intimacy between audience and performer and makes the experience richer for both. However, designers of theaters don't have to perform in them. Most artists want the audience in their sight all of the time but shun physical contact with them. Theater-in-the-round may be an intimate experience for the audience, but it is an intimidating one for the performer. Intimidating or not, however, that's what the Judds faced in Cleveland.

The Judds liked the idea of a band backing them up, as was the case on their minialbum and at their Omaha performance. All RCA would provide was Don Potter, the Judds' key backup-guitar player, and two others with acoustic instruments that did not give the full-throated sound of a band and robbed the Judds of the musical and emotional support they needed. They went onstage and enchanted the audience with their own harmonies and stage presence, again collecting good notices.

RCA knew what it had and was going to exploit it for RCA's and for the Judds' benefit. They started booking them on various TV and radio shows in what has, over the years, developed into a symbiotic arrangement by which celebrities appear for scale in exchange for a few minutes to plug their latest movie, song, book, tape, or whatever. One knows that when stars are on Jay Leno or David Letterman, it is not to discuss the meaning of life, how migratory animals find their way home, or if the United States should return to the gold standard. They are there to promote their latest commercial enterprise or themselves.

So it was that the Judds started appearing on *Entertainment Tonight*, *The Bobby Bare Show*, *Music City USA*, *That Nashville Music*, and *Hee Haw* to promote their minialbum, which was making the rounds of disk jockeys around the country. Moreover, RCA was booking the Judds as an opening act for other stars and talking about another, full-fledged album for which the Judds already had a title, *Why Not Me?*

As the singing Judds were beginning to leave the launching pad, Larry's musical career was not doing nearly as well, and his prospects didn't appear to be getting any better. It was that old macho bugaboo again, where the woman is successful and the man is not.

The health of Naomi's father, Glen, began to deteriorate, and when Naomi learned that he had been admitted to the hospital, she flew to be with him. She sat with her father for hours at a time, telling him about how well the Judds' singing career was progressing and sharing with him anecdotes of the shows they were on and the people they met. It was both interesting and bewildering to Glen, who couldn't quite comprehend what his daughter and granddaughter were doing. Later, he was admitted to the medical facility at the University of Kentucky and seemed to be getting worse, to the point that his wife and his two sisters remained at his side, trying to help and comfort him.

While Naomi was visiting her father, she decided to attend her twentieth high school reunion. The next day, she got a call asking the Judds to open for Ricky Skaggs, that is, to warm up the audience by entertaining them before the star comes onstage. She immediately agreed to do the gig. It was a bittersweet time because her father was deathly ill and there was nothing anybody could do to save him. On July 4, 1984, Glen Judd died. Four days earlier, Naomi and Wynonna had opened for Ricky Skaggs.

After the funeral, the singing Judds flew to Memphis for another gig and opened for country star Lee Greenwood. Naomi tried to pull herself together and present a happy face for the audience, even though she had just buried her father four hours earlier.

Larry had been playing in Nashville, and the night the Judds opened for Thomas Conley, in Rome, Georgia, Larry drove there, picked up Naomi and Wynonna, and drove them back to Del Rio for a steak barbecue. When they arrived home, Naomi played back her telephone messages on her answering machine while Larry listened. They heard the incredible news that "Mama He's Crazy" had moved to number one among country songs.

Both Larry and Naomi stared at each other, a freeze-frame moment as the two just stood there, not knowing quite what to do or to say. There were no hugs or kisses or jumping up and down. There was only stunned silence. Then, slowly, Larry stood up, left the room, and shut the door behind him. The last thing Naomi heard was Larry's car being driven away. Naomi knew it was the end of their relationship. Larry couldn't handle having a star for a girlfriend.

The next day, she waited, hoping that Larry would change his mind and come back to her. He never did, and she ended up going out with Wynonna's boyfriend, dancing at a club called Chevy's. She thought it was amazing that she could dance the night away with a broken heart.

Naomi decided to throw herself into her work. She began to write more songs, starting with one appropriately entitled "Mr. Pain" that she coauthored with Kent Robbins. Robbins also helped with several other numbers, including, "Love Is Alive," "Girls' Night Out," "Baby's Gone," and "Drops of Water." By now the Judds were becoming a popular act and opened for the legendary star Conway Twitty several times. When Naomi got a check for ten thousand dollars from her father's estate, she bought one of Conway's Cadillacs. The Twittys and the Judds became friends and began to hang out together.

Now RCA booked the Judds for more road appearances. They were given the mandatory touring bus. They christened it the Juddmobile and turned it into a place for the crew to gather and enjoy themselves. While the bus took them from place to place (except for long runs, when the Judds would fly; the bus would catch up to them later), they would often spend the night in hotels.

They were becoming more popular and had to hide from fans and autograph seekers, so they made a game of registering at hotels under kooky names, such as Barb Wire, Ben Dover, Sue She, and Bertha Dablues. In their off time on the road, the Judds enjoyed swimming, bowling, and miniature golf. Don Potter, who guided them through some of the potholes on the road to success, was getting tired. He loved the Judds, but he wanted to be with his family, so he returned home. He was replaced by two guitarists,

Mark Thompson on rhythm and Steve Sheehan on lead guitar.

For the first time in her adult life, Naomi was doing well financially. She used some of her newly earned wealth to send Ashley to the Sayre School, a private school in Lexington, Kentucky. After touring, Wynonna returned to her apartment in Franklin, where she seemed to relish her privacy. In contrast, Naomi went back to her now-empty home at Del Rio. To help, Ken Stilts, her manager, who was nervous about Naomi being alone in that house, would have Odell, a crew member, stay in Ashley's room. Her loneliness grew when she learned that Larry was now living with a younger woman. Just as her success had pushed all his buttons, he knew how to push hers. That was, she thought, another good thing about being on the road. She would be too busy to think about the breakup with Larry.

There were other problems, too, that had to be faced now that the Judds were on and off the tour circuit regularly. For one thing, Wynonna and Naomi would fight when they were living in close quarters. Their screaming matches were quickly known to everybody in their troupe. In one dramatic instance, they were close to going onstage, and a battle royal erupted, with shouting and demands and threats flying furiously. Ken Stilts told them there were several thousand people who had paid a lot of money to watch a wonderful Judd show and that the yelling must stop. Before they did anything more or said anything further, their manager said they must decide what they were going to be: professional entertainers or a gigantic disappointment to everyone, including him. They went onstage and poured all that energy into singing and making the audience happy.

Nitty Gritty Dirt Band, Roy Orbison, Eddie Rabbit, and Ronnie Milsap were added to the list of acts for which they had opened, and now the country-music industry was paying attention to the Judds. In a rare honor, the Judds were nominated for three separate awards by the Country Music Association: Best Single ("Had a Dream"); Best Group of the Year; and the Horizon Award, which goes to the most promising new act of the year. All of these honors came to two singers who had yet to produce a complete album.

18

The Man She Loves Returns

WITHIN TWO YEARS, FROM 1983 TO 1985, the Judds went from obscurity to stardom with four hit singles on their album *Why Not Me*. Naomi said they weren't an overnight success; they were an over-coffee-break success.

The album went gold and then platinum, and while Naomi was pleased as could be with their success, she said that the Judds getting the Horizon Award focused attention on them and sent them into overdrive. Their success was further enhanced by their increasing number of gigs around Nashville, and then around the country, including a trip to Manhattan to appear on *Good Morning America*. Once they arrived in New York, the Judds understood why they loved Kentucky and Tennessee. To them New York seemed noisy, overpriced, and hectic. Naomi wondered what terribly important things all these hurrying people did when they finally got to where they where going or even if they knew the answer themselves.

Reporters kept swarming around them seeking a story. Jamie James, of *Life* magazine, interviewed them, and photographer William Allard, of *National Geographic*, took their pictures. *National Geographic!* thought Naomi. Are we supposed to carry spears, be topless, and grunt about life in the wild hinterlands of Tennessee? They just kept rolling on in the Juddmobile, and *NBC Nightly News* correspondent Douglas Kiker, traveling along as they toured, did a "day in the life" story on them. Then they debuted on Canadian TV with the *Tommy Hunter Show* and met Hank Snow, the famous *Grand Ole Opry* star who was a native of Nova Scotia, of all places. They also appeared on the *Family Brown Show*.

In February 1985 the Judds came off tour and were back for the Grammys; they had been nominated for Best Duo with Vocal, Best New Artist, and Song of the Year ("Mama He's Crazy"). The exciting part of being chosen in the category of Best New Artist was that a country singer hadn't been nominated for that category since 1968, when Jeannie C. Riley was nominated for "Harper Valley P.T.A." The Judds walked away—or perhaps danced away—overjoyed that night with a Grammy for Best Duo with Vocal. Their career was moving faster than the Wabash Cannonball barreling down a steep grade with no brakes.

In fact, they were booked months in advance at top prices. That meant the Judds were only getting three thousand dollars to open for the likes of Kenny Rogers or Ronnie Milsap. More important, however, was the exposure to ever-widening audiences that would buy their records.

One of the Judds' favorite bands they opened for was the Oak Ridge Boys. They all loved to horse around and play little pranks on each other, such as the time after the Judds finished their opening routine when one of the Oak Ridge Boys, Joe Bonsall, asked the audience what they thought of Wynonna and Naomi. Bonsall was rocked back when the audience exploded with applause and cheers. Then he turned around and saw the rest of the band laughing and Naomi and Wynonna parading across the stage holding up a big Applause sign.

The Boys were not going to let a prank like that just slide by. Naomi tells of their revenge on the last night, when the Judds were singing their final song. The Judds were just finishing when the audience burst into wild laughter and yelling. Naomi and Wynonna turned around and saw the Oak Ridge Boys and the crew all decked out in flamboyant women's clothes and heels doing a chorus-line number. Naomi and Wynonna refer to that experience as "Transvestites' Night Out."

Now that the Judds were taking off, they decided they had to extend and expand their stage wardrobe beyond the ready-to-wear, off-the-rack fashion level. Naomi found a clothing stylist in Nashville she liked, Vanessa Ware, who could put together the wardrobe they desired. Naomi, in particular, wanted to look glamorous and enchanting. One of her favorite outfits produced what she called her Rita Hayworth look, after the legendary photo of the actress kneeling on her bed in the World War II *Life* magazine pinup photo. It was a clingy, full-length nude gown with black lace covering it. It was only one of many outfits the two of them had made for their stage appearances.

In another milestone of their growing success, in March 1985, Naomi bought a condo in Brentwood, Tennessee. Although she was a minor celebrity and making lots of money, she had absolutely no credit history, and Ken had to cosign the loan for her. It was a nice feeling not to have to go to secondhand shops and look for bargains. Instead she could buy wallpaper and drapes and silverware that matched.

Soon afterward, when Wynonna and Naomi were recording their second album, *Rockin' With the Rhythm*, Naomi got a call from Larry at the studio. It was his birthday, and he was alone and lonely. He told her that he still loved her and that he missed her and the girls. At this time, Naomi was dating somebody exclusively, but she was still in love with Larry and they let it go at that for the time being. Another important man in Naomi and Wynonna's lives was having troubles of his own. Ken Stilts had suffered another heart attack and required a triple bypass. Naomi had grown very close to Ken; from the start, he had believed in them and she and Wynonna truly loved and respected him. It wasn't long before Ken was out of the hospital and on the road with the Judds again. Because of his incredible will and strength, Naomi nicknamed him Mr. Big. Mr. Big decided that it was time to hire a bodyguard for the Judds. His name was Bill "Snipper" Snyder, and Naomi and Wynonna adored him.

The Judds' schedule just seemed to get tighter. On May second they were in the Kentucky Derby parade; then they flew to Los Angeles for the Academy of Country Music (ACM) Show. Once again, the Judds walked away with top honors—Top Vocal Duo and Song of the Year for "Why Not Me." That night, when Wynonna and Naomi returned to their hotel room, they were given a reminder of days gone by. They looked out the window of their room and saw their old house on Larrabee Street and the health food store where Naomi used to work. They had come a long way since then.

A few weeks later, the Judds appeared as part of the Music City News Awards in Nashville. It was the first time that they had performed at an awards ceremony, and they not only gave a wonderful performance; they won Star of Tomorrow and Duo of the Year. The Music City News Awards are fan voted, like the People's Choice Awards. After the show, tents are set up at the fairgrounds, and various country artists sign autographs, perform, and mingle with their fans.

After Nashville, Ken surprised the Judds by buying them a $350,000 customized Silver Eagle touring bus with a living room, a booth for dining, three bunks, bath, microwave, TV, refrigerator, full-size bed, vanity, sunroof, and much more. Naomi named this magnificent bus Dreamchaser and hired a driver, Gaylon Moore, and a road manager, Wayne Smith, who used to manage the Charlie Daniels Band. The Judds and their Dreamchaser then went hitting every outdoor fair they could find. They nicknamed it the "Mud and Dust Tour." They traveled through Ohio and into Illinois and picked up Jack "Hawkeye" Hurst, a reporter from the *Chicago Tribune*, who stayed with them for two shows, ate the staple food—corn dogs—and wrote a long article about them.

Some of the more unique audiences included prisoners in Huntsville, Texas, Hell's Angels in Pleasanton, California, the FBI in Missouri, and some nuns in Maryland. All the concerts went off without a glitch. Although there was gossip that the head of the FBI, Judge William Webster, and Naomi had started a romance, Naomi denied it. In New England, Naomi became seriously ill after eating at a cafe in Boston and had to go to the hospital with extreme stomach cramps but played in Hampton Beach, New

Hampshire, the next day. However, she put on the brakes and canceled their show in Van Wert, Ohio, when she discovered that Wynonna had a dental malady called "dry socket." It was one thing when Mom was sick and another when it happened to one of the children, so Wynonna had her wisdom teeth pulled, and they took some time off while she recovered.

Meanwhile, like everyone else, Ashley was reading about her mom and sister in newspapers and magazines. Ashley formed an extended family with some friends from her school. When summer came, she joined her mother and her sister. Naomi paid Ashley ten dollars a day to clean the bus and made sure she spent at least two hours doing algebra for a correspondence class she was taking. When fall came, Grandma Polly and her husband, Wib, insisted that Ashley live with them and finish out her senior high school year in Ashland. For the first time since she was born, Ashley enjoyed a normal family life.

Ashley would go to school and come home to a "mother" who always had a snack waiting for her and someone to talk to who cared about what she was doing. It was also nice to have her clothes washed and folded and someone to fix and pack her lunch. It was almost like being in a real family home! Polly would talk with Ashley about books they read—Ashley was a voracious reader— and they would go on trips together to museums and art galleries and nearby places, such as a weekend in Washington, D.C. At school, Ashley studied hard, got good grades, and became a homecoming princess.

Meanwhile, Naomi had her hands full with Wynonna, who was now twenty-one and beginning to get into activities that her mother didn't approve. One night some fellow invited Wynonna to a fraternity party, and Naomi approved, since one of the men on the Judd crew would be escorting her. It was agreed that Wynonna could stay out until 2:30 A.M., which was when Dreamchaser was going to leave on the next leg of their tour. But when the hour arrived, Wynonna was nowhere to be found. By 3:30 A.M. Wynonna was still a no-show. Naomi was both angry and worried, as most parents are in this kind of situation. Finally, when a carful of frat boys dropped Wynonna off, Naomi lit into Wynonna, accusing her of being irresponsible to the crew. They had to be in the next town by a certain time so they'd have enough time to set up. Wynonna shot back that she just wanted to hang out with people her own age. Thus ensued a huge argument that came to be known as "the Battle of the Titans."

As brutally and ruthlessly as the Judds fought with each other in front of others, beneath all the yelling was an incredible amount of love, forgiveness, and loyalty. That night, Wynonna slipped a note under Naomi's door that said: "I love you, Mom." Naomi wept, deeply touched by her daughter's ability to say "I'm sorry," first, which she did most of the time.

After this big brouhaha, Naomi began to rethink her relationship with her eldest daughter and slowly realized that they were both getting older. Naomi at thirty-nine was foolishly trying to keep everything the same in the relationship as it was when Naomi was the grown-up mother and Wynonna, now twenty-one, was still the teenager. It wasn't that way anymore, and Naomi had to accept that fact. She finally realized that her role now was "to be her mentor, not her tormentor."

The Judds also realized each time they had a fight that the crew of thirty men had a look on their faces as if they weren't sure the Judds would be together the next day or if they would have a job. It was unfair to their crew to subject them to such volatile situations. In addition, they understood that a lot of moms and their daughters were looking at the Judds as role models. They would get letters asking for advice or questioning them as to how they got along so well. Naomi said, "We began to be kinder and more patient with each other."

When the Judds were in Memphis, they attended the recording of the Reunion of '55 Album at the legendary Sun Studios, where Elvis began his career. Naomi remembered stories Larry used to tell her about Graceland and Elvis, particularly the one about how Elvis gave Larry some of his stage outfits after he gained weight. Then she thought about how Ken Stilts was such an Elvis fan, and wouldn't it be great to have a wax figure of Elvis made wearing the outfit he gave Ken, which she could give him for Christmas. Naomi had to call Larry to see if he would be interested in selling one of his Elvis suits.

Naomi says her hands were visibly trembling as she picked up the phone. It had been a year since that fateful night when they listened to the news that "Mama He's Crazy" had become the number-one country song. Earlier he called her and wanted to get back together. Naomi said that if Larry agreed to give her an Elvis outfit, it would mean he was still holding a torch for her and wanted a reconciliation. Larry was pleasantly surprised to hear from Naomi and agreed to sell her an outfit for two thousand dollars—a bargain. When Larry asked when she could come to his apartment and pick up the clothes, she told him she was too busy and that she'd put him in contact with her personal assistant, Vanessa Ware, whom Naomi had hired in 1984.

The next crisis occurred when Marlboro offered to sponsor several concerts. Ken became excited because of the exposure it would bring to the Judds, but Naomi, a nurse, understood the effects of smoking and didn't want to promote tobacco on any level. Ken finally convinced Naomi to accept Marlboro's endorsement, but only under certain conditions: She would never say the word Marlboro, she would give a percentage of the profits to food banks, and she would visit the centers to create publicity for them.

Meanwhile, work on the album continued. The Judds collected songs from songwriters, including Paul Kennerley, Jamie O'Hara, and, of course, Brent Maher. The critics raved about the new album. On October 1985, the Country Music Association announced that the Judds had been nominated for three awards: Vocal Group of the Year, Single of the Year, and Album of the Year. They won Group of the Year and Single of the Year for "Why Not Me."

Even with this great news, the Judds were not going to sit around and rest on their laurels; the tour must go on. They went to Yakima, Washington, where Naomi swears they almost froze to death, and then they flew to Amsterdam for a European tour. They toured London and then Switzerland, which Naomi says was her favorite country. In fact, they loved it so much that they decided to have a shooting session in the Alps for the cover of their holiday album. Unfortunately, during the shoot the driver almost caused the sled to go off a steep cliff, and the photo session was cut short, but they did come away with a beautiful, serene picture for their Christmas album.

When the Judds returned to America, they were scheduled to do a TV taping every day of the week. There was *Dick Clark, Rockin' New Year's Eve, Hour Magazine, Solid Gold*, and *The Tonight Show* with Johnny Carson. The Judds' visit on *The Tonight Show* was special fun because one of the writers, Bob Smith, had been Naomi's classmate in Ashland. Ken told them, "You girls could bust your butts out on that hard road for a solid year and not be exposed to as many people as you'll reach on this one TV show." It was such a big deal that they decided to fly Ashley to Los Angeles to be with them.

Back in Nashville, Naomi and Wynonna went to a benefit concert for one of their secretaries whose husband was paralyzed in a hunting accident. The day before the show, Larry called Naomi and asked her if he could come to the show and watch, since he still had never seen them perform live. She hesitantly agreed. Though Wynonna concurred with her mother's decision, she was concerned that Larry's presence would interfere with her performance. It didn't.

Afterward, Larry walked right up to the bus and stood before his two ladies. Wynonna immediately threw her arms around him as though nothing had happened. Neither Larry nor Naomi moved toward each other. There was some desultory small talk, and then Larry looked into Naomi's eyes and asked what she was doing tomorrow. It was an electric moment, heightened by the fact that Wynonna was standing next to them, looking back and forth at these two grown-ups who were acting like lost children.

They both loved each other, and they both knew it, but neither could make the big move. Then Naomi told Larry to come to her condo the following night for supper. He did, and they went shopping for ornaments for her Christmas tree. The reunion was strained, but Larry, a perfect gentlemen, did not even try to hug her.

The week before Christmas, the Judds were scheduled to play Vegas, which is a place that Naomi doesn't like because she can't stand the thought that people go out there and gamble away their hard-earned money. The main topic of conversation revolved around winning or losing money, and it proved to be too much for these country gals. On top of all that, Merle Haggard, for whom they were opening, appeared to be distracted and drinking heavily. The management considered dumping Haggard and making the Judds the headliners, but Haggard made it through to the end of the week. It was an omen of something to come.

Larry and Naomi were officially together again and would show up at social gatherings as a couple. Naomi says that while the sight of the two of them caused a stir, people were genuinely glad to see them together again. For Christmas, Larry went home to spend a few days with his family in North Carolina. Naomi and Ashley went to Polly's in Ashland, and Wynonna flew there in a private plane to meet them. Friends and neighbors stopped by. Naomi has very fond memories of that Christmas. After all, now she had medical insurance, life insurance, three burial plots, and money to take care of her children. What more could anyone ask?

19

Aboard the Dreamchaser

THE JUDDS HAD BECOME AN AMAZING SUCCESS. When Naomi turned forty in January 1986, the night they won their second Grammy, she returned to her hotel room and got another surprise, a call from Larry that was reminiscent of a lyric from some of the songs played that night at the Grammy ceremony about a love and a life gone wrong and a broken man begging forgiveness from his woman. Larry poured out his heart to Naomi. He said he was trying to alter his behavior—bedding every female over twelve who came within a mile of him—and that he felt as though he had been getting nowhere in his career and his life. He complained that he had been having panic attacks, had been hospitalized, and wanted to get off his personal, fear-induced merry-go-round. He summed things up by telling Naomi he needed to find some peace and happiness and thought Naomi and God, in that order, could give it to him.

Naturally, Naomi loved hearing this outpouring of Larry's feelings, but like many women in love, she failed to grasp the focus of Larry's mea culpa. All he was talking and thinking about was himself—how he hurt and how he needed peace, but nothing about what he could bring to the table for the woman he wanted to save and comfort him. Naomi had to think over what Larry said. In the meantime, Wynonna, now 22, had grown into a young woman and had been dating quite a few musicians whom she'd met on the road, such as Gene Miller, the bandleader from Barbara Mandrell's band; Gary Smith, who was Ricky Skaggs's keyboard player; and Dwight Yoakam.

Professionally, too, life was sublime for the singing Judds. In February they would play the Houston Astrodome for the first time. Even though the Astrodome is a huge arena and its size precludes the one-on-one personal intimacy that exists in smaller sites, Naomi still made a point of connecting with the audience. She spoke of an occasion when she met a fan, David Brown, before the concert who told her how he had met his girlfriend, Susan Perot. It was at a club after he got up the nerve to ask her to dance with him while the DJ played "Mama He's Crazy." Now, he told her, he was trying to figure out how to ask his girl to marry him. During the concert Naomi and Wynonna stopped before singing "Mama He's Crazy" and pointed to the area where they knew David was sitting. Naomi said, "Hey, Susan Perot, David wants to know if you'll be his wife?" This was the kind of at-home interplay that helped make Naomi so popular with her fans.

The next big arena in which the Judds performed was Ranger Stadium in Arlington, Texas, in front of a crowd of thirty-eight thousand. Naomi likes to fool around during a show, and Ranger Stadium proved to be no exception when she batted an imaginary ball with her microphone and ran the bases, meeting Wynonna amid thunderous applause at home plate. Then they were off to New York City and the famous Radio City Music Hall, where the mood was a little more restrained, but the shopping afterward wasn't when Wynonna and Naomi checked out Saks Fifth Avenue. It was an experience and a half because they had never been inside a store with so many goodies they wanted to buy. Suddenly, they broke loose and were enjoying the first high-style shopping binge of their lives.

Neither one of them would ever forget the experience, even though Ken, their manager, was a little put out by their extravagance. Naomi says she also learned a lesson, namely, "Never loan your credit card to someone you've given birth to."

Not that this was the end of their Manhattan experience. They loved the wonderful restaurants and further shopping in other stores on subsequent days. They were also kept busy by the press and TV. They did *The Today Show* with Jane Pauley, and after that they appeared on *Phil Donahue*.

When they weren't doing TV shows or shopping or eating, they were back in their hotel room. One time, a reporter, Jon Bream, of the *Minneapolis Star Tribune*, came to Naomi's room to interview the Judds for the first time and walked in on one of their now-famous arguments. He taped their entire banter and then printed it, along with his commentary, in a story entitled "Judds: Precious Innocence Is Part of Their Charm."

Another reporter caught in the middle of a Judd battle was Kurt Osslinger Jr., of *Country Song Roundup*. During an interview, he sat and watched the Judds argue back and forth about room temperature, which segued into an argument about Wynonna's age and maturity, which is something parents and children love to harp on, as if children were always children and adults were always adults. At that point, Wynonna was twenty-one and had been dating Dwight Yoakam. They made a good pair; they understood each other's lifestyle, background, and goals, and Naomi was crazy about him, which is not always a plus in a relationship.

In the end, Dwight and Wynonna's mutually demanding schedules left little time for them to be together. They agreed to be good friends. Of course, all the details of their affair were relevant to the press and their fans. As the Judds' popularity grew, the interviews changed from questions about their background and their rags-to-riches story to boyfriends and romance. Wynonna knew what she was looking for and made that very clear from the start: "We prefer everyday men who aren't afraid to get their hands dirty." She found it mildly amusing and a little disconcerting that a lot of people assumed that the Judds were celebrities, successful, and with a lot of money, which would make them prefer dating other celebrities, tycoons, or playboys. In fact, both mother and daughter preferred ordinary men. Naomi's taste was undoubtedly shaped to some extent by her father and the men she grew up observing and interacting with at the Judds' gas station in Ashland.

The Judds soon had a corps of male groupies, with guys sending the usual candy, poems, and marriage proposals. One outrageous fan, Dave Scheibe, promised his daughter a new Corvette if she got him a date with Naomi. With mother and daughter constantly working together, socializing, and traveling, an unusual atmosphere developed. There was also the unspoken contrast between mother and daughter, with most people—men, in particular—visualizing Naomi as Wynonna's older and prettier sister. It must have been strange to witness men going after your mom or your daughter right before your eyes.

Of course, their relationship was pretty unique. Often Naomi would discover how Wynonna felt at press conferences when Wynonna complained to journalists about her controlling ways. Bob Allen, a writer from *Country Music*, tried to sum up their relationship when he described Wynonna's impulsive behavior, her need to rebel against her mother, and at the same time the need for Naomi's approval. Naomi commented on the Allen article, saying she understood the need to be sensitive to her daughter's feelings, because of their particularly ambivalent relationship. Musically, they were equal partners, each enhancing the other's talent to produce entertainment that was superior to what either of them did alone. However, their professional relationship aside, Naomi would not abdicate her role as Wynonna's mother. The trick was to keep the two roles and the two identities separate.

They are also distinct personalities. Naomi and Wynonna are opposites, and while Naomi is controlling, prepared, and concerned about what others think of her, Wynonna is carefree, says what she means, and doesn't seem to care about what others think. Naomi says, "Our music was bigger than both of us: the glue that bound us together, the motivation to be more patient, the inspiration to try to get along."

The critics agreed as they toured the country and exposed their talents to tens of thousands of fans everywhere. The concert reviews kept getting better and better: "Simply put, there is no finer country singer today than Wynonna Judd..." Walter Tunis wrote in the *Lexington Paper*. "Music of the spheres," declared James Tarbox of the *Pioneer Press Dispatch*. "Wynonna Judd will go down in history alongside Patsy Cline," wrote producer Gail Davis in an interview with *Newsweek*.

Even with all the accolades, at this point Wynonna never got a big head, nor did she want any special treatment. One night, Wynonna was standing in line at the Bluebird Club in Nashville for a Dan Fogelberg concert when it began to rain. The manager recognized Wynonna and told her to come inside. Wynonna declined his offer, instead choosing to stick it out with the rest of the paying customers.

The only trouble that the Judds experienced on the road was Wynonna's asthma. After a show in Austin, Texas, Wynonna had such a horrible attack that she had to be rushed to the hospital; the next day's show was canceled. She took her Marax pills and brought her inhaler everywhere they went, but sometimes it just wasn't enough. Even so, she and Naomi kept touring and singing until one concert blurred into the next. Suddenly it was time again for the American Country Music Awards show. This time, when the Judds won for "Top Vocal Duo," Naomi did something that surprised everybody, maybe even herself. She grabbed daughter Ashley from the audience and introduced her as the third, unsung Judd. Then she and Wynonna left on a Canadian tour with Vince Gill as his opening act and did a show practically every night. When they weren't giving a concert, they would arrange to visit a local record store to promote their albums and to meet and chat with the patrons. The schedule was hectic, but it was also part of what the life of a successful star is all about.

Back in Ashland, where she had been living with her grandmother, Polly, and Polly's husband, riverboat captain Wib, Ashley graduated from Paul G. Blazer High School on May 27, 1986. Senior year in high school was one of the happiest of her life. She said, "It was the first time I was in a traditional family. It really calmed me down."

Flying back home to watch Ashley graduate from her old high school produced mixed emotions in Naomi. The last time Naomi was officially a student at Paul Blazer High was when she was pregnant and the object of cruel gossip. Now Naomi was the returning queen, an award-winning country-music star who had achieved her dream. She was the grown-up version of the little girl who had lost her way but who now, twenty years later, had found it again.

Naomi describes how she felt: "The last time I'd been there they'd stared at me in pity. Now they stare at me and that baby-turned-star every chance they get." Naomi clearly felt vilified two decades before and now got a secret thrill when she presented the Brian Judd Scholarship to a young man—Noel Quade—for "academic achievement under trying or adverse circumstances."

While in Kentucky, the Judds sang at a fair. Ashley accompanied them and agreed to give an interview to Bob Dollar from the *Kentucky New Era*. Once again, Naomi learned something about a daughter that she didn't know through a newspaper article. In the interview Ashley expressed interest in being an actress. The thought made Naomi cringe, for she knew the rigors and emotional war games that such a career would involve, but Ashley had grown into a person with enough self-reliance to spare—because of her upbringing or in spite of it.

It was a short, bittersweet jaunt to Kentucky to see home, Ashley, and Ashland and then back to Nashville, where the Judds began to work on their third album, which would follow the others as a commercial success. The three singles on the album became number-one hits: "Turn It Loose," "Maybe Your Baby's Got the Blues," and "I Know Where I'm Goin."

It is an interesting insight into the critical importance of radio stations and their program directors—not the disc jockeys, since they often play what they are told to by the program directors—to see what happened to the fourth single, "Don't Be Cruel," pulled off this album because the stations wouldn't play it. It had been an Elvis Presley favorite, and some radio stations thought it was an insult or disrespectful to the memory of "the King" to play a song made popular by him. The music business is a very personal one in which friendships are critically important. As they went out on the road more and more, Naomi and Wynonna would not only make appearances at record stores and talk with fans and the store buyers, who decided what they would stock and how they would display them; they would also stop at radio stations whenever they could and chat with the program director, disk jockeys, and other people there.

When they were recording an album, the Judds made it a practice to meet writers of the songs they were using so they could share a sense of the meanings of the songs and how they might best be performed. Naturally, God hasn't made the writer who doesn't like that kind of ego message, especially when delivered by two beautiful, flirtatious Southern women. Naomi and Wynonna loved making albums and the process of working in the studio because it gave them a chance to be totally relaxed—no make-up, no hair spray, no fancy clothes; not that they were scruffy, just not glamorous. They loved the camaraderie and the creative process of putting a song together with that special Judd flare.

When their third album was completed, they couldn't decide on a title, so they thought about it for a while, during which time they had to start back on tour again. Then, one night when the Judds were playing on the Vegas Strip, Naomi returned to the Hilton to find a letter from her mom with clippings from two local Kentucky papers, the *Courier Journal* and the *Big Sandy News*. There was one story about a town called Waddy, Kentucky, "where the Union 76 truck stop played Loretta Lynn, Randy Travis, and the Judds." Naomi immediately felt a connection with the small-town mom-and-pop diners and country stores she read about in that article; she had encountered enough of them in her travels. She decided to write an open letter to the town to tell them that she'd rather be back in the heartland. With Brent's approval, the third album would be called *Heartland*.

Before you could blink an eye, they boarded their new bus, Dreamchaser, and were "back on the road again," in the words of the Willie Nelson song. They would drive all night, then arrive in different towns anywhere between breakfast and lunch. Naomi says, "Sometimes we'd awaken to find ourselves parked at the curb of some busy downtown street. Wynonna and I would bump into each other in our jammies on the way to the bathroom."

Outside the bus, of course, oblivious to the Judds inside, were the townspeople, going about their work and their business. For the Judds, work and business came at night. During the daytime,

Naomi loved to explore each new town and soak in some of the local atmosphere. She would take a cab out to the edge of town, walk around, and chat with kids on bikes or folks mowing their lawns. She observed their lifestyles and wondered what her life would've been like if she had fallen in love, gotten married, and decided to be a housewife.

In some ways there was always a tinge of guilt about Ashley, for Naomi, while she knew she did what she had to do to hold things together and support herself and her children, felt on some level that she had abandoned her youngest daughter. Although they frequently spoke on the phone, Naomi was physically absent from Ashley's life, which would have a lifelong effect on her youngest daughter. Ashley claims that her mother's vagabond lifestyle enriched her life, but you have to wonder, Is that her head or her heart talking? Naomi did all she could to pass on that self-reliant gene to Ashley. Both Ashley and Naomi agree that it's okay to leave a young girl at home while Mom traipses around the country in search of her dream.

What a dream it was! The Judds were now headlining shows and getting bigger with every song, and while they didn't get booked with a lot of female acts, when they did, they loved it. Some of the women included Patty Loveless, the Forester Sisters, Tanya Tucker, and Marie Osmond, and it was a chance to share war stories, talk about men, and even trade beauty secrets. After sound checks of the audio equipment, there was usually a dinner of some sort provided by the local catering company and a chance for the acts to get to know one another and the crew to share a few laughs or stories. Often there would be pranks and jokes. A popular prank was for everyone in the band and crew to tell the caterer not to serve crew-member Odell any beans. Odell apparently had a gas problem that everyone became quickly aware of after he consumed beans. Finally, he gave up asking and vowed to keep the bus a fresh air environment.

Naomi established the "Judd Annual Cuss Day" because profanity bothered her and everyone had to watch what they said. Naomi was aware that everyone tried hard not to swear, so she declared a day of pure, unadulterated swearing, with two exceptions that were always forbidden around Naomi: the "f word" and taking the Lord's name in vain.

In time life on the road got pretty routine, as is normal with almost every human endeavor no matter how exciting, glamorous, or dangerous it appears to outsiders. It consisted of driving all night, waking up, eating, phone calls or interviews, doing a sound check, relaxing (sort of, because you never really relax before a show), and then getting ready for the show. At some point, Naomi and Wynonna checked into a hotel so they could bathe and rest easier, but by 7:00 P.M. the women usually left their room, and that's about when the butterflies started to collide. They would walk their dogs, sign autographs, and then get back either to the hotel, the bus, or the dressing room to wait for the arrival of their bandleader, Mark Thompson.

When Mark arrived, they would all go over the song list and agree on which songs would be performed in what order and any other details they might want to cover. Then it was on to the auditorium or arena stage, where the shows were performed with all the energy and verve they could muster for the thousands of fans. That was what audiences came to see and hear. When it was all over a few hours later, it was back to business; exhausted, they rolled down the highway to the next concert location, where they began the process all over again.

Sometimes when Ashley joined them on the road, the Judds would watch TV, or Ashley would read out loud to Wynonna from either of her favorite books, *A Prayer for Owen Meany* by John Irving or *Victory of Japan* by Ellen Gilchrist. Sometimes they would play a Bonnie Rait CD and dance and sing around the hotel room.

One Fourth of July, 1986, the Judds headed for Lake City, South Dakota, to do an outdoor concert. There they received the news that Mama Ciminella had suffered a serious stroke and was in the hospital back in Ashland. The Judds flew there immediately, even though they had to be back in South Dakota in a few hours. Naomi heard that the man promoting the concert had mortgaged his farm to bring them to Lake City and felt obliged to fulfill her obligation. Luckily, Ken lined up a Lear jet to fly them back so they could appear on time.

On August 9, as often happens in life, somebody else's mistake or tragedy became the Judds' opportunity when they were supposed to open for Merle Haggard at the Universal Amphitheater in Los Angeles. When they arrived, they learned that Haggard had apparently become depressed and withdrawn or possibly had gone on a drinking binge, which left the Judds with two days of sold-out concert dates. Earlier the Judds won a Grammy for Best Country Performance by a duo or group with "Why Not Me?" and at the American Country Music Awards, they won the Hat Award as top vocal duet, but all this time they had been opening for other acts on the road. The promoters of the Universal concert tried getting other acts, such as Willie Nelson, but couldn't on such short notice, and so overnight the Judds became the main act.

Ken Stilts broke the news that they were going to have to be the headliner and that they would quickly have to find a local opener, which they did in the person of the band South Pacific, from Malibu. As noted earlier, opening acts are important to warm up the audience and make it more receptive to the headliners. They were all set, except that there were thousands of people seated in the Universal Amphitheater who had come expecting to see and hear Merle Haggard, not the Judds. The announcer explained to the audience that Merle was ill and couldn't perform that evening but that they were pleased to bring them, instead, the Judds. Understanding that some of them might be disappointed, the management would happily refund the admission of anyone who wanted to leave.

In their dressing room, Naomi and Wynonna dressed apprehensively, wondering how many thousands of people were lined up at the box office that very moment asking for their money back. Naomi thought to herself, What if there's no one in the theater when we run out onstage? Isn't it nervewracking enough traveling, doing a show, without all this extra drama? They had been opening for Kenny Rogers and Conway Twitty, but the Judds had never, in those last two years, been a main act. They had been very successful at what they did, but they had not yet achieved star status, and doing opening acts and building a following were all part of the apprenticeship everybody went through in show business. However, they came across as stars that night. Nobody asked for his or her money back. For the concerts that followed, they changed the theme of their performances, consistent with what they had said when receiving awards in 1985 about theirs being a dream-come-true kind of success in show business. They were overwhelmed by the loving reaction of their audiences and kept emphasizing that everyone should hold on to his dream.

What happened next was not a dream but akin to a potential nightmare that could change Naomi's life forever. Like most women who draw ever closer to the edge of middle age, Naomi, now forty, was concerned about her youthful appearance. This concern was not only personal but professional. She had always been told she looked like Wynonna's sister instead of her mother. According to many (including Naomi), part of their appeal was their looks. What would happen if Naomi's looks started to fade even a little?

Naomi decided to get collagen injected into her laugh lines. Many of Naomi's female acquaintances had used it and were satisfied with the result. So Naomi took the usual skin-test injections to see if she would have any allergic reaction. The Country Music Association Awards of 1986 were approaching, and Naomi went to get the injections four days before the big event. She received ten painful shots on each side of her face, but on the way home, Naomi knew that something was wrong. Each injection site started to swell up like tiny bee stings. She had suffered a severe allergic reaction to the collagen and immediately returned to the doctor. She had tested extremely well for any allergic reaction, but one thing that disputed what "everybody" and science said was that she had such a bad reaction. Everybody and science were wrong, and Naomi's body was right.

Fearing a malpractice lawsuit, the doctor quickly gave her an injection of hydrocortisone, an anti-inflammatory drug, and Naomi wore a heavy base makeup to cover the redness and swelling, but if you had gotten close enough to her, you would have known that something weird was going on. That night, they won the Vocal Group of the Year Award, and Naomi lived through her freakish skin problem, but the problem wouldn't just go away. In fact, it may even have been one of the factors that ultimately ended her career.

During this time the fights between Naomi and Wynonna occurred less frequently, but they were meaner and more destructive. After struggling for so long, Naomi felt that their success and their glamorous life were going to Wynonna's head. Naomi would irritate Wynonna by reminding her how far they had come and that Wynonna had been a secretary just three years before. Don Potter, who toured with them, was a stabilizing influence. "He has been a major blessing in my life," Wynonna admitted, but it was a blessing that would not accompany the Judds every time they toured. He didn't like going on tour and stayed home; the Judds only saw him when they returned to Franklin.

Wynonna liked to party, but she came from a religious and stable home that restrained her at times. She had been seeing a man named McCord, but as she grew more sophisticated on the road, he became less appealing, and they drifted apart. Still, people noticed that Wynonna was growing up and Naomi was becoming more self-confident. For the second consecutive year, in 1986, the two received the County Music Association Award for Best Vocal Group.

Ashley, who was largely abandoned at fifteen when her mother and sister started touring seriously, left Franklin and moved to Ashland with Polly. Then she moved to Lexington to live with her father. In time, she graduated from Paul G. Blazer High School and enrolled at the state university. After that, she pursued an acting career in Hollywood, and that promised to bring the three Judds back together, which might heal some old wounds between the sisters. "Ashley and I have a very love-hate relationship," Wynonna admits. Wynonna believes Ashley thinks she is melodramatic and spoiled, and Wynonna thinks Ashley is full of baloney. "It's really wonderful to sit in the room and watch the three of us go off on one another—and that's exactly what happens."

At one point 20th Century–Fox conceived the idea of bringing these three women together in a TV comedy. Naomi liked the idea.

Doing a show together would serve as a form of private reconciliation; they would also be paid well. They met with the network executives but in the end decided to pass. Naomi said the thought of spending so much time in Hollywood was unappealing to them. She also expressed a major reservation to the people at Fox, that none of them could actually act, although Ashley would eventually develop into an actress. The project never reached the stage of being turned into a pilot.

Something that made more sense, at least for Naomi and Wynonna, was to produce another album, which they set out to do with Brent Maher, their producer. They both wanted to include an Elvis Presley song, "Don't Be Cruel," because they are big Elvis fans and because Naomi believes it was the dead Elvis who brought her together with her boyfriend Larry Strickland. Larry sang bass with the Stamps Quartet and hung around with Elvis and as a result got some of his clothes. Naomi had not seen Larry Strickland for about a year after he came by on the propitious day that "Mama He's Crazy" hit number-one on the country charts and she was a very happy lady. Larry had some of Elvis's clothes, and Naomi wanted to buy an outfit from him to use in her performances. As noted earlier, when he came over to talk about it, they got together again.

The second significant thing to happen in 1986 was that Naomi's nursing license from the state of Tennessee lapsed on the last day of the year. She had decided not to renew it, making a total commitment to being a country-music entertainer. It was a commitment that she would not have been comfortable making several years earlier. About the only nursing that Naomi figured on having to do from here on out was to control Wynonna's allergies and tension problems on tour.

20

The River of Time
Keeps Flowing

THE YEAR 1987 brought the Judds two more honors from the American Music Awards; Country Single of the Year and Best Country Video, both for "Grampa (Tell Me 'Bout the Good Old Days)." Afterward, the Judds went straight from the public bathroom, where they had changed from their stage outfits into street clothes, and hurried to the airport, where they then flew to France.

The Midem International Music Festival had taken over the beautiful town of Cannes—as does its film festival—and the Judds walked around wide-eyed as they mingled with international music stars. What strongly impressed animal-loving Wynonna was that dogs were allowed everywhere, even in restaurants. The Judds performed at the festival, which was broadcast live to 300 million people. They then flew to Monte Carlo and London to perform at the London Palladium. At first, Wynonna was too petrified to sing before a British audience; she had heard rumors that they were harsh critics. Her fears vanished, however, when the Brits gave them a standing ovation, and the *Record Mirror* even warned of Juddmania!

Naomi continued to take massive daily doses of prednisone to relieve her asthma. It resulted in terrible insomnia, and she paced the floor all night, causing her to almost fall asleep during interviews the following day. They had come to Europe to promote their new album, which was number one there and in England. The demand for interviews was staggering. Naomi felt that she wasn't getting the results that prednisone promised, plus her cheeks still felt chubby, and she seemed to be getting worse. She also discovered that extended use of prednisone causes Cushing's syndrome.

Naomi was very concerned about her physical health, which was pivotal to the continued success of the singing Judds. Because steroid medicine, such as prednisone, is commonly prescribed, Cushing's syndrome is also common, and among adults it is mostly found in women between thirty-five and forty-five. Naomi was taking prednisone for her asthma, and her gender and age were strong risk factors. As a nurse, she knew that Cushing's could increase her blood pressure and add pounds to her stomach, face, and upper back as well as make her skin fragile and sensitive. Even more disturbing to an attractive woman like Naomi, it can have a masculinizing effect on women, including growth of facial hair and loss of hair on the head. Other signs include fatigue, weakness, depression, mood swings, increased thirst and urination, and lack of menstrual periods in women—a very unpleasant situation, particularly if you make your living looking beautiful, traveling great distances, and working long, stressful hours. If Cushing's syndrome occurs and withdrawal of the medicine is not monitored, the disease can ultimately require the removal of the entire pituitary gland. If medicine withdrawal works, it can still take two to eighteen months to completely get over Cushing's, during which time the patient suffers dizziness, weakness, nausea, and loss of appetite. So Naomi had to monitor the medicine, which proved difficult, since she was always pushing and driving to succeed.

Although Naomi was concerned about her condition, mother and daughter found some small comfort in the fact they could walk the streets of Europe and not worry about being recognized. It felt great to be able to sit at a cafe and enjoy their meal without

A happy Ashley at the thirtieth Academy of Country Music Awards ceremony, Universal Studios Amphitheater, Studio City, California, May 10, 1995 (Gregg Deguire)

Ashley Judd with brother-in-law Arch Kelley III at premier of the movie *Nick of Time*, Academy Theater, Beverly Hills, California (Tammie Arroyo)

Naomi poses with daughter Ashley at the thirty-second annual Country Music Awards, April 23, 1997. (Gregg Deguire)

Naomi in svelte white gown holds up greeting sign, "Hi, Wy," for her older daughter, Wynonna. (Gregg Deguire)

Naomi gets an unexpected lift from the men of Diamond Rio. (Gregg Deguire)

Naomi on the set of the TV miniseries *The Judds*, Pasadena, California, January 18, 1995 (Ron Davis/Shooting Star International)

(*Left*) Ashley Judd as a blonde for her role as Marilyn Monroe (Nancy Kaszerman/Shooting Star International)

(*Below right*) Naomi kisses her Academy of County Music Award at Universal Studios ceremony in Studio City, California. (Gregg Deguire)

(*Below left*) Wynonna at the Peninsula Hotel, Beverly Hills, California, with her two dogs, Tammy and Wynette (Ron Davis/Shooting Star International)

(*Above*) The Judds in concert (Marc Morrison/Shooting Star International)

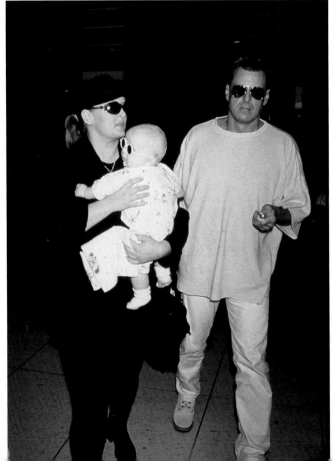

(*Left*) Wynonna, husband Arch, and their son, Elijah, at Los Angeles International Airport, June 21, 1995 (Bob Scott/Celebrity Photo)

The apartment where Naomi, Wynonna, and Ashley lived in West Hollywood, California, just off the Sunset Strip, on Larrabee Street (Karen Erbach)

The Sunset Strip just a half block from where Naomi, Wynonna, and Ashley lived on Larrabee Street (Karen Erbach)

Naomi's first California home, in Sylmar, where she lived with husband, Michael Ciminella, and daughter, Christina (later named Wynonna). The family was living in this home when Ashley was born. (Karen Erbach)

Providence Holy Cross Medical Center where Ashley was born in Sylmar, California (Karen Erbach)

worrying about being disturbed every five minutes. She realized that when you finally become famous, you learn it is not easy to cope with the attention.

Beyond that, Naomi had an artistic concern: Being thrust into a glamorous celebrity life can strip a country artist of the very thing that made him or her a success, namely, empathy with the ordinary crises and nuances of country life. It's easy to be the recipient of oysters and champagne in a $500-a-night luxury hotel suite. One can easily forget what it meant to haul ice-encrusted wood to the stove or to sit in a drafty outhouse with veils of snow swirling around outside, sad and depressed because your lover has gone.

Naomi and Wynonna soon returned to their own country, and while they enjoyed their sojourn to Europe, it was good to be home, tooling around the highways on tour in their favorite bus, Dreamchaser. They had played almost all fifty states, and as they passed through them, Naomi said she tried to teach Wynonna the state capitals and historical facts. In the process, she, too, was getting an education of her own about the lives of ordinary people, whom she had understood partially from growing up where she did.

Still, the Judd family wasn't poverty-stricken, and Naomi lived in a relatively comfortable middle-class environment. She was surprised to see how the majority of Americans lived. As they drove around the country, she was impressed by the changes month to month and year after year, with shopping malls springing up where family farms had once been cultivated and with tract houses replacing open fields or dense woods. Naomi recalls when they performed at Dave Murdoch's ranch in California for then President Reagan, she wanted to grab him and say, "Wake up! Wake up! American's in danger!" Ashley came to Dave Murdoch's ranch, too, and when the Judds drove past the Secret Service, they were simply waved on. Naomi figured that they either recognized the Judds or knew that Naomi was good friends with Judge Webster, now head of the CIA.

When the Judds returned to Nashville, they rented studio space and began to put together their show for 1987. Theirs was a treadmill existence: preparing for a road tour when home, then on the road for months, and finally back home to prepare for the next road tour and the next album. These rehearsals proved increasingly difficult for Naomi; she was popping the prednisone pills like a junkie and they were making her irritable and tired. It got so bad that during one rehearsal she walked out, went home, closed the drapes, and told Larry, who was living there, that she didn't want to be disturbed. Everyone was concerned, but Naomi convinced them that her condition was temporary, even though she knew enough about the pharmacology of prednisone to be aware of the danger of contracting Cushing's syndrome.

Somehow they made it through the trying months, and the Judds were ready for what they christened their Heartland tour. They had a new production manager, Tim Rogers, Kenny Rogers's nephew. Their opening act was the new country heartthrob of the moment, Randy Travis. The premiere show was a huge success, but Naomi wasn't herself even though the Judd gang tried to cheer her up by buying her a 1956 T-bird convertible with the vanity plates Hillbilly. Naomi appreciated the effort, but it was becoming obvious that something was seriously wrong with her.

During the 1987 Grammys, Wynonna became concerned about her mother's sleeping and her irritability when she was awake. Naomi may have been sick, but one would never have known it by all the awards the Judds kept taking home. They received a Grammy for Best Country Performance by a Duo/Group. The only mistake, if you could call it that, was Naomi's dress, which was about two inches too low at the neckline. She was reprimanded by RCA and Ken. The Associated Press ran a photo of the revealing dress, and Dennis Miller from *Saturday Night Live* even joked about the photo on the show. Naomi naively explained that the dress had arrived only two hours before show time and there wasn't time to fix it—which is a good story if anybody believed it, and it's doubtful that anybody did, including Naomi, who loves to be looked at almost as much as people love to look at her.

Often the Judds' lyrics were a bit unusual for country singers; traditionally, female performers have always sung about their man treating them badly or how much they have suffered. The Judds' lyrics were about strong females, family values, and independence.

Some writers, among them Ken Tucker of the *Philadelphia Inquirer* and Mark Crawford of the *Reno Gazette*, labeled the Judds a new breed of feminists. Whatever label anyone gave the lyrics the Judds wrote, the women in their audiences loved them, even if they bewildered some of the men in the world of country music.

Naturally, with the soaring popularity of the Judds came offers to endorse products, such as feminine hygiene and junk food. Naomi and Wynonna weren't interested in endorsing products they didn't believe in or being on TV shows that they found ridiculous, like *Life Styles of the Rich and Famous*. They turned down repeated offers by *Life Styles* because Wynonna couldn't fathom the idea of a TV crew following them around their house. The products the Judds did endorse were AT&T, Kraft Barbecue, Target, and Oldsmobile, all of which they used and enjoyed.

Some wags said they should endorse AT&T because that's who Ashley thought was her mother, since her only contact with Naomi for weeks at a time would be from some phone booth at the side of an interstate highway. Naomi recalls a pretty hilarious story about an Oldsmobile commercial she and Wynonna made. Wynonna would drive Naomi down a country road, and when she got to the curb, Wynonna was told to accelerate just at about the spot where Oscar-winning cinematographer Gordon Willis (*The Godfather*) and his camera crew were set up. It was an extraordinarily hot day, and Naomi noticed that Wynonna was guzzling down what she thought was beer from brown bottles stashed in the cooler. Naomi says she was horrified that Wynonna was drinking beer in front of policemen while driving a new car that wasn't hers.

Gordon put a walkie-talkie into Wynonna's lap so that she could hear him when he yelled "Action." Gordon has a reputation for being an overbearing and in-charge director. Most people around him are afraid of offending him. They were preparing for the shot when Wynonna suddenly grabs the walkie-talkie and snaps into the microphone, "Shut up, you brick brain, or I'll make you an offer you can't refuse!" while pushing the gas pedal to the floor. As the new car lurched from zero to sixty miles per hour, the blood drained from Naomi's face.

Naomi thought Wynonna was driving drunk. She had just

insulted a very important film director. She wasn't going to make that turn up ahead and would end up killing the two of them plus the director and his six-man crew. Naomi did what she has done all her life—acted. She reached over and grabbed the wheel enough to run the car off the road and save everybody—or so she thought.

Everybody came running, and Wynonna was almost speechless—a rare occurrence—but she was able to blurt out that her mother was nuts. As the absurdity of the situation instantly dawned on the two women, they reacted as they frequently did to life's funny happenstances. By the time Gordon and the alarmed crew reached the Judds, they found two beautiful female country singers sitting in a ditched car laughing uncontrollably. It all turned out well, and as compensation the Judds each received a brand-new car, but they ended up giving them away.

Before Ashley was shipped off to the University of Kentucky, Naomi flew her out to Los Angeles so they could just hang out together for a rare attempt at mother-daughter-daughter bonding. When Ashley arrived, Naomi hired a limo, and they went shopping on the then-trendy fashion street of Melrose Avenue, which is trendier and not as uptight as fabled Rodeo Drive and would also become the locale of a TV nighttime soap opera. As they spent the day relaxing, Ashley told her mother and sister about school and how she would be carrying a double major— French and history. Later, on Ashley's summer break, the girls and their mother spent their vacation fishing on a rented houseboat on Lake Sidney Lanier near Atlanta. It was one of those rare occasions when the Judds actually behaved like a traditional family.

After Ashley returned to school and the summer was winding down, Naomi knew that she had to see a doctor about her physical condition, which seemed to be worsening. She called a physician she knew in Franklin and described her symptoms: mild headache, low-grade temperature, insomnia, and a general sense of foreboding. They performed a few blood tests—white blood count, mono, and SMA12. Soon the doctor called Naomi with the bad news: She had CMV—cytomegalovirus. CMV is similar to mono. He told her it would take five or six months for the illness to pass; she would just have to wait it out, since there's nothing one can take for it.

The doctor explained that somewhere between 40 and 100 percent of adults have come in contact with CMV but have developed antibodies for it. Normally it is not contagious, but the doctor pointed out that because Naomi was taking prednisone, her immune system had been compromised and she was more susceptible to it. Naomi was concerned, and being a nurse, she did some of her own research and requested that her test results be sent to her. She discovered that her ALT (alanine aminotransferase, the enzyme that shows liver damage) was high. The test reading is based on the number of units per liter, and the normal range is from 1 to 21 units per liter. Naomi's was in the hundreds!

When she asked her doctor about this high number, he told her that it was probably nothing, just stress or muscle strain. There was no further testing, which proved a huge mistake. Naomi kept her illness to herself because she knew there was nothing anyone could do and she didn't want to worry anybody. Coincidentally, when the Judds played Lake Tahoe, Naomi learned of a new disease that sounded similar to hers that had appeared in Incline Village when Naomi and Wynonna had played Reno, which is very close to Incline. The Center for Disease Control (CDC), based in Atlanta, sent medical investigators to check into the strange new illness that was making half the town sick. They would later identify it as chronic fatigue syndrome.

While Naomi waited out her illness to see what would happen, she tried to enjoy life to the fullest, and their time at Tahoe turned out to be fantastic. They rented a villa, went swimming and parasailing, had barbecues, and relaxed. Later that summer, when Naomi and Wynonna were in northern California, they drove to Marin County and checked out the old haunts. They to visited Wynonna's old school, Sir Francis Drake High, and then drove by the College of Marin.

When the Judds returned to Nashville, they found a condo in the Green Hills area and settled in for a while. Shortly thereafter, the Judds left their handprints in wet concrete on the Starwalk in

Nashville; they were now authentic stars. With stardom come the paparazzi, and soon enough their faces were plastered on the tabloids with such headlines as "The Battling Judds."

Naomi took the news well, but Wynonna was upset and cried. She felt that she and her mom had already worked through so many of their differences and now, after all their hard work, some "inside source" was claiming that they were still fighting. Naomi tried to reassure Wynonna that sensation-seeking articles are written about every celebrity and that she shouldn't take them too seriously.

She pointed to a recent article written by Patrick Carr of *Country Music* magazine, who had spent a day with them on the road. In his article he commented on how well the mother-daughter team got along. The previous story was the Judds' first taste of the sleazy tabloid world, and they decided to ignore it and continue to deal with legitimate reporters and publications. After all, the media had been good for the Judds' career, and in turn the Judds were more than generous with their time with the press. Often they were too generous with information, to the point that they were constantly getting memos from RCA or receiving a reprimand from Ken about talking too freely and giving out too much information. The Judds didn't really see it that way. This was who they were. Take them or leave them.

Apparently, people were more than willing to take them. They won Group of the Year at the Country Music Association Awards, and Wynonna told the audience, "I want to thank you for allowing a twenty-three-year-old to feel what I feel tonight and for allowing Mom to enjoy a second childhood!"

Even though they were mother and daughter, the singing Judds were unique people who dressed differently and were perceived variously by their fans. The press, for example, labeled Naomi a Barbie doll because of her size-six dresses and the flattering outfits she wore, while they called Wynonna Elvis because of her black pants, rock-and-roll rhinestone jackets, and matching boots. Naomi says she called Wynonna "the Countess of Hip," and Wynonna called her "Country Music's Miss America."

The frequent extended road trips interrupted the regular flow and growth of friendships for Wynonna and Naomi, and most of the intimate celebrations were shared with the crew and band members—their extended family. Being on the road allowed the Judds to catch up with out-of-state relatives and friends. They were able to visit Naomi's brother, Mark, who was a now a Baptist minister in Colesburg, near Elizabethtown, Kentucky. They also visited Margaret in York, Pennsylvania. She is a pianist, a dental technician, and a mother, too. Still, Wynonna went from early teens to adult performer without seeing youngsters her own age. Instead, she was constantly in the company of musicians. She never really got to enjoy that once-in-a-lifetime opportunity to be a regular girl.

On Veterans Day, 1987, thousands of veterans and their families and friends were standing near the Vietnam Memorial in Washington in the blinding snow to honor those who had died for their country. In the stillness of the cold and silent snow, Naomi and Wynonna sang "God Bless America." It was a day that everyone present would never forget, including the Judds. Later that night they gave a benefit concert with Bob Hope to raise money so that more names could be added to "the Wall."

The military was the theme for the next couple of weeks as the Judds, along with Ashley, who was on school break, went on a USO tour. They spent Thanksgiving at Guantanamo Naval Base in Cuba, where they mingled and cheered the men stationed there, and when Naomi was asked to give the Thanksgiving prayer, she quickly agreed. After dinner, Naomi, Wynonna, and Ashley made it a point to visit briefly with all the men who couldn't leave their posts and who had missed the dinner. It was a typically thoughtful and gracious thing for the Judds to do and a mark of what is inside them. Then it was back to Nashville, where they went to see the Irish band U2, who were big fans of the Judds, a feeling that was mutual. When the lead singer, Bono, spotted them in the audience, he waved them to come up on the stage. Wynonna joined him for "People Get Ready."

As 1987 wound down, the Judds began preparations for their holiday shows and a special one-hour radio program. After their album *Christmas Time With the Judds* was released, the girls went to Ashland to spend Christmas with Grandma Polly and Wib. Naomi remembers sitting at the kitchen table listening to an old radio when suddenly the Judds' program came on. Old emotions welled up inside her, making her feel as though she were in a time warp as she listened to Wynonna's voice on the radio and remembered all the past Christmases they had spent together—some of them not so joyous or lucky at this one in 1987.

At the beginning of 1988, the Judds appeared at Caesars Palace in Las Vegas; a stand-up comic named Jay Leno opened for them. The Judds went from Vegas to being ringmasters for Ringling Bros. and Barnum & Bailey Circus for a CBS TV special. During this time, Wynonna bought herself a dream home just outside Franklin. It was registered with the Historical Society, and most important, it was big enough for her animals. Not only did she have six dogs and almost thirty cats, but Ken bought Wynonna a horse for Christmas to add to her menagerie. Wynonna had a passion for animals, particularly those in need of love; every time Wynonna saw a stranded animal, she would rescue it.

Meanwhile, Larry seemed to be settling down into a lifestyle that suited him. He was a changed man from the time he first met Naomi. He was now devoted and faithful to her and her children and shared her bed, but the time had come to make a big decision. Larry and Naomi were attracted to each other because they held the same values of family and fidelity, even if Larry had been careless about observing them at the beginning of their relationship. He had wanted to marry Naomi, but she wasn't sure or was scared. Finally, Larry was determined to lay down a marriage ultimatum. He proposed and demonstrated his serious-ness with the presentation of a little velvet box containing a ring. There was no question about her answer.

The next emotional moment occurred days later when the singing Judds' contract with RCA expired. The RCA executives figured that the Judds needed them more than they needed the Judds, so thry insisted they renew with the same terms as their original contract. Ken Stilts simply walked them over to the competing MCA record publisher and got them the deal they wanted. However, there had been a lot of tough negotiating with

RCA before they joined MCA. The state of Ken's health finally brought him to Naomi's door to tell her that he wanted to resign.

The thought of Ken's leaving stunned Naomi, and she tried to convince him to stay with them, but only if he quit smoking and took more time off to be with his family. The three of them held hands and vowed, "Till death do us part." Later, feeling indebted to Ken, Naomi wrote the only song that the Judds would never sing in public; it was a personal song for Ken called "The Ballad of Mr. Big." Wynonna and Naomi recorded it and then put it in a beautiful Wurlitzer jukebox. They also made a personal *This Is Your Life* for Ken in which she hired an actor that resembled Ken, had him wear Ken's clothes, and then had him behave in ways that Ken never would.

At around this time Wynonna started dating Tony King, the lead guitarist for Vince Gill, and Larry, Naomi, Wynonna, and Tony would often double-date—go to movies or bowling or even take a trip to the Taco Bell drive-through.

A new project arose when Tony Eaton, a film producer, contacted the Judds to do a documentary on them. Unlike others with ideas for projects, Tony had the backing of CBS and had lined up director Bud Schaetzle. So Eaton, Schaetzle, and their film crew followed the Judds around America while they made their Across the Heartland tour. The show later aired as a one-hour special and also introduced Ashley to the public, playing herself as an "inside" filmmaker getting behind the scenes footage of the real Judds. Ashley was so comfortable in front of the camera, it seemed natural for her to want to be a film actress. The critics were kind and gave the Judds' TV special a warm reception. Clark Parsons, of the *Nashville Banner*, said that he felt as if he "had a visit, not just a show." Because of all the fine reviews, Ken decided to make the tape available for home video. Later, they took some footage from the video and incorporated it into a music video for *Give a Little Love*, which won *Cable Guide's* Video of the Year.

Before they realized it in their busy lives, it was time to start on the third album, with the usual hunt for songs and collaborators. One of the new changes for the album would be the use of an electric guitar. Up to now all the music they performed had been acoustic, but Naomi recruited Carl Perkins to play electric guitar on "Let Me Tell You About Love." Once again, Naomi couldn't think of a title for the album, and once again, as corny as it may sound, she sought out divine guidance, which she has done all her adult life, without making a big show of it. One night when she was driving back to Ashland, she stopped at a lake to meditate and ask God for inspiration. Some words came to her, and piano player John Jarvis put them to music in a song they called "River of Time."

Naomi told her family that the song was about her brother Brian and the process of grieving over such a devastating loss, and they named the new album after the song. That song and the album would mean more to the Judds because it would somehow heal many wounds in the Judd family in ways that can't be fully explained but may well have begun with the illness and death of Naomi's brother Brian.

Coincidentally, one day soon after, Naomi got a letter from Jimmy Lett, an old friend of Brian's. Jimmy was one of Brian's pallbearers and wanted Naomi to know that because of his friendship with Brian and having suffered watching him live with an incurable disease, Jimmy decided to become a doctor. The letter touched Naomi deeply because she secretly sensed that her own future was becoming more and more uncertain due to an illness that nobody understood.

21

Let Love Be a Bridge

WYNONNA AND NAOMI grew to love their little band-family and to interact with the audience, often responding to comments or shouts farthest away so that those fans did not feel left out. They tried not to take themselves too seriously.

The only blot on Naomi's feelings of complete happiness was her bout with CMV. Her health had not improved, and when the Judds arrived in Las Vegas for their biannual show at Caesars Palace, the illness struck again; she came down with a terrible sore throat. Naomi had slowly weaned herself off prednisone, and sometimes she would visit different doctors to get further opinions about what was happening to her. She would also try nonmedical solutions to alleviate her physical discomfort. After arriving in Vegas, she bought a humidifier and some Vicks ointment and tried to get a full night's sleep. The next day, she discovered that the humidifier had apparently melted away the wallpaper paste and that all the wallpaper was falling down. Naomi felt so bad that she had to cancel their Superbowl Sunday show, one of the biggest events in Vegas.

Later, the Judds appeared at another scheduled show in Utah. Naomi was still sick but refused to cancel the show at the Centrum

Arena and agreed to be interviewed by Rob Weller of *Entertainment Tonight* after the show. Larry had joined Naomi and Wynonna on the road so that he could speak for her and she could save her voice. That night, Larry came along, and when Weller asked who he was, Naomi said he was her fiancé. The next thing the Judds knew, *Entertainment Tonight* was advertising its interview with the Judds, saying that Naomi was leaving the stage to be with her husband. This made the Judds furious because it was the kind of blockbuster news every performer wants to carefully control if it's true and not be reported at all if it's not. The change in a top performer's marital status can seriously affect his or her popularity and an audience's attitude. At that point, it wasn't true that she was engaged.

The Judds complained, and the producers of *Entertainment Tonight* discovered that Weller had hyped up the story and distorted it so that it looked as if he were getting a hot scoop. The technique of shading a story to make it more sensational or pumping up basic information into inflated "facts" is something some reporters do to get that competitive edge. *Entertainment Tonight* offered a retraction the next day; as usual, it was too late for worried fans and promoters. The Judds' business people and managers were inundated with calls, wondering when Naomi would leave the group. Why had nobody called them, and who would pay for this mess? In time, it all got sorted out, and yet it was a precursor of what was to come.

Soon after the *Entertainment Tonight* incident, the Judds went off to Europe again. The first stop was Germany and then Ireland, where Wynonna said she felt a rush of sentimental feelings and the mythical stirring of blood when she walked in the land of her forefathers. She was deeply affected by the appearance of bomb squads and the threat of violence everywhere they turned. In Dublin they played for a relatively small audience of three thousand in an old boxing arena that had a rather musty smell, but they loved it. Somehow, it felt like home. After the concert, members from the band U2 took them to the home of Adam, the bass player, where they were pleasantly amazed that the band had arranged for a surprise party. Wynonna drifted off with the drummer, Larry Mullen, and Naomi hung out with Bono, from the band. Finally, as dawn appeared, the four of them found themselves outside on the patio.

While they were standing there, Naomi said that Bono turned to her and said, "Naomi, are you aware that you are an angel? Do you quite understand that God has put you on this earth to help people?" Naomi says she's not sure why Bono said those things to her, but she is glad that she can call him her friend. Years afterward, in 1996, when Naomi was reminded of this episode, she responded, "I'm no angel. I'm just a red-headed, boogie-woogie babe from rural Mars." Later, when it was time to leave Ireland, Wynonna and Naomi sadly bid farewell and headed home to a busy schedule. They had concert dates scheduled every day until Naomi's marriage, which was now finally going to happen.

Larry and Naomi wanted to have a beautiful, family-oriented wedding that would not turn into some media circus. They wanted their friends and family—who were traveling some distance—to feel comfortable and pampered. They arranged to have them stay in nice hotels with all the amenities—even their dentist from Nashville was invited. A friend of Naomi's, Jo Stilts (Ken's wife), gave a wedding shower, and it was a huge success. Naomi's wedding dress was a blush pink taffeta gown with lace; she said it was her fantasy design. The rehearsal dinner went well, and now all that remained was the wedding.

Naomi and Larry were married at Christ Church on May 6, 1989, in what was the kind of fairy-tale wedding that all young brides dream of, with soft, live music and in a candlelit church. Even though Larry and Naomi had been together for so long, Naomi says she was shaking with excitement that she was finally marrying a man she loved and who loved her in a ceremony that seemed aeons away from that pathetic, embarrassing wedding she had endured with Mike Ciminella in Pearisburg, Virginia, a quarter of a century before. The Judds had covered a lot of ground in those twenty-five years.

Bud Schaetzle, the director, was hired to film the wedding, and Robert Oermann, a family friend, was the only journalist invited. The matron of honor was Naomi's sister, Margaret, and the bridesmaids included Wynonna, Ashley, Naomi's sister-in-law,

Middy, and her niece, Erin. Ken Stilts walked Naomi down the aisle and gave her away. Larry's best man was his brother Don, and the groomsmen were his younger brother Reggie, his brother-in-law Gene Boone, and his friends Ed Enoch, Tony King, and Guy Penrod. Ashley was one of the speakers at the ceremony, and she read from Scripture. While Naomi was getting ready for the wedding, a messenger delivered a letter from Wynonna that touched Naomi deeply that she wanted to share it with loved ones at the wedding ceremony. The wedding went off without a hitch, and the reception was held at the antebellum Redd Mansion, where folks danced to the bluegrass band the Dillards.

More surprises continued to fill their lives. Larry found a dream farm with a two-story house on several hundred acres for the new Mr. and Mrs. Strickland to share. Located on Old Hillsboro Road in Leipers Fork, a small community south of Franklin, it was not far from Wynonna's home in Peaceful Valley, where she kept an estimated twenty-five cats, seven dogs, and three horses. The next surprise was Wynonna's sudden determination to shed that extra weight she was hauling around and hire a personal trainer to take on the road and guide her so she could lose twenty-five pounds. Naomi's marriage was predictably followed by Wynonna's becoming engaged to Tony King, which made everybody around her, including her mother, ecstatic.

Meanwhile, Ashley, the somewhat neglected daughter, was going through her rebellious stage, wearing baggy clothes, acting smart and getting her nose pierced. She also became politically active and at one point was on the cover of a paper, protesting, with the NAACP, against something she thought was racial. Ashley also volunteered at the local soup kitchen, taught French to children, and ran the women's radio program on campus.

Somewhere around this time, Naomi decided to go back to Ashland for her twenty-fifth high school reunion, "Feeling nostalgic," she says, "and fostering a guarded hope that they wouldn't treat me any differently than when they had known me back when." That probably was exactly the opposite of what she felt. "Back when" in her senior year they treated her as a promiscuous, fallen woman carrying a child out of wedlock. Actually, it is more likely that Naomi, with her new name and her new star status, wanted to go back and do a little flaunting in front of her old classmates as in "You treated me like dirt back then and look at me now." Anyway, she said that she had a great time and that everyone was really nice to her. She was even highlighted in the hometown newspaper, and they interviewed her mother for a story.

Naomi has a huge capacity to empathize with the underdog, the person who has nothing or the person who has lost everything. She has known what that's like; she's been there. She's sensitive to the troubles that plague ordinary people and seems to have an intuitive understanding that her positive contribution should come from music. In Oregon she came upon a homeless man that would inspire the song "Love Can Build a Bridge," which also became the title of her autobiography. The first words came to her as she lay in bed that night, but after that, she was suddenly stuck.

One night she and Larry invited Paul Overstreet, a Christian singer, over for dinner. They were casually sitting around the table talking when Paul noticed a postcard from Ashley, who was visiting the Grand Canyon. As he studied the photo, he turned to Naomi and said, "Sometimes the only way we can cross life's great divides is to let love be a bridge." Immediately, Naomi knew this was the part that she needed to complete the song. John Jarvis wrote the music, and they shot a video in the Grand Canyon.

From the taping in Arizona, the Judds went to Hawaii and then back to Nashville for Christmas vacation. Ashley had returned to France after the Grand Canyon experience, where she was studying at the École des Beaux-arts in LaCoste and majoring in French. Naomi was expecting Ashley on the morning of December 21 on a Pan Am flight and suddenly had a terrible scare when Polly called to say that she had heard that a Pan Am airplane had crashed after a midair explosion over Lockerbie, Scotland.

When the Judds turned on the TV they heard the grim news that no one had survived. The entire family was paralyzed until they found out it was not Ashley's flight. Actually, she had been booked on the doomed Pan Am flight 103 but had spent the night in a youth hostel in Frankfurt and was late getting up. She missed the flight by twenty minutes. Naomi says that it was a very strange Christmas. She didn't care about a Christmas tree or presents; all she could think about was how happy she was to have her arms around Ashley. That Christmas the Judds were truly grateful for God's gifts.

22

A Heartbreaking Decision

NEW YEAR'S DAY, 1990, just ten days short of Naomi's forty-forth birthday, did not bring good health or cheer for Naomi. She had to drag herself to the Bob Hope Christmas taping a few days before, and on the afternoon of New Year's Day she was so tired, she napped, which was not like her. During recording sessions Naomi didn't even have the strength to sit in a chair. She had to lie down on the couch.

In a way, it was lucky that Ashley got sick at about this time. While Naomi wouldn't worry enough about her own health, she insisted that her child see the doctor right away. She figured that Ashley probably had the flu, but she wanted to make sure. She took Ashley to the doctor to get a white-blood-count test, and on an impulse, while Naomi was waiting in the office, she asked a nurse to check her blood. The Judds were scheduled to go on tour in a few days, and Naomi wanted to make sure she was well enough to do so. She wasn't. The test results confirmed that she had hepatitis. The doctor informed her that there was damage to her liver but that she had tested negative to both hepatitis A and B. He needed to do a hepatitis C test in a week. He also told her that he knew of no medication that she could take to get better, and he doubted if she was contagious. The irony was that, years before, Naomi's mother, Polly, had been felled by liver disease for a time, and now the same thing seemed to be happening to Naomi.

Hepatitis is an inflammation of the liver caused by certain viruses and sometimes, other factors, such as alcohol abuse or medications. Certainly in Naomi's case it was not due to alcohol. Hepatitis is not a serious threat to health if treated properly. Otherwise, the disease can become chronic and can sometimes lead to liver failure and death.

A small percentage of people with hepatitis go on to develop the most serious complications of viral hepatitis: cirrhosis of the liver, liver cancer, and immune-system disorders. This was the danger with Naomi, who, because she neglected herself by denying she was sick, was in danger of developing cirrhosis of the liver. She resisted the doctor's instructions to stay in bed. She had a tour, and people were counting on her. Wynonna had come with her to get the blood results, so she knew everything, but, she was unaware of the impact her mother's illness would have on her own life. It was something her mother made Wynonna pledge to keep secret from the public and their fans.

When Naomi returned home, she could barely stand up through a costume fitting. She may have sworn her daughter to secrecy and was determined to keep silent herself, but her body rebelled. It was screaming to Naomi to do something about her condition. She was trying not to listen, but at least she had the good sense that night when Larry came home to tell him what was going on, even if he didn't have the good sense to understand how serious it was. She insisted that Larry go straight to bed while she finished packing, even though she felt as if she were moving in slow motion. Naomi tried to sleep through the night. When morning came, reality had finally sunk in. She realized she was in no condition to travel. She reluctantly called Ken and told him about her illness and that they were going to have to cancel a week's worth of shows.

The one thing that Naomi did not want to cancel was the American Music Awards. She had been asked to cohost the show, a great honor for any performer, but especially a country musician.

She begged Ken to keep that gig open for her and promised to stay in bed the entire week to build up her strength. Ken agreed and even arranged to have a Winnebago parked nearby so that she could rest in between rehearsals. Naomi kept her promise and remained in bed all day.

It was slow torture for her as the guilt started to overwhelm her. She kept thinking about the canceled shows, how much money her absence would cost her, and how disappointed her fans would feel. She saw promos of Wynonna and herself for the awards show and wished that she had the same kind of energy as her daughter. She felt that her life was out of control.

When the week was over, Naomi and Wynonna flew to Los Angeles to prepare for the show. Organizer Dick Clark had set up a small tent for Naomi to rest during breaks in the rehearsal. Several people began to notice the absence of the bounce and energy for which she was famous. She decided to tell a few people, including friends Anita Baker and Dwight Yoakam, the reason for her sluggish behavior. They both offered encouragement, and Baker even sent Naomi some flowers that night.

It was an immense struggle to get through the American Music Awards show, but Naomi managed almost entirely on guts. The next day, she went to see a gastrointestinal specialist. After taking a battery of tests, the doctor told her that an elusive virus was about to explode inside her body. The final verdict was that Naomi had non-A hepatitis, which tends to be chronic.

Naomi was stunned. This disease seemed to come from nowhere. If it was chronic, what would that mean for the future of the Judds? Naomi recalled that after she left the doctor's office she walked around in a daze, all these questions and what-if scenarios swirling around in her head. She had always taken the initiative and solved her problems, but she didn't know what to do now, and she didn't want to follow her doctor's advice. She had come a long way, struggling to make it as a woman alone and a single mother, and now, as she was enjoying the sweet taste of success, it was being snatched away from her by the unpredictable virus inside her body. She also knew that if anything happened to her Wynonna probably couldn't make it on her own just yet. Much as they still clashed on occasion, they were still mother and daughter. Wynonna was not quite ready to be her own woman.

Despite the bad news, the Judds went to work on their next album. Naomi and songwriter Don Schiltz had written a tune entitled "Rompin' Stompin' Bad News Blues." Bonnie Raitt, who had long been an idol of Wynonna's, agreed to do some vocals on the album, so it was a very special treat to have her in the studio. Bonnie and Wynonna got along famously and joked around with Bonnie's current boyfriend, Michael O'Keefe. The three women talked on and on about Hollywood and how they were glad they didn't live there, after which Wynonna and Naomi returned to Nashville uncertain as to what the next few weeks would bring. As it turned out, Naomi was unable to get out of bed, and they had to cancel more shows. Wynonna continued to record at the studio, laying down her lead vocals. Often she would play them over the phone for Naomi, to get her opinion.

In the meantime, Larry kept busy building a horse barn and restoring the home in Peaceful Valley, trying to get it ready so that they could move in within a year. Larry also decided to become something like a big brother to a needy child from their church. He met with a single mom whose seven-year-old son, Casey Robertson, needed a male role model. The mother worked in a factory and was barely able to pay the rent. Casey started hanging out with Larry, often spending weekends with the Judds.

Meanwhile, Naomi found herself visiting the doctors and taking more blood tests. The doctor admitted that he was uncertain of her disease, but he was sure she wasn't contagious. Neither knew how she contracted the illness, but the doctor speculated that perhaps she got it from an infected needle when she was a nurse. Naomi went to see a nutritionist and was instructed to give up caffeine, fried foods, and junk food. She cut down on red meat and replaced it with chicken, turkey, or fish. She began to research nutritional therapy and found that there could be a significant benefit to taking vitamins and supplements. She also got as much sleep as she could to build up her strength because she really wanted to appear at a scheduled show in Austin, Texas, with Ricky Van Shelton.

Naomi arranged to be flown into Texas, while Wynonna and the crew traveled on the bus. Naomi even arrived a day early so that she could sleep longer, just in case. However, while Naomi was at the airport, she was deluged by fans requesting autographs. She began to think she had made a mistake committing to this concert because she couldn't even stand to sign autographs. Even sitting exhausted her. She was so desperate to be alone, she excused herself and sneaked into the ladies' room to rest in a stall. Had she made a mistake? Her answer came at the Austin airport when she was waiting for her luggage. A man stepped up to her and said, "Hi." At first she thought he wanted an autograph, but she soon learned that he had just gotten off the road so he could take his family to see the Judds. She knew she had made the right decision.

As she had promised, Naomi stayed in bed the whole day and gave very specific instructions to one of her assistants, Gaylon. She told him to keep a keen eye on her and to get her if she signaled. She also told Wynonna that if for any reason she had to leave the stage, Wynonna should continue on without her. Wynonna refused and said she would leave the stage, too, in that event. That put even more pressure on Naomi to hang in there; she didn't want to disappoint the fans who had paid to see them. It also underscored Wynonna's inability to perform without the artistic and emotional support of her mother, which reinforced Naomi's conclusion that her daughter was not ready to continue her career alone. Naomi also devised an instrumental to pass the time if she felt she wasn't able to sing and needed a break. They had thought of everything.

Finally, the curtains slowly rose. A sea of fans erupted into loving applause and sent their energy to the stage. For a time, Naomi felt revived. The show progressed off without a hint that anything was wrong. The Judds were their old dynamic selves. That night, Naomi fell into bed and slept fifteen hours. The next show was scheduled for Midland, Texas, on February 10. This time, Tim McGrath, a crew member, got golf carts so that Naomi didn't have to walk from the bus to the stage. Naomi felt it was a bit much, but McGrath insisted.

Then it was back to Nashville and a new doctor to get a second opinion. It was as if Naomi were determined to find one who would tell her what she wanted to hear. She didn't. He firmly explained that she was very sick and was going to die if she didn't take care of herself. He was cold, firm, and definite. Naomi was stunned, depressed, and uncertain.

Still, she wasn't doing what the doctor warned that she must do to save her life, and her body continued to punish her. After the doctor's visit, Naomi went straight to bed again and remained there, but only until she was scheduled to do a weekend show in Indianapolis. A lot of thoughts whizzed through Naomi's head before she went to sleep that night in her private bedroom on the tour bus to Indiana. She couldn't believe the ugly and insensitive way the doctor casually talked about her dying. As a nurse, she would never talk that way to a patient and was appalled that he undoubtedly spoke to all his patients that way.

Such thoughts were weighing heavily on her mind as she tried to sleep but couldn't. She was filled with stress and worry. Then she was startled out of her sleep with a terrible sense of foreboding. Her heart was pounding as if it would crash through the wall of her chest. She was gasping for breath. She struggled for air and felt icy with sweat as she verged on hysteria.

Naomi staggered into the bathroom to wash cold water on her face. She wanted Gaylon to help her, but she didn't want to wake Wynonna. Eventually, her symptoms subsided. She had just experienced her first panic attack. Naomi was shocked. She said she couldn't believe it could happen to someone as centered as herself. Mark and Middy, who had come to visit Naomi upon hearing of her illness, were there to comfort her. They tried to help her understand that everyone is susceptible to panic attacks, that she had been under a lot of pressure. She was suffering from an illness no one could control.

Despite the fatigue, anxiety, and panic, Naomi strutted up onstage in front of an audience of 22,500 and sang her heart out. She gave a soulful performance that night, almost if she were back to her old self. It was a great show, but the truth was, Naomi was not her old self. It was time to call a meeting with the crew and bring them up to date. She would do that soon; meanwhile, she was getting blood tests every week now. Wynonna affectionately called her Pin Cushion.

On the agenda was next one of the Judds' favorites, the Houston Livestock and Rodeo Show at the Astrodome. Naomi claimed she was up to it. This time, though, there would be some traveling adjustments. Normally, when their destination was longer than ten hours on the bus, the Judds would fly. Only now, moving through airports and dealing with fans and reporters proved too strenuous, and so the Judds traveled on the bus. Just after the Judds had checked into their hotel room, Naomi got a phone call from her doctor. His tone was serious and urgent. He told her that her ALT levels were at an all time-high and insisted that she come home so that he could perform a liver biopsy immediately. Naomi was truly shaken. Where was all this going? she wondered.

Naomi looked at herself in the mirror as she prepared for the Texas concert. She knew that this would be the last concert for a while; how long, no one knew for certain. What Naomi did know was that she was going to give this audience of forty-four thousand everything she had, wherever she could find it. She and Wynonna gave the Lone Star fans a run for their money and pulled out all the stops in giving a foot-stomping, belly-aching, throat-parching concert.

Then things got worse. The symptoms mentioned earlier began again, and Naomi says that she got an onslaught of symptoms that included fever, weakness, nausea, vomiting, muscle aches, headaches, and abdominal pain. She felt miserable, and because she felt miserable, she became depressed. She would lie in bed all day with only the dogs to keep her company. Larry was becoming the picture of health and fitness, while Naomi looked and felt worse.

One day Larry saw Naomi, disoriented, walk into a wall. He called Ken, who immediately canceled the upcoming shows in Vegas. Naomi was well aware that canceling two sold-out weeks in Vegas would cost millions of dollars. It would also affect a lot of the crew, who made their living and supported their families working for the Judds, a fact that only made Naomi feel worse. Ken knew that Naomi would start to feel guilty and quietly assured her that the payroll would continue for the Judd organization.

So Naomi was left to lie in bed for weeks to come. Sometimes too tired to read or unable to do so because of terrible headaches, she was forced to watch a lot of bad TV. She lay there and had, she says, internal monologues: I'm trying to make a comeback, and nobody even knows I'm gone. It was as if Naomi, who had struggled so long and yearned so much for the fame she and Wynonna now had, were being sentenced to solitary confinement away from all the people, places, and performances she loved and needed. The best year of her life was quickly becoming the worst. She said that she "hardly knew herself anymore." In a real sense, Naomi was twins during this trying time. First she would be the upbeat, positive person she had grown up to be, and then she would be the other person, desperately depressed and ill, barely hanging on.

One of the things that Naomi did while in bed was read everything she could find on liver disease. She discovered that one of the causes of hepatitis was CMV infection, with a compromised immune system. Perhaps, she wondered, she could have gotten it when she was taking all that prednisone. The more she read, the scarier her future looked; one book stated that people with her illness usually live three years. She says she threw the books down and prayed for God to help her heal herself. She put the books away and never looked back. She did call her doctor to discuss the connection between CMV and also the short time she had to live that some books claimed. Dr. Mitchum advised her to go to the Mayo clinic as soon as possible.

Now Naomi had to find a way to tell Larry. She scheduled an appointment with a psychologist. Larry thought that they were going to talk about the physical pain of her illness and was completely shocked when Naomi told him that she might die within three years. Larry promised to do everything in his power to help her. Then Naomi flew to Rochester in a private plane and was admitted to the Mayo Clinic. She prayed that she would find a decent doctor, not just a man who knew medicine, but also the human heart. She was surprised to learn that her doctor had trained under her brother Brian's hematologist.

The next day, the team at Mayo began their battery of tests, starting with a liver biopsy. Dr. Dalton informed Naomi that her illness probably began in 1986. They were going to start her on an experimental interferon therapy to stop the virus from replicating. The interferon nurse met with Naomi and Larry, and they discussed some of the side effects of the drug, how Naomi was going to have to inject herself three times a week, and how faith would be as powerful as medicine at this point. That night, Naomi suffered tremendous side effects from the therapy. She said the pain and discomfort were almost too much to bear, and she was only allowed one Tylenol because her liver wasn't healthy enough for anything stronger. Larry was at her side all through the night, rubbing her down, playing choir tapes, just being there.

What felt worse than the pain was talking to Wynonna over the phone long distance. It was hard for Naomi to tell her not to come to Rochester; she knew that would only upset her more. It takes a special person to sit in an oncology room filled with people who have cancer and be cheery and supportive. At least Wynonna would be with Tony and he could comfort her. Ashley, on the other hand, was kept completely in the dark while she finished her final year at the University of Kentucky. In spite of earlier claims to the contrary, she never did graduate.

Finally, after some stressful days in Rochester at the Mayo Clinic, Larry and Naomi returned to the farm in Tennessee where Naomi was to recover. Larry took Naomi on little trips around the countryside to distract her from the headaches that plagued her now. They would sit by the bridge they had built and look at all the flowers that were given to them for their wedding instead of traditional presents. They reminded Larry and Naomi that "love can build a bridge" and that love also grows. Naomi's mom came and took care of her as well.

Then, one night, when Naomi's headache seemed unbearable, Wynonna came over, and Larry called the doctor. The doctor instructed her to go to Nashville's Vanderbilt Hospital to get another blood test. To their astonishment, Naomi's ALT levels had dropped to normal range. The doctor had been worried that he was going to have to take Naomi off interferon because of the severe side effects, but it was clearly working. He instructed Naomi to continue the medication. Naomi had passed through the worst of it and was on the long road to recovery.

Once again, Naomi became strong enough to work in the studio. She could lay down harmony, which reassured Wynonna and gave her the emotional boost she needed. When the Judds started to record, Naomi decided, against the advice of her doctors, to go on the road again. She justified her decision by saying the interferon had worked and she was feeling better. Naomi really missed the road.

The first show was in Billings, Montana. The Judds were a little off their game, but everyone in the crew was so happy they were together again that it didn't matter. Naomi says that she felt a bit draggy, as if she had a minor flu, but the enthusiastic crowd carried her through the show. The interferon became a minor inconvenience because it's made from human protein and needs to be kept chilled at all times. If the Judds weren't on the bus, Naomi would have to pack some into a cooler with dry ice and syringes. It often caused raised eyebrows at airport security gates.

Significantly, Naomi and Wynonna's time together took on a different tone; they began to have more heart-to-heart conversations. They talked about what was really important in life, and while money was nice, they agreed that it couldn't buy health or happiness. They were richer now than they had ever been, but that couldn't rid Naomi of the virus that dogged her. On another dimension, the Judds expanded their group of acquaintances to include people outside the music field, among them humanitarians and scientists. Moreover, a new and gentler side of Larry was emerging as he took charge of all the family matters.

In June 1990, as the Judds were on their way to a gig, Naomi began to feel ill. She had been taking interferon for three months, and the side effects should have disappeared. Naomi said she became alarmed when the side effects seemed to be returning again. She was being interviewed by Neil Pond of *Country America* when she began to have trouble concentrating and couldn't finish her sentences. She had to do a show that night, and once again she managed.

Soon after the Judds appeared in Evansville, Indiana, for a show, Naomi felt a lump in her breast. She told no one until she returned to Nashville, where she could have a biopsy done on the tumor. On July 10, 1990, Naomi had a breast biopsy and the usual blood-test workup. The blood test showed that her ALT levels had risen again, and the doctor instructed her to double her interferon injections. Getting the biopsy proved a hair-raising experience. Naomi could not take anesthesia, so they just used a topical, lidocaine. During the biopsy, Naomi's blood pressure plummeted, and it seemed she might go into cardiac arrest. Naomi was completely conscious during the procedure and saw exactly what was happening. She said she felt as if she were losing consciousness. Eventually, she was stabilized, and they completed the surgery. Thankfully, the tumor turned out to be benign.

Major changes in their family relationships were now occurring, such as the breaking up of Naomi and Wynonna as a performing duo as Naomi's illness got worse and Ashley's launching a career of her own. Naomi decided that she and Wynonna should seek counseling. A friend recommended a therapist who had been practicing for thirty-five years, and both Wynonna and Naomi immediately felt comfortable with her. Seeing the therapist helped them deal with the changing relationships in their lives, and taught them about understanding where they were in their lives and how they should focus on the here and now and not the could-have-beens, might-have-beens, or should-have-beens.

Meanwhile, Ashley was getting on with life on her own, as she had been forced to do for a long time. She wasn't sure if she wanted to join the Peace Corps, be an anthropologist, or become an actress. She packed her bags and headed for Los Angeles to either bring the local natives surcease, study their culture, or become a part of it. For her own reasons, part of Naomi did not want Ashley to go to Hollywood. She didn't know what was happening with her health and wanted her family nearby. In the end, she had to let her children follow their destiny. The day after Ashley moved, the

Judds flew to Canada to perform at the Calgary Stampede Rodeo. That night, when Naomi returned to her hotel room, she felt completely exhausted. The next day, she and Mike McGrath went to a clinic and had her ALT checked. The levels were quadruple the norm. The interferon wasn't working anymore.

Obviously, Naomi needed some time to do some serious thinking, not only about her future but about Wynonna's. She took a trip to the country by herself. She had come so far from the one-room shacks and minimum-wage jobs; she had wished for something and made it come true; she had taken harsh words of criticism when she was younger and turned them into words of praise. She had come a long way. Yet it seemed that her destiny would not continue down that path anymore. That night she had to come to terms with that fact, and she did.

The next day, through tears, she told Ken that she had to quit. She needed to concentrate on her health. Running around the country would only make things worse. She begged him to tell Wynonna. She said, "I simply can't say the words *It's over*. It's the hardest thing I've ever had to do in my whole life, and I cannot bring myself to do it by myself." Instead, Wynonna and Ken showed up at Naomi's hotel room. Ken came into the room first and then opened the door for a bewildered, hesitant Wynonna, who just stood there uncertain as to whether she should enter the room or run away. It was a moment all three of them would always remember because of the tension and the importance of the decision they had to make. Ken struggled with the words that Naomi wanted him to say and the words that Wynonna was terrified to hear, but he finally got them out. As the realization of what her mother's decision meant to her own life sank in, Wynonna was filled with sorrow and depression. The three of them then just sat still for almost an hour.

Finally, the old Judd fire rose, and Wynonna spit out her own determined decision. If her mother was quitting, so was she. It was exactly what Naomi had dreaded, and the sparks flew between them when Naomi said she wouldn't hear of it. She had worked too hard and gone too far for Wynonna to give it all up now. Wynonna was unresponsive and appeared adamant, but she was terrified of performing alone. She needed her mother there with her. Further talk settled nothing, and when Wynonna and Naomi returned to Nashville, they headed straight for the therapist's office. She told them that they were going to have to cut the chord that bound them so tightly, even though their bond was very strong.

Finally, they both understood that it was time for Wynonna to be free of her mother's embracing emotional nest. As mother and daughter discussed the inevitable split, the therapist told them that such breakups produce emotions similar to those triggered by death: denial, shock, numbness, anger, disorientation and bargaining, depression, and finally acceptance. She went on to tell them that fear was the most useless and harmful emotion of all. They should not fear but embrace a new, unexpected future, perhaps a good one.

Ken wanted to get the Judds a new bus for the final days of their touring. He asked Naomi to remove all her personal belongings from the old one. She grabbed two hefty garbage bags and started filling them up. It was a gut-wrenching experience for her because Dreamchaser had been their home, their security, and their promise of a bright future. Now it was just another bus. Naomi fought hard to be strong through the following weeks and had to consciously battle the fears that kept haunting her. She fought hard to keep hope in focus.

23

To Sing or to Live

THE ADJUSTMENT TO THEIR NEW LIFE would not be easy. Naomi knew about Wynonna's terrible nightmares, since they kept the door between their rooms open when they were on tour. It was disturbing for Naomi to hear her daughter cry out in her sleep. Their work was part of the cause and it was also part of the cure, so that in the midst of the confusing emotions each woman was experiencing, performing onstage at night became a calming force. Eventually, they would have to tell the world what was happening.

The seventh Country Music Awards were set for October 8, 1990. Because the Judds did not want to detract from the show, they decided to make the announcement a week afterward. During the show, when some of the crew asked Wynonna why she seemed so tense, she put them off with a cute retort that worked for the time being. "Let's just say, until you've walked a mile in a man's moccasins, you can't imagine the smell!" Ironically, in Naomi's acceptance speech at the Awards show the previous year, she said, "One of the most important Scriptures is 'And this, too, shall pass.'" She said this to help people appreciate the good times and realize that the bad times do not last, either.

Meanwhile, when not in the public eye, Naomi and Wynonna

were talking about the important values in their lives. Naomi didn't believe that excellence and success were synonymous. She felt success was superficial. Conversely, she believed excellence can be defined as a private struggle to be true to one's own heart.

Naomi was not the only person on the tour who was having health problems. Ken suffered another heart attack while Naomi was making her acceptance speech, but he didn't want her to know until she received the award. Afterward, Naomi and Wynonna rushed to the hospital and prayed with Ken's family for his recovery. He survived but later went to the Mayo Clinic for surgery.

A week passed. After a show at Caesars Palace in Las Vegas, the Judds returned to Nashville and decided it was time to inform the band about Naomi's battle with hepatitis. In addition, Ken was arranging a press conference, with Naomi reviewing the newspeople who would be invited to attend. Then the two Judds and Larry were taken by limo to the old MCA office for the conference. The office was rather dreary. It consisted of a room with no carpeting, no heat, and old folding chairs. Because Naomi had looked a little weak at the Awards show, rumors had been churning in the tabloids, and the press conference was designed to quiet the rumors, but as is often the case, it had the reverse effect.

Naomi told the assembled reporters that she had to stop performing because of a serious health problem, which she explained in general terms. She said that a liver transplant was the last option because it was a dangerous operation, required a donor, and left the recipient dependent on drugs to suppress the body's natural need to reject the new organ. Then she thanked everybody for coming and excused herself so that she could go home to rest and recover. Everyone received the news solemnly and left to file their stories, while all three Judds (Ashley was there for the press conference) and Larry headed for a nearby restaurant.

In a stunning demonstration of the swiftness of bad news, the radio in their car broke in with a bulletin announcing that much-admired Naomi Judd at forty-four was forced to end her career because of a serious, life-threatening liver aliment. They had just pulled into the restaurant parking lot, with Wynonna alongside their vehicle in her truck. Naomi looked over at her oldest daughter to see if she, too, had heard the announcement on the radio; clearly she had. She was crying. The two of them remained outside to share the moment together while Larry and Ashley went inside to get some food. Through her tears, Wynonna told her mother that she felt as if she were dying. Later, they drove the back roads almost aimlessly and finally reached Naomi's home. As they did, the radio station's phone lines were jammed with Judd fans, to whom the Judds' music meant so much, calling in to ask if the terrible news about Naomi was true. In a surreal way the words of support and admiration, mixed with their own grief, made it more bearable. The next day, it got worse. The front page of many newspapers had stories about Naomi's illness and her departure. It was time for Naomi to go back to the Mayo Clinic for another examination, since it had been three weeks since her last dose of interferon.

Naomi, the nurse and the involved patient, was never content to sit quietly no matter what was happening in her life. She was proactive and wanted to participate in the decisions that affected her. This critical time was no exception. At the clinic she told her physician that she had been studying about the immune system and the mind's role in good health. These discussions were a continuation of her longtime interest in alternative medicine, which was fostered by her nurse's training in Marin County. However, the doctor said he had been busy with a heavy patient load and was not familiar with psychoneuroimmunology (PNI), to which she was referring.

PNI is the study of how the mind influences the body in sickness and in health, because the mind can stimulate or suppress the immune system. This means thoughts can have a powerful effect on the immune system. Beyond the stress caused by actual events, our emotional reactions to those events also cause additional stress and can adversely effect one's physical well-being. If we have a physical injury or illness that is stressful, our mind's reaction to our injury or illness can make it worse. Examples of the impact of the mind or the will on the body are the many documented cases of terminally ill patients who strive to postpone dying until some event of sentimental importance has occurred: for example, the arrival at the patient's bedside of a distant relative or the completion of some important event. In this instance, it is believed that the dying person wills the delay of death until he or she has the emotional fulfillment of being alive for that special event.

Even more impressive, some patients have experienced inexplicable remissions of illness that could be due to improvement of the emotional response to internal stress. Several tests on the effect of laughter on the sick have shown that funny movies, for example, can help a sick person improve because of the emotional impact it has on him.

Naomi learned that attitudes and emotions trigger chemical or hormonal reactions in our bodies that affect physical parts of the body. Blood chemistry, heart rate, and the speed with which wounds heal are all affected. To learn more, she studied books on the subject, such as *Mind, Body, Medicine* by Daniel Coleman and Joel Gurin as well as *Who Gets Sick* by Blair Justice. Dr. Justice explains the work of Candace Perth at the National Institute of Mental Health, who studied the message of the emotions, chemicals called neurotransmitters, and neuropeptides.

All of this studying developed into a routine for Naomi, starting with meditation every morning, because it has been shown to reduce stress. Naomi got into a regime that included walking, "listening to her body" as she says, and focusing on positive things to help herself relax. She was also fascinated by the work of Deepak Chopra, a pioneer in mind-body medicine in America since his arrival from India years ago. He combined his medical knowledge with ancient Indian Ayurvedic healing techniques, which he says are based on the body wanting to heal whatever is wrong with it if we only give it a chance to do so and some help. To illustrate, Stephen Rosenburg, chief of surgery at the National Cancer Institute, had a patient suffering from large, aggressive cancerous tumors in the stomach, liver, and lymph systems who went into spontaneous remission by use of these mind-body techniques.

There are many such documented cases, and Naomi believes in this approach to healing. It is important to put such beliefs into perspective to fully understand Naomi and the Judd women. On a personal level, Naomi became close to Steve Shima, who was diagnosed as having a huge brain tumor that couldn't be operated on. Most doctors, with the exception of Robert Cantrell, wrote off his chances of survival. Dr. Cantrell was impressed by Shima's strong belief that he would conquer the cancer and that he thought surgery might help. Cantrell and Shima went ahead with brain surgery. It is a bizarre story, but when they probed into Shima's skull, the tumor was gone!

The doctors and nurses in the operating room panicked for a moment for fear that they may have operated on the wrong patient, which has happened before. They quickly checked the X-rays and CAT scans of the person lying on the operating table; astonishingly, it was the right patient, but there was no cancerous tumor. Steve Shima went on to become an ordained minister (who probably had a reinforced belief in miracles) and hasn't had an indication of cancer since then.

Mind-body medicine was the kind of therapy that Naomi was embracing. If she could bring her emotions and internal stresses under control, she could help her body defeat the hepatitis and prevent it from becoming life threatening. There was only one thing standing in the way: Naomi herself.

Most normal people in Naomi's situation would have immediately withdrawn from the public scene, and begun round-the-clock therapy and rest, but as we know, Naomi Judd is unlike most normal people. Her plan was to first say goodbye to all her fans around the country and to make sure her daughter, Wynonna, was really prepared to be on her own. That was the birth of the Farewell Tour. Dalton wanted her to rest, but Naomi had other plans. She felt it would take a year for Wynonna to work through her grief and get used to the idea of being a solo artist. It would also take that long for Naomi to relinquish what was soon to be her former life in a business she loved.

Bowing to the inevitable and the invincible, Dalton said that Naomi could go on tour even though he wished she wouldn't do so. When she returned to Nashville, she sat down with Ken and agreed to be booked to play 120 cities during the next twelve months. Not quite what Dalton was thinking when he said she needed rest, but off the Judds went, starting with their first concert in Fargo, North Dakota, where the airport was jammed with reporters and TV crews and the concert hall was filled with the Judd fans.

Naomi realized that she had to keep a positive focus on this Farewell Tour so that it didn't become the Funeral Tour. She needed to keep everything upbeat. That's what her head said, but it wasn't what her heart was telling her. As mother and daughter sang their songs for the enthusiastic audience, the reality began to creep in that this was goodbye. As the tears welled up, Naomi took a quick break, stepped to the back of the stage and sipped a glass of water, and secretly hid her tears. Then she spun around with renewed determination and enthusiasm and told the audience, "You all are our guardian angels now. The Lord is my doctor, and the fans are my medicine."

From this point on, questions from the press and the public about her illness and the possible consequences were constantly posed and discussed wherever Naomi went. Naturally, disaster-oriented reporters would open interviews or press conferences with frighteningly painful questions. At first, Naomi wasn't ready for such blunt, emotional queries. However, she quickly developed a routine for answering them, drawing partially on her sense of humor or giving philosophical-religious responses. Once, when she was on TV's Phil Donahue's show and somebody posed a question about her chances of her recovery, she replied, "Don't worry, honey! It's not my tombstone; it's a stepping-stone." When she gave interviews, she always mentioned that vaccines for hepatitis B were available and that the American Liver Foundation had made her their spokesperson, which elevated the discussion.

At Thanksgiving, everybody converged on Naomi's mother's place in Ashland, where old wounds seemed to be healed. Naomi felt the security of being back in the old neighborhood where her mom had lived for forty years. That feeling prompted her to reflect that she, Wynonna, and Ashley had never lived in any one place longer than five years, so the familiarity of being "back home" was comforting. Afterward, when Naomi and Wynonna were back on the road, the grieving process for their life and their singing career together would sometimes depress her; she knew she was singing some of the songs for the last time.

Always searching for spiritual support, Naomi found another book she liked that helped her through this time, *Releasing the Ability of God* by Charles Capps. The premise of the book is that words—how we define and describe things—are very important because they shape our image and perception of the world. It's called "semantic realignment." She discovered that she could fight the negative forces and negative thoughts that sometimes assailed her by rethinking the words and redefining the situation. For example, Naomi and Wynonna concluded that they should never pray over the problems they encountered in life, but, rather, over the solutions and focus on what they wanted for their lives rather than complaining about what they didn't want. Instead of praying about the inflammation of her liver, Naomi thanked God for the healing, the uplifting experience of their Farewell Tour, and the reuniting of her family.

As the tour progressed, it was heartwarming that so many people sent or brought advice and home remedies to the Judds' trailer or bus. It was also a little bit scary to be constantly talking with people about the pain she endured and its possible outcome, but she tried to acknowledge everybody's good wishes and support as best she could. She and Wynonna would try to turn these encounters into something positive, particularly when people would visit their tour bus and bring their own sick children with them.

24

The Farewell Tour

FOR THE JUDDS' FANS, the Farewell Tour was an exciting opportunity to share something they could never experience again. That gave great importance to the tour and assured that ticket prices would be skyrocketing all over the country. For MCA and the tour promoters, it was obviously an opportunity to profit handsomely from Naomi's misfortune. For Wynonna it was the last training flight before she was pushed out on her own to fly solo—if she could—and that made it scary for her. For Ashley, it meant another hundred nights or more that she would be a country-music orphan, with her mother and sister checking in for a few minutes by telephone from someplace on the road.

By far the most complex aspect of all was that the Farewell Tour motivated Naomi to embark on a journey of inner discovery more extensive and probing than any she had previously done. Her focus was changing from Farewell Tour to Hello, My Inner Being, and she immersed herself in an introspective type of therapy that would help guide her through the enormous transition. She would take Wynonna by the hand spiritually, but mostly she was her own Magellan.

For example, Naomi got caught up in Thomas Moore's book

219

Care of the Soul and its philosophy of infusing daily life with the soul's qualities: character, expression, and integrity. Moore contends that these qualities give authenticity and meaning by touching the heart, stirring the emotions, and evoking sentiment. He preaches that each person must discover his or her own individual inner voyage, which is the way to reclaim one's soul.

Naomi's physical condition forced her to slow down and adopt a less glitzy style that would provide meaning to her life. She began to see her body as a recipient of the messages her soul was attempting to give her. She consciously decided to take the time and pay attention to choosing the form of self-expression she would use that day.

Naomi and Wynonna began to study Native American culture while they toured in the Southwest and found that since all of life is an expression of art, then art and function are linked. Naomi and Wynonna believed that this concept described their music—functional as well as emotionally moving. This discovery lead Naomi to research the effects of music on the human body, which is a subject that has intrigued scientists for many years, since we know that music affects us in many ways, particularly emotionally. However, science has still not determined how this connection occurs. If one embraces the concept of mind-body interaction that posits that our physical being is affected by our mental and emotional state, then the nexus between music and the physical body becomes obvious. Naomi believes she discovered that every organ, bone, and part of the body resonated to a certain frequency specific to that part. Therefore, knowledgeable health practitioners used this musical connection to heal the mind, body, and emotions. For example, calming music could be used with patients in mental hospitals to give some measure of peace to troubled minds.

Naomi also drew from the teachings of Carl Jung, the Swiss psychologist, who dealt with the many symbols in life. Each person has what he called a "shadow." This is a part of oneself that represents dark, suppressed subconscious choices. Naomi found a demonstration of this view of the world by looking at a dream she had several times a week for many years about the house where she grew up. She finally realized that being forced to leave home and grow up at such a young age had created within her a feeling of loss. She shared these feelings with her mother, especially about the time she went home for a visit and found the door locked for the first time. That moment emphasized her loss of connection to the safety of home. Her mother immediately fished into her purse and gave Naomi a house key. That event became a powerful symbol that told her she could reclaim her life.

Wynonna also began to understand dreams, particularly those she had of not being respected as a solo artist. She learned that if she believed in herself, others would believe in her, too. Naomi used the time to get Wynonna to understand that she could be whatever she imagined, so she should imagine herself to be the very best. Wynonna also struggled to develop her own singing style so that she could perform solo, without the nuances and harmony contributed by her mother's voice and style. The songs she chose for her first solo album would prove critical as to how she would be accepted as an artist. Inevitably, how she performed on her own would be compared to the albums and songs she had done with her mother. Although Naomi wanted to help bolster her daughter's confidence, only Wynonna could successfully accomplish that.

For many reasons, including personal, Wynonna decided to leave Brent Maher and Don Potter at Creative Recording. Tony Brown, Wynonna's new producer, had known Wynonna since the first audition in 1983, when she was with RCA. They got along well. Wynonna went to visit Brent and his family one day and gently broke the news that she was going to work with Tony. While sad about the change, Brent understood the need for a new environment for Wynonna. They agreed that they would still work together in other ways.

At about this time they learned the terrible news about Reba McEntire's band. It was on a Sunday morning that song writer and country singing star Vince Gill told them that all seven members of the band and Reba's tour manager were killed in a crash that came on the heels of losses to Naomi's own band. A very serious car wreck badly injured the keyboard player, Larry Miller, and he had to be replaced by John Glazer. Because a band is like a family, the rest of the band had to make adjustments not only to John himself but among themselves. To add to the strain, John's mother died right before the band was to appear on *The Tonight Show*. Naomi decided to sing "Guardian Angels" that night to give John support during the performance.

Three different acts took turns opening for the Judds during their Farewell Tour. In addition, several dates were scheduled with Garth Brooks, even though he was destined to become a headliner himself. At every stop of the Farewell Tour, the place was filled, even auditoriums holding thousands of seats. Still, there were moments that helped to keep Naomi's ego in perspective, such as the Dr. Blair Justice incident in Houston. When she saw that they were going to play at the Houston Astrodome, she immediately got in touch with Justice, who lived in Houston. He was the author of *Who Gets Sick*. She wanted to consult him about psychoneuroim-munology. His book would prove influential in Naomi's new approach to her life. At first, Justice did not know who she was. Initially he thought she said she was "the judge." By the end of their telephone conversation, he still didn't know her correct name. He did understand that she was a musician performing at the Astrodome while suffering from hepatitis C. He wanted to meet her, whatever her name.

Justice attended the concert with his wife and met with Naomi afterward. He noted right away that she was definitely helping to heal herself by drawing love and support from the audience. She thanked him for the insights of his book, and they talked for a time. They both believed that feeling good does as much for the body as it does for the mind—and there has been much research to support that view. An example could be found in the case of Norman Cousins, the longtime literary star and editor of the *Saturday Review*, once one of the most important literary magazines in America. He became ill and went to UCLA Medical School, where he joined in experiments on the effect of laughter on illness and pain. He wrote extensively about the results. The study showed that a positive emotional state releases hormones known as endorphins into the brain and that these hormones make us feel happy, lower blood pressure and heart rate, and boost the immune system.

At times it was only natural that things would become dicey

during the Farewell Tour, particularly during intense discussions between mother and daughter. To lighten the mood, Naomi occasionally composed silly lyrics and would make up songs like "My Liver's Gone Bad and I'm So Mad."

In September 1991, Ed Morris, of *Billboard*, wrote a story that everybody was trying to be supportive of Naomi to the point that somebody had started a rumor that Naomi was not sick at all! According to the rumor, her sickness was just a promotional gimmick to boost concert and record sales and that later there would be a joyous announcement that Naomi was cured. Naturally, this upset Naomi. She was sick, and she had never been a money-grubbing prima donna who would lie and cheat her fans. The rumors were hurtful, but they could only deny them, which they did.

The personal relationship between Naomi and Wynonna continued to improve, and on Mother's Day, Wynonna surprised Naomi with an article about it in *USA Weekend* magazine. In this interview, Wynonna said that the public airing of her feelings toward her mother was a secret gift. She talked about how much she had learned from her mother's courage in dealing with her career-ending illness and how her mother had worked so hard to make their dreams come true. She was grateful to her mother for the good Christian values and virtues she had instilled in her daughters. Her mom, she said, would always be singing through Wynonna's voice and music. Naomi was overwhelmed by the beauty and sincerity of this public display of Wynonna's love.

There were also private expressions of their love for each other, such as a small, heart-shaped stone that they often passed back and forth between them. They also wrote each other often, sending little notes, cards, and letters when talking was difficult. For example, Wynonna's first recording date for her first album as a solo artist occurred the day before her twenty-seventh birthday, and because it was such an emotionally charged day, Naomi sent a little note instead of attending the session. Besides, it was Wynonna's session, and her mother shouldn't be hanging around kibitzing. The next day, she brought to the studio an armload of gifts and a cake for everybody in the new band and crew.

At this time the American Country Music Association invited them to perform in the finale of the awards program with the International Children's Choir, singing "Love Can Build a Bridge." Ken was afraid that because it was the last time the two Judds would be singing at the ceremony, emotion might interfere with their performance. Naomi pulled herself together and gave Wynonna a pep talk; it helped because she was flustered as they ran through the rehearsal. Naomi asked for a break and reviewed what she wanted to have happen at the end of the song, namely, to tell the audience that she believed the most important words in life are love, faith, and hope.

Naomi found that the continued support from her fans was important. She gathered strength from letters telling how music had assisted them with serious problems. Some fans told Naomi facts about their own experiences that she thought were helpful with her own illness, such as taking thymus supplements. Dr. Carson Burgstiner of Georgia was sick with hepatitis B and began taking thymus supplements available from his local health-food store, with the result that the function of his liver returned to normal. Naomi began taking the thymus supplements, and to her surprise and that of her doctors at the Mayo Clinic, it improved her ALT level.

Naomi continued to talk every chance she got about alternative medical approaches that could be used in conjunction with traditional medicine. She did so in a cover story on her in *People* magazine. It was seen by Dr. David Green, who called to tell her that a study at Wayne State University in Detroit showed that patients with hepatitis B had significant improvement from thymus injections and that the improvement seemed to have a lasting effect without negative side effects.

During a break in the Farewell Tour, while Naomi and Ashley spent some time together, Wynonna left for a few days to attend Bonnie Raitt's wedding. They had decided to visit Marin County and stopped at one of the restaurants where Naomi had worked as a waitress while attending the nearby nursing school. Coincidentally, as they sat at the bar, the jukebox played "Lazy Country Evening." It was symbolic because it was a song that Naomi had written. When she worked there ten years before, she said that one day that jukebox would be playing her songs.

Later, the singing Judds were invited to visit the White House when President George Bush awarded the Medal of Freedom to one of their friends, Judge William Webster. Naomi decided it would be too much for her to attend and stayed home, but Wynonna did go. It was an exciting experience for her. She was feeling more and more neglected on the Farewell Tour, since Naomi always seemed to be the center of attention. In time, Wynonna became irritable and began to snap at people. She either withdrew or easily became angered. People were starting to call her Godzilla.

Ken decided to join the tour to take her in hand. They had known each other for years, and she had always respected him, but now even he was only partially successful in calming her down, at least until the time came to talk about the grand finale of the Farewell Tour, which Ken said would occur on December 4, 1991. That show would be televised nationally. Wynonna and Naomi didn't like the idea. The concert, they said, was too personal for TV, but Ken said that thousands of their fans who supported them were unable to attend any of the concerts on the tour. It was the only way to include them and say, "Thank you."

Beyond that, the final concert would appear on pay-per-view cable and would not be interrupted by commercials. Ken didn't focus too much on the fact that it would also make lots of money. He thought that such a justification would turn Naomi off. The Judds said they wanted to think it over. The proposal of such a final concert had a strong effect on Wynonna. She couldn't sleep that night, but finally did so during the next day. It was an omen of darker days to come.

However, a very bright day occurred on September 28. The Judds were performing with Merle Haggard, at a concert in San Bernardino, California. They sat inside their own bus, pulled up next to the stage with the lights out, listening to Merle perform. Afterward, he joined them in their bus, and they could see that there was something he wanted to say but was having trouble saying it. Finally, he said that he thought Naomi had been dealt a bad hand of cards with her illness, and turning to Wynonna, he declared that she was the finest girl singer he had ever heard, even with all the new ones coming onto the scene. It thrilled Wynonna to hear such a star say these things about her. He then turned to Naomi and sang his mother's favorite song just for her. It was made all the more touching by the fact that Merle's mother had recently passed away.

Later, the Judds appeared at the Country Music Awards in Nashville, the last award ceremony they would ever attend as the singing Judds. To their delight and the delight of their fans, the Judds were named the top-grossing music act of 1991 and the best country duo for the eighth year in a row! This made them the most successful duo, with the most awards, in the history of country music. They had come a long way from that cold fishing hut in Kentucky with no inside plumbing. On a personal level, Naomi had some good news of her own when she took another ALT liver blood test. Her levels had remained about the same, so her condition had not gotten worse, as she feared it might.

Then they were back on the road with the Farewell Tour, and while it had been a wonderful musical tour professionally and an exhilarating time for Naomi as she explored her inner self, Wynonna at twenty-seven found herself living a nightmare.. By November 1991, as they neared the end of the tour, Wynonna had stopped laughing, socializing, or even leaving her little private area in the tour bus. She would stay cooped up in the dark, windowless room, never seeing the sun or leaving for any reason except to do the next show. One day Naomi came to the bus shortly before it was time to leave for the show. Wynonna was still in her pajamas. When Naomi asked why her daughter had not yet changed into her clothes, Wynonna flew into a rage. She had broken up with her boyfriend Tony King that day and was brooding over her mother's abandoning her at the end of the tour.

Wynonna had spent much of her life with her mother, and Naomi, in turn, was always there, guiding Wynonna and taking care of business, even if they fought from time to time. Now Wynonna felt that her mother was deserting her. She didn't feel she could make it on her own. When Naomi tried to comfort her, she stomped off into her little room and shut the door. Naomi thought Wynonna was just having a hard time adjusting to changing circumstances, but even so, it could mean that the show that night would be in jeopardy if Wynonna refused to dress and come onstage to perform. Then something strange happened.

A preacher showed up at the door of the bus. When Naomi answered his knock, the preacher said he had come all the way from Slidell, Louisiana, to deliver an urgent message. He said he only wanted a few minutes of Naomi's time. She invited him in and heard him say she that was about to be put to a severe test. He asked that she remember that she was a faithful child of God and that God, in turn, was faithful to her because she lived according to his will. He told her to remember that when she sings "Love Can Build a Bridge," love and Jesus are the same. He said a quick prayer and then was gone. Immediately, Naomi went back to Wynonna's room and told her what had just happened, and they cried together. That's when Naomi took to occasionally calling her eldest daughter Hurricane Wynonna.

25

From the Queen
of Everything to the Queen
# of Quite a Lot

NOVEMBER 23, 1991, ARRIVED. The sun was hiding behind a slate-colored, overcast sky, and the rain had drenched everything below. It was a day for contemplation. That's what Naomi was doing. The end of the Farewell Tour was approaching, and she was thinking that she was too young to abandon the fabulous career she was finally enjoying after serving all those orders of chicken-fried steak and emptying bedpans. Now she was a star. Actually, more like a shooting star who had enjoyed a brilliant but brief eight years arcing across the country-music sky but was destined to plunge into the darkness. Naomi snapped out of her depressed mood and reaffirmed her determination to move on.

Before a concert, the performers and technicians go through a sound check to make sure that all the audio systems and instruments are working correctly. This time, during the sound check, the families of the band and crew started dropping by to say farewell to Naomi. They all sat in a circle on the stage to share a few memories about the tough times as well as the good ones and what they all had to go through with each other's help. Finally, the time came to rehearse. Naomi declared she was passing her scepter as "queen of everything" to Wynonna, who thus became the "queen of quite a lot." Later on, as show time neared and Naomi watched from an unseen place as the crowd began to drift in, she felt very warm and fulfilled.

A reporter once asked her one of those silly questions that they ask when groping for something significant to write about. What was her favorite gift? She replied that it was the feeling of friendship from the audience. Both she and her fans felt they were friends. She said that her inner strength had always come from being an inspiration to people and hoping that they considered her one of them.

An extraordinary irony became apparent one night when Naomi realized that she was quite unlike most people—at least in her life situation. She sang about family but was far from them most of the time. Her two children were separated from their father, and she and Wynonna had been apart from Ashley during the last few years. She sang of home but lived on a bus. She wrote songs about security and stability but more often than not ate meals in different towns. The neighbors she talked of in her music were in reality strangers met on the road. She wrote lyrics about good old folks rocking on the front porch, but her companions were rich and famous. It was the paradox of her life, but it was a life that freed her from waiting tables and tending sick people. Back in those bad old days she couldn't dream of what she had now because then she had no insurance, little money, no husband, and darn little emotional support. Success with country music gave her financial security, good friends, a wonderful husband, and an internal feeling of peace in spite of her illness.

The mother-daughter differences between Naomi and Wynonna made for fun onstage, and their antics brought pleasure to the audience. They bonded better onstage than anyplace else, and the fans knew it and loved it. However, the Farewell Tour had been going on for so long, Wynonna renamed it the Infinity Tour. Happily, it was winding down, but the big challenge was still ahead of them: the televised, pay-per-view final concert. To prepare for it emotionally, Naomi decided to employ a biofeedback specialist to work with her on guided imagery, which is using the imagination to train the nervous system into desirable reactions. Many studies show that the nervous system reacts the same to real or imagined events, and this knowledge has led to athletes receiving sophisticated training using visual imagery. In other words, by creating the image of what is supposed to happen, the nervous system trains itself to respond in a certain way to achieve the desired result. It is, in effect, a rehearsal of what the performer will be going through and getting the body to respond so as to produce what the performer wants. Then, when the body starts experiencing the real event, the nervous system is "trained" to know what it should do.

Naomi used imagery for some years to prepare for coping with stressful situations, and this time she wanted to be sure her immune system operated correctly so that she could make it through the December fourth final concert, set for the University of Tennessee's Murphy Center in Murfreesboro, before twelve thousand fans.

All the seats were sold in seventeen minutes. People came from around the country, and many camped out for several days waiting to get into the concert hall. The farewell concert was going to be huge, as would the attendant anxiety.

Naomi's hands were full as the time began ticking down to the night of the big show and farewell concert. First, there was the business of keeping Wynonna's shaky spirits up, even though she complained that she felt like a little bird with a broken wing. That's when Naomi kept telling Wynonna she was no little bird but an eagle, that she should soar into the swirling storm and spread her wings so that they would carry her high above adversity. This kind of pep talk often brought Wynonna around and improved her spirits. Then, on the Friday night before the concert, both Larry and Ashley came down with the Beijing flu. Naomi knew that she had to move to a nearby hotel to avoid becoming sick. She took Wynonna with her.

It continued to rain, and the hotel room seemed dreary—as

cheerless as the thoughts Naomi had about no longer being able to perform on stage before thousands of people. She began to feel isolated and sensed that a panic attack was gathering momentum. She quickly began slow deep breathing, turning her mind to other thoughts by reading the Bible and focusing on the positive aspects of her life. Her fears were soon under control.

As they checked the song list, the costumes, and the other details, Naomi sensed a roughness in Wynonna's voice. By the next afternoon, during a final rehearsal, Wynonna could hardly talk, much less sing. Naomi called their family doctor, who prescribed a regimen of oral prednisone and some other medications. Unfortunately, it was the long holiday weekend following Thanksgiving, and they couldn't find a pharmacy that was open. The rehearsal was called off, and everybody went home early, hoping Wynonna's voice would improve with a little rest.

Naomi was also concerned that in her weakened condition Wynonna would be susceptible to the flu, which would have made the concert impossible. Happily, that didn't happen, but her voice didn't improve at all, and at rehearsal Monday afternoon, Wynonna had no voice at all. She communicated with her mother by writing on a magic slate. Her first message: "I'm scared." Naomi nodded in understanding and told her they would work something out. She told the crew not to talk to Wynonna so she wouldn't strain her voice even more. The concert was forty-eight hours away, and the worst was yet to come.

Worried about Wynonna and the concert, Naomi remembered that Larry Gatlin knew a doctor who helped him through a voice crisis. Not only did he visit Wynonna in the middle of a cold December night, but he had an associate open the Vanderbilt Clinic in Nashville, which meant Wynonna had to go there. Wynonna felt terrible that she was the cause of all this fuss, but Naomi insisted she visit the Vanderbilt Clinic. Naomi stayed behind in case she had to perform alone.

The next morning, while Wynonna was in Nashville, Naomi was conducting several media interviews to publicize the concert, trying to be cheerful while making excuses for Wynonna's absence. Most of the reporters accepted Naomi's explanations at face value except Dick Heard of *Entertainment Tonight*, because he knew the two women and had interviewed them before. He suspected there was something seriously wrong because he had never seen Naomi and Wynonna apart on the eve of a concert in all his years of covering them. When he probed privately for the truth, he found out that Wynonna had no voice at all and that the impending concert might prove a disaster.

Meanwhile, Naomi called the doctor after her last interview with a sick feeling about what was happening and her inability to control the situation. The doctor reported that he had inserted a small scope into the back of Wynonna's throat and could see that her vocal cords were red and swollen from what they believed was gastric reflux. He explained that this condition occurs when stomach acid slips through the valve that separates the stomach and the esophagus. When the acid escapes upward into the esophagus, it irritates the area, causing asthma, heartburn, sore throat, and other problems. Asthmatics like Wynonna suffer more side effects than most people. Medications such as Zantac are typically sold over the counter to relieve the irritation and burning, but other measures can be taken to relieve the problem, among them sleeping with the head up, not eating within two hours of going to sleep, and avoiding acid-generating foods.

Naomi listened to these comments but wanted to concentrate on Wynonna's specific problem. Finally, the doctor told her that Wynonna was suffering from a combination of gastric reflex plus swollen glands and tonsillitis and was having a recurring attack of asthma. They were now managing all her symptoms and he wanted to keep her at the medical facility overnight to treat her again in the morning and then before the show. Cautiously, the doctor said that he frankly didn't know if Wynonna would be able to perform. They would have to wait until tomorrow. Nothing further could be done until then.

Naomi was stunned into disbelief. On the biggest night of their career, the singing Judds were about to self-destruct. Suddenly, an idea flashed into Naomi's mind, and she picked up the phone and dialed her therapist to see what she thought. Operating on the theory that she has held ever since her discovery of mind-body medicine, Naomi believed that often the symptoms and ailments we display are a means by which the mind and the body communicate distress. Naomi asked her therapist if Wynonna's inability to speak was a subconscious way of not having to say goodbye to her mother and their dual act, that she was fearful of having to sing their last song together. The therapist agreed that it was a possibility. She said she would work with Naomi to help overcome the problem.

The next day, December 4, Naomi had yet to receive a report on whether Wynonna could sing. The day was gray and rainy as Naomi dressed and went over to the Murphy Center. Her spirits were lifted a little when she stopped to chat with some fans who were hanging around. Then she entered her dressing room and waited.

Finally, Wynonna and the doctor, with two assistants, came through the door. Toting a load of equipment and medicine, they set and started to treat Wynonna. She was still whispering, and the doctor said she would be able to sing in a limited way—only middle-range notes. Wynonna confided that the concert was terrifying to her because it was the end of her identity as she had known it and she felt she was right on the edge. She would try to bluff her way through it because she and her mother had always made it through somehow. Then the call came for them to appear on stage.

The singing Judds walked out onstage. Wynonna was actually trembling. They were greeted by a barrage of flashbulbs and cheers from their ecstatic fans. They were now in familiar territory and knew what they had to do. Even though Wynonna's voice sounded husky, it was still in harmony as they opened with "The Sweetest Gift: A Mother's Smile," the first song they had ever learned together when Wynonna was barefoot and in overalls at age twelve. While the performance was far from perfect, the two of them managed through the next eighteen songs. At least they were giving a good performance, which was more than Naomi dared hope for when she woke up that morning. Each song brought back recollections of important moments in their lives. Finally, when they harmonized on "Grandpa," Naomi could hear Wynonna's voice start to give out. Wynonna asked the audience to bear with her while she took a break for a sip of hot tea, and then she began to cry. Naomi knew they had gone as far as they could. It was time to say goodbye.

Mother and daughter joined in harmony for the last time with the spotlight on them, and both experienced a precious moment of bonding with each other and their thousands of enchanted fans. Then the music ended, and Naomi told the audience that she and Wynonna were blessed to have traveled America and shared their music with such wonderful people. She closed with "I believe in the power of love, and I believe that there is always hope," and the two of them walked arm in arm off the stage.

Backstage exploded with emotion as people poured in to talk about how much the audience loved the Judds and were still in their seats unwilling to leave. They couldn't believe what they had experienced, and they didn't want to go home. The ending of Naomi's singing career brought sadness, which was diminished by the delight they felt at how well Wynonna sang in spite of her throat problems. The Judds were exhausted, but as always, they stayed long enough to thank the entire crew before heading home to rest. Later that day, the news reports came in that this concert was the most successful pay-per-view music program in the history of cable television. The next day, they gathered the family and the crew at the farm for a glory party.

When the Farewell Tour was actually over, the Judds took some criticism in the media because it seemed like an endless goodbye punctuated with tear-jerking emotions, excessive medical reports, hand wringing, and possibly phony posturing, but Wynonna lashed out at the critics. She said it was all sincere and it was important for her mother to say goodbye to all the people who had made them a success.

Later, Naomi would tell Richard Harrington of the *Washington Post* that her career had been oxygen to her and that leaving it had affected her profoundly. Then she dipped into Greek mythology to draw the analogy of Naomi sacrificing herself on the Farewell Tour so that Wynonna could find her own life and be able to continue on her own. It was, she said, like Persephone being kidnapped and taken down into the netherworld, after which her mother, Demeter (Naomi), sacrifices herself in an attempt to save her child.

26

Turning Country Music
Into a Money Machine

Music Row was once a fashionable residential address of Nashville society, as evidenced by the ornate architecture, but it became Music Row in the 1950s when Owen Bradley, then head of the Country Music Division of Decca Records, opened a recording studio in a military-surplus Quonset hut on 16th Avenue. Other music-publishing companies followed, for example, Hill & Range Music and Cedarwood Music, attracted to the area by the cheap real-estate prices due to by the flight of older residents to the suburbs.

It was to Music Row that a disgruntled New Yorker came in the mid-1970s who would change the way country music was marketed. His arrival occurred at a propitious time for Naomi and Wynonna because several years later he took them under his wing in a special way that would give them the chance at success they needed. His name is Joe Galante. Previously, a country artist would usually be marketed by his or her publishing company through traditional means, such as a kit with an eight-by-ten black-and-white glossy and a demo that was mailed to radio stations.

As progress and technology advanced, the need for country-music artists to be photogenic and telegenic became almost as important as their musical ability. The business moved into the 1970s, and the old-fashioned photo press kit was soon history, replaced by what was nicknamed the EPK, the electronic press kit. It consisted of some printed material, but more importantly, a videocassette with the artist performing plus some insider interviews with the artist and a CD from which the radio station could play at least one of the artists' new releases.

Allen Butler, of RCA/Nashville, Naomi and Wynonna's first big-name record publisher, says, "There was no marketing at that time in Nashville. Radio was your sales mechanism." That is partially still true today, but in those days it was the only sales mechanism.

When Joe Galante arrived in Nashville, he wasn't a happy man. He began with RCA records in 1973 in New York, first in the finance department and then in record promotion, where he was assigned to work with some of the label's slower-moving artists, such as David Bowie—long before Bowie made it big in the 1980s. Galante relished his role with RCA, but then he was transferred to Nashville, which came as a shock. In the 1960s and 1970s, Nashville record operations were considered the Siberia of the recording industry. He worked hard to fit in with the local scene but was regarded as an outsider because he wasn't from the area and had no family or history there. He wasn't a Nashville person. Apparently, somebody in New York failed to explain it to him, but they had recognized his talent for developing young artists and that's what RCA needed in its Nashville operation, and so they sent Joe. Although he worked diligently, he really had no affinity for country music, or its world, or for that matter, the young country artists of the time that he was supposed to develop.

However, that situation began to change in 1974. That's when Galante met Waylon Jennings at his Nashville studio near the RCA building on 17th Avenue. After that, he met Dolly Parton, which led to his meeting Ronnie Milsap. Galante's feelings about country music began to change dramatically through meeting these three artists. He recalls: "I began to like what I was hearing. It was country with an edge, an attitude."

Galante remembers that the first artist he started marketing in a modern sense was Ronnie Milsap. Joe was working to improve the marketing of country albums. In those days, the stock routine was to send out the standard, tired press kit and wait while stations played it for a few weeks and then send out another cut to repeat the process. In time, they might then release the album from which these cuts were taken and hope people would buy it. The whole process was catch-as-catch can. As Galante says, "Nashville didn't market the records. They promoted them."

In contrast, Galante wanted to develop a deeper, more lasting process by creating an identity for country artists when he signed them to an RCA contract—the first step in creating a market strategy and campaign. "I wanted to sit down with *People* magazine and explain the artist in a paragraph. Once we had an image in mind, we could have a campaign in mind." Later on, this is exactly what he did with the Judds. The strategy grew out of the process he perfected with Ronnie Milsap's 1977 album *It Was Almost Like a Song*.

While working in tandem with Milsap's producer and publisher, Galante had every marketing aspect of the new album reworked through less conventional and more innovative means, ranging from the photography to the graphics and artwork. Even other nontraditional marketing means were used, such as positioning him at the American Music Awards, which was outside his normal environment. As a result, *It Was Almost Like a Song* became Milsap's first platinum album.

With every new signing by Galante, each project became more focused and refined. Eventually, he said, "we imagined the artist in terms of a logo. All of the advertising had a special style to it. The Judds—that one was the first that we really worked the media hard for. They had a story to tell—mother and daughter who had been through adversity. You swore she [Naomi] had been through life fifteen times. It was like putting the Ivory Snow commercial on the cover. We took the fabric of what they were and wove it into the media."

Throughout the process, the rules of marketing country music were changing as well. As Galante would say, you can run around the country booking your artist onto a hundred radio stations, but if you can get them one appearance on *The Tonight Show* or *David Letterman*, you have accomplished the same thing with a lot less effort. Actually, you haven't done the same thing; you have done better. With country music it is a matter of reaching people, and you reach them through the most efficient conduit in the world for doing that—the media. Galante's style was successful, and the artists he signed during his tenure at RCA proved that.

Galante recognized that he had brought about a definitive change in the marketing of country music, but there had also occurred a constant change in country music itself. Back in 1974, Galante saw a different style of country music, with acts like Waylon Jennings, Dolly Parton, and Ronnie Milsap, which paved the way for a new attitude about country music while also attracting more fans. Sure, the new sound—the Nashville Sound—brought country music closer to rock and to pop music, but all records, including country records, were selling more than ever before. He saw the changes in country as making it strong and with a wider appeal. Galante noted: "While it was never regarded as a sexy format, in recent years it's become one."

Both the Judds and Garth Brooks, country's latest star, are testimony to that. Garth Brooks was found performing at Nashville's Bluebird Cafe in 1988 at a time when the Judds were doing very well. Brooks's first album, *Garth Brooks*, for Capitol Records, was a success, and one single from the album sold 200,000 copies, a huge number. What set him apart from other country-music stars was something that the Judds did with great success but that a lot of stars wouldn't do. Namely, the artist got involved directly in the promotion of his works by visiting radio stations and retail stores and doing interviews—lots and lots of interviews—all of which amounts to priceless publicity. He was doing what pop music stars did, and as the Judds knew, it worked. Wynonna was now going to have to start doing it by herself.

27

Wynonna Alone

IN 1992, NERVOUS AND INSECURE, Wynonna, now twenty-eight, took the big leap into the music world as a solo artist, competing with the act she herself helped create: the Judds. She and her mother had a tumultuous eight years together, but they also had eighteen country hits that went to number one on the charts, six Grammys, and seven Country Music Association Awards in a row as Best Vocal Group of the Year. Naomi had not only been the perfect harmonizing voice; she had been the lighthouse, the rudder, and the safe harbor in rough seas who nurtured, protected, and guided Wynonna. Now that Naomi was no longer there, Wynonna had to make it on her own. She told Mary Murphy of *TV Guide*, "I felt terrified. I felt frustrated and resentful of the fact that—bam! My mother was gone. No one really understood the insecurity I had to overcome."

One way Wynonna overcame insecurity and let off steam was to hop on one of her Harley-Davidson motorcycles and leave a trail of dust and worries behind her. So she added a new six-hundred-pound Harley to her collection and subtracted a boyfriend, singer-songwriter Tony King. Wynonna said she needed more time alone, and being engaged to Tony was getting in the way, although they might still date. Their engagement, which Wynonna said she was sorry she had ever announced, lasted approximately twenty months, and Tony's best composition, "I've Cried My Last Tear for You," may have said it all about their fizzled romance.

Then it was pedal to the metal and straight ahead for Wynonna. Her first solo album was released in 1992, *Wynonna*, and turned out to be one of the most successful albums ever produced by a female country singer. *New York Times* critic James Hunter said, *"Wynonna* is a faultless '90s country album...it demonstrates that a country performer can explore vibrant pop, deep gospel and straight-forward rock and still make sense even to country traditionalists." Hunter's enthusiasm was mirrored by the fans who bought four million copies of *Wynonna*. Out of the album emerged three distinct hit singles: "She Is His Only Need," "My Strongest Weakness, " and "I Saw The Light." The album clearly established the solo Judd as a major music star. *Rolling Stone* labeled the album "the most important release by a country artist so far this decade... powerful, stirring, ennobling."

Still, there was the strange experience of going out on the road again, this time alone, to promote the album before 110 different audiences over the next nine months. Beyond that, Wynonna was haunted by a nightmare that she kept having several nights every week, "Mom dies and comes back and dies and comes back." Nevertheless, in April she opened in Midland, Texas, with fans standing and cheering throughout the concert as they pelted the stage with flowers. Afterward, Wynonna said it made her feel ecstatic and reborn until she got back to her room at the Holiday Inn, where she suddenly felt alone and afraid again. At every stop, people would ask where her mother was. Would she be appearing at the performance, too? They had done the Farewell Tour, but America was still unwilling to let go. They remained devoted to both Judds.

Ken Stilts wanted Wynonna back on the road; he felt she would end up a bigger star on her own than as one of the singing Judds. She would gain experience in running her life and her career and acquire the self-confidence she still didn't have. Wynonna began to shine in the solo spotlight, but her self-confidence was still lacking.

Like many women, she felt that validation could come only through having a lover, or better yet, lovers. Thus, there were men all along the way, but the most significant one turned out to be Arch Kelley III, a forty-one-year-old boat salesman from Nashville, whom she met on a plane trip to Los Angeles.

While one Judd daughter was launching her new career alone, the other Judd daughter, the one who didn't sing, was pushing ahead with hers. Naomi and Wynonna had made it to Nashville via Kentucky and California, Ashley to Hollywood via Kentucky and France, where she had attended art school. When Ashley was a child, it seemed that her mother was always loading her and her sister into some car or U-Haul and taking off to another location. Ashley was living close to where she was born in the San Fernando Valley when she finally returned to Hollywood to pursue a movie career. She remembers: "We grew up in the back of a car asking, 'Where are we going now?'"

Ashley recalls, too, that she didn't have all the attention or normal childhood things other kids had. Perhaps that helped her grow up independent and self-reliant, which is reflected in her constantly making lists of things to do and spending a lot of time by herself when she was at her home in Malibu. Well, not entirely "by herself." She does have three constant, loving, and loyal companions, her cats, Charlotte and Emily (presumably named after the Brontë sisters), and her rabbit, Stinkerbelle. Of course, some of her independence doesn't particularly please her mother, for two of her favorite recreations are skydiving and bungee jumping, neither of which Naomi will countenance. Naomi summarized the difference between her two daughters when she said that Wynonna was born with clenched fists and is always trying to arm-wrestle with God. In contrast, Ashley was born with open hands.

Looking back on that horrendous year of the Judds' Farewell Tour in 1991 sends a shudder down Wynonna's spine. It was a trying year of 120 concerts and 120 goodbye-to-momma scenes for the fans in every locale. For Wynonna, still emotionally insecure about being a solo performer, it was like planning the funeral for a corpse that wasn't dead yet. In the years since 1982, when the singing Judds began their professional rise to stardom, mother had been the boss. All Wynonna had to do was show up at curtain time ready to sing. Naomi took care of everything and everybody—made all the decisions, dealt with all the problems, handled all the stress—and now that was suddenly dumped in Wynonna's lap. That's why Wynonna called 1992 Survival Year; she was just trying to make it through the tour.

Life improved in 1993. Wynonna attributes the change to the strong sense of who she is instilled in her by her mother, who constantly preached about the strength of the Judd women going back generations. While a part of Wynonna loves the public adulation, glamor, and money success has brought, deep down she would really like to be a farmer and spend her time sowing, tending, and reaping. She bought a farm not far from Naomi and Larry's spread and dreamed of someday plowing the dark soil, but for now she was out on tour again.

After completing the promotional tour for the first of her solo albums, Wynonna created a second album called *Tell Me Why* for release in 1993, demonstrating a refinement of the unique Judd sound, as it has come to be called in the business, a blend of country, blues, 1940s jazz, rock, folk, and gospel. *Tell Me Why* went platinum in just two weeks on the market, causing Chuck Dean of *Rolling Stone* to comment, "Wynonna has let her guard down and what we get is a half-country, half-soft-rock album comfortably packed with more emotion than most mood rings can handle." One of the numbers was "That Was Yesterday," a bluesy number cowritten by her mother. Tony Scherman, of *People* magazine, underscored his enthusiasm by saying that the album "establishes her as one of the finer pop voices of the young decade."

The end of 1993 was not great for Ashley. First, in the middle of November, Ashley's Malibu bungalow burned down, and a month later, at Thanksgiving time, when she was horseback riding in Franklin, she was thrown and ended up in the hospital with a fractured right ankle.

28

A Stunning Confession

KEN STILTS HAD BEEN the Judds' manager and general factotum since 1982, the beginning of their success in Nashville. Stilts had launched the singing Judds, but Wynonna began to resent his presence. She wanted more control over her life and career. She began seeing Stilts as a man who cared only about the money she could make as a commodity, to be marketed along with the CDs, T-shirts, and other memorabilia. For example, Naomi and Wynonna were surprised when they discovered that Ken had sold the TV rights to Naomi's autobiography, *Love Can Build a Bridge*, without telling her. Ken shot back that the allegation was "a bold-faced lie." Even though it turned out to be a great success—it was on the *New York Times* bestseller list for ten weeks—Wynonna felt Stilts may have overstepped his authority.

Early in 1994, Wynonna fired Stilts and hired in his place John Unger, who knew little about managing artists. As a result, Wynonna invited a massive lawsuit from Ken Stilts. Nashville musician Eddie Bayers has known both Wynonna and Ken Stilts for a long time, and he's not sure what happened: "From my end, Ken was a fantastic manager. He never let anything stand in the way of everything being top-notch. I mean, he really saw that everything was handled, but he had no say over the artists, such as the musicians in the band. Some thought Wynonna fired Ken because Naomi wanted to manage Wynonna, but I don't think so. I think it was just another evolution. You finally get to the point where you say you can handle yourself or somebody in your family can do it because nobody knows family like family does. Of course, Larry, Naomi's husband, is managing her. So I think because of that, they've created their own little management group, and that's the way it is."

Still, that doesn't explain why Wynonna hired John Unger. After graduating from Princeton, Unger attended Vanderbilt Law School in Nashville. He knew little or nothing about the music business, the management of celebrities, or where he wanted to go with his own life. He quit his law firm and became Wynonna's manager for a straight salary, as opposed to a percentage of the income, which is standard for managers. Wynonna said she wanted Unger to create a team of people who would help her be a success and who would always tell her the truth.

Soon after, on September 1994, 30-year-old Wynonna, now five months pregnant, took time off from touring to prepare for the birth of her son. She spent a few minutes with Oprah to explain why she had rejected the idea of an abortion. She was afraid if she did, the abortion would come back to haunt her because of the reaction from her conservative fans. According to author Larry Leamer in his book about Nashville, *Three Chords and the Truth*, Wynonna became pregnant several years earlier, in 1987, while dating and having sex with several different men and had an abortion under the name of Connie Sims.

Four months later, in December, Wynonna went into labor in Nashville Baptist Hospital. She told a friend that she was surprised and comforted by the vision of an angel in a churchyard, assuring her all would be well. She said that during the weeks before, she was getting more and more depressed and at the same time felt a magnetic pull toward the church that she and her mother attended. She drove to the church and went into what her mother calls the Meditation Garden. There she sensed an angel telling her that God was keeping an eye on her. The experience lifted her spirits, and she got in touch with her mother, with whom she had been feuding again, and they reconciled.

Then, early on the morning of December 23, she felt the contractions start, and her fiancé, Arch Kelley, rushed her to the hospital, where they were joined by Naomi and Ashley. Even though they had heard of the angel's reassuring words, Naomi and the doctors were very concerned because Wynonna's weight had ballooned to 270 pounds. After she had been in labor four hours, they decided that the angel probably meant it would be best to take the child by cesarean section, and they did.

Elijah Judd Kelley, all eight pounds and fifteen ounces of him, arrived in Nashville Baptist Hospital two days before Christmas, 1994. To everyone's horror, his umbilical cord was wrapped around him three times and could very easily have strangled him. Naomi and Ashley were present, along with the father, Arch Kelley III.

It was a replay of most Judd gatherings. The three women dominated and the rest of the world played walk-on roles. As Naomi's husband of six years summarizes such gatherings, "When the three of them walk into a room, they can soak up all the oxygen." Typically, Naomi was fluttering around the hospital room trying to put up a hospital screen to shield Wynonna from curious eyes, and Wynonna kept telling her mother to please stop!

Actually, they continued to fight over Wynonna's disorganized life—always late, always messy—her eating habits and weight, her taste in clothes and men, and her headstrong attitude. For example, she and Arch had yet to marry when Elijah arrived because Wynonna didn't want to just yet. She announced that as soon as she left the hospital, she was going to a fat farm and drop all the excess weight; then she would be married in white. Meanwhile, Wynonna's staff was concerned that her illegitimate child would send a message to her fans that she didn't share their values.

The healing of the rift between Wynonna and Naomi made Naomi feel better about her possible future son-in-law, Arch. She saw how caring and tender he was with the newborn child and with Wynonna. Naomi rethought her opinion and now accepted him because he seemed genuine. She still wished the two of them had married before Elijah was born. Wynonna said she was thinking about a Valentine's Day wedding, but only after she dropped some weight. She said she didn't want to be a bulging bride.

The three Judd women were to appear together on the Oprah show to promote the NBC-TV miniseries based on *Love Can Build a Bridge*, but Wynonna decided she didn't want to do it. Chris Smith, writing in *New York* magazine about Ashley, offered this insightful observation about the Judd women: "Naomi and Wynonna clawed their way out of a plumbingless Kentucky hollow to an eight-year run as the queens of Nashville. For Ashley, the nonsinging Judd, carving out her own identity has required just as strong a will."

Meanwhile, Ashley pursued her professional life in Hollywood and appeared for three seasons in the NBC-TV series *Sisters* playing Swoosie Kurtz's daughter. Ironically, Ashley had never seen the show *Sisters* when she auditioned for it in 1991. She said, "I was raised without TV. I was raised on imagination and books, for which I am eternally grateful." After several seasons she left to do film roles in *Heat* with Robert De Niro and *Smoke* with Harvey Keitel and Stockard Channing.

Wynonna was also doing well on her chosen path except for a pothole here and a dead armadillo there. She knew, for example, that everybody wanted her to marry, but at this point, she said she wasn't ready. She admitted that she has felt shame because of the baby, but with that strong-minded Judd streak, she put the feeling aside as unimportant. She and Arch were in love, and they would eventually marry, but only when they were ready. In the meantime, motherhood had created new vistas for Wynonna. Having a child, she says, was the most important event of her life. Even if she were never to sing again, she would be happy.

Wynonna's in-your-face style fit in with the rise of strong women's music during the early 1990s, in what may be described as a country-music version of feminism. The male-oriented country songs tend to talk about a woman who isn't willing to put up with a man's infidelity and drunkenness, issues that did not resonate with women. Strong women songs deal with problems facing women, such as being part of a harem, or such songs as Reba McEntire's "She Thinks His Name Was John," about being aware of AIDS. There was also Patty Loveless's lament about family bonds, "How

Can I Help You Say Goodbye," plus the harsh tale of violence in the privacy of home and love portrayed in Martina McBride's "Independence Day," about burning down her home with herself and her abusive, drunken husband in it. These songs go beyond the traditional role of a woman's being a good girlfriend or a good wife.

From a commercial viewpoint such songs appeal to women record buyers because they make a statement and take a stand. Lyrics have made the transition from something like "I dream of being a cowboy's girlfriend" to "you treat me right or get out." There had been a precursor of such songs back in 1952 with Kitty Wells's ballad about how infidelity in men encouraged faithlessness in women, "It Wasn't God Who Made Honky-Tonk Angels," but the new attitude didn't take hold until later, and now it fits the style of a Wynonna solo.

In spite of the tough feminine talk, Wynonna kept thinking about marrying Arch and losing weight so that she could be a Valentine's Day bride. Unfortunately, the will was weak, and she couldn't seem to lose the unwanted pounds. Finally, she said there would be no Valentine's Day wedding because she weighed 240 pounds instead of the 150 everybody—including herself—thought she should be.

Meanwhile, the most recent diagnosis of Naomi's condition made it clear that she was suffering from hepatitis C, which was not good news. This form of the disease posed a greater possibility of developing into liver cancer, which, of course, is what she had feared all along. Her condition, required that she rest and avoid the hectic pace at which she had been living when she was in the music business. She sorely missed the excitement and rewards of performing but reconciled herself to the joys of grandmotherhood and a more relaxed life on her Franklin farm. She did have installed on the farm the so-called Mom Line, an unlisted number known only by Wynonna and Ashley. Aside from that, she trashed her alarm clock and goes to bed when she's tired and wakes up whenever she wishes.

Her morning starts with sipping decaf coffee, reading about mind-body medicine, and listening to the kind of tapes that encourage relaxation and meditation. When husband Larry is home from his work as a manager of several pop and Christian music groups, they go for long walks. In general, she is doing all she can to help her mind and body heal.

Of course, the Judd tempers continued to erupt from time to time. Once, a couple of years back, the two sisters refused to speak to each other for almost six months. As always, peace was ultimately restored. The memories the three cherish most are the ones Ashley and Wynonna share, such as the time when Ashley broke an ankle while riding a horse in the winter of 1994 and stayed with Wynonna until it healed. They slept together in the same bed for two and a half months. Ashley recalls that it was like when they were kids sleeping together and always fell asleep holding each other's hair. More recently, Naomi was delighted when the three of them were sitting on Naomi's turquoise couch with their arms around each other.

In May, NBC-TV aired the miniseries based on Naomi's autobiography, *Love Can Build a Bridge*, which prompted one critic to say that the Judds' life story could never have been sold as fiction. It would have been rejected as melodramatic and unbelievable. In some ways that may also have been the opinion of Naomi's mother, sixty-seven-year-old Polly Rideout, who watched an advanced tape of the program. Naomi thought it was important for her mother to see the tape in advance because it did cover some of the painful times in her life as well as Naomi's, such as the death of Brian from Hodgkin's disease. Naomi let her mother view the tape alone, after which she returned to Naomi's farm. The two spent the next three days together.

The same month NBC-TV broadcast the miniseries, Mike Stevens, a farmer from Mill Valley in northern California, told the *National Enquirer* about his romance with Naomi. Mike Stevens, a guitar player and publisher of *BAM* (Bay Area Music) magazine, said he knew Naomi in Marin County, California, when she was just starting out. According to Stevens, they did a lot of things that were not mentioned in Naomi's book, such as smoking pot around her kids and lying about Wynonna's age so she and Naomi could get a job singing in a small local saloon.

Neither of those great "revelations" seems too outrageous in today's society, nor do they reflect that badly on Naomi, if that was Mike's objective. To tantalize the readers, he said that Naomi was heart-stoppingly beautiful, with "luscious lips and a voluptuous figure, and she was an expert at pleasing her man!"

Mike said that Naomi told him she had breast implants because of an accident she had had as a girl and, more importantly, that she was pregnant with Stevens's child. However, she told him she already had two children, didn't want his, and would have the pregnancy "taken care of." Mike claims he drove her to a free clinic and waited outside while they were "killing my child" inside.

Probably the most believable part of Mike's story is that Naomi is clairvoyant and hot-tempered. To illustrate the former, he said that one night he cheated on Naomi with a quickie affair. The next night, she informed him that her ESP told her he had been unfaithful. Stunned, he says, he broke up with her a few nights later, but she grabbed the keys to his car and refused to let him leave. So he began walking down the road when she started chasing him in his own car. He said she was hysterical and yelling. She was never going to let him leave her. In desperation, he hid in some bushes while she drove up and down, honking, yelling, and blinking the lights, looking for him. Finally, she gave up, and went home. Reacting to the story, Naomi said that Mike walked out on her because she was too much woman for him to handle.

In July, Michael Ciminella told the local Ashland newspaper that he was not Wynonna's biological father. He said the real father was Charlie Jordan, an Ashland high school classmate of his and Naomi's. Ciminella said he believed Naomi deliberately tricked him into marrying her because she calculated that his family was richer than Charlie Jordan's.

He told the newspaper, "She has spent her career saying what a horrible person I was when she, in fact, is the one who didn't stand up and do what is right. She let me take the rap for something I did not do." Soon after Naomi's second child, Ashley, was born, Ciminella said he began to get suspicious that Wynonna (then called Christina) was not his daughter, and he confronted Naomi (then called Diana). She admitted she had also been sleeping with Charlie Jordan and that he was Wynonna's biological father.

Ciminella says he is finally speaking out because Naomi has kept saying unflattering things about him and he was getting tired of hearing them.

Michael told the author he wanted to say more about this relationship but ultimately decided not to further embarrass the Judds. In his last letter to the author (November 4, 1997), Ciminella wrote: "I received a rundown of the topics you are interested in regarding my daughter. There is no new ground to be broken here, and therefore I don't think I have much to add. If, however, you ever decide to take a genuine look at the 'inside' of how this 'phonom' came to pass, I might be willing to talk at length with you."

Although the author said he wanted to hear Michael's side of the story, Michael decided later to remain silent. Wynonna wrote Michael saying that as far as she was concerned, the relationship between them was no different than it had been in the past and that as far as she was concerned, he was still her daddy. Privately, she believed that her mother kept the truth from her to protect her. While she understands that, she was saddened by it. She wants to meet her biological father someday, but not while there is all the publicity and headlines. She says she wants to meet him in private and not on Oprah.

In autumn 1995, Wynonna was trying to shed those pounds so that she could get married in the kind of designer gown she wanted to wear and not something, as she would say, from the Nashville Tent, Camp and Awning Company. By the end of September, she was making good progress and had lost one hundred pounds through a combination of diet and spiritual workout under the supervision of mind-body-medicine guru Deepak Chopra. Her goal was to lose a total of 150 pounds.

In the meantime, as a spokeswoman for the American Liver Foundation, Naomi made a TV public-service announcement warning the public that many people may be infected with hepatitis and not know it. The announcement was widely distributed, and more than an estimated 13 million people have seen it.

29

Finding the Fun in Dysfunctional

ON JANUARY 11, 1996, Naomi Judd, retired former showbiz star, turned fifty. However, although she may no longer be making music with her guitar, she does appears on the lecture circuit, talking to scientists, battered women, social workers, and others about the one thing she knows best. In January 1997 she addressed a Columbia, South Carolina, audience of five hundred. She said she would be fifty-one in a few days and was proud out it.

As a result of her illness, she enjoys meeting with researchers and doctors to learn more about what she prefers to call complementary, as opposed to alternative, medicine. She talks and listens and enjoys thinking about what she has learned during long walks in the woods on her Peaceful Valley ranch in Franklin, Tennessee. These walks remind her of the time she was a young girl ambling through the Kentucky forests around her grandparents' home.

Her inspirational talks revolve around that theme, and her lectures are about keeping alive and active, even though the hepatitis lurking inside her might flare up without warning. She still wants to do things, go places, and be with people. At one point, she suggested that she might volunteer for the Peace Corps on her sixty-fifth birthday.

It was a Saturday in the middle of January 1997, just a few days after Naomi's fifty-first birthday. Most women in Wynonna's situation would have focused on her wedding, about a week away. Instead, Wynonna was on the stage of the legendary Ryman Auditorium, used by the *Grand Ole Opry* to broadcast their shows. She was getting ready appear on the Nashville TV Network. It is clear that she is in charge of herself these days and has adopted a cocky presence. That attitude comes across in her performances, and for many women fans, it is the feminine independence that they like.

For many other women, however, Wynonna's out-of-wedlock pregnancies are troubling because of the example they set for their daughters. Wynonna does not feel that any of this is her problem. She isn't going to be responsible for the moral upbringing of other women's daughters. Naomi tries not to be too judgmental, but she knows that such posturing can hurt Wynonna professionally.

Audience and critics, for example, who see her performing regularly at Caesars Palace in Las Vegas like her image. One critic, Michael Paskevich of the *Las Vegas Review-Journal*, labels Wynonna's music as an "aggressive blend of country and other American roots music that has led to a crossover commercial success." He cautions everyone to be sure to pronounce her name "Y-nona" and quotes her about her attitude. "If you're looking for glitz and glamour, you're in the wrong place." If you want attitude, says Paskevich, you're definitely in the right place, or as Y-nona herself says, "It all comes down to me, my red hair, and my big mouth."

At this time, Wynonna's mind was probably not focused on her upcoming marriage, the fact she was pregnant a second time, or her mother's attitude. Rather, she was concerned about her next album, *Revelations*, her first one in the last three years and due out in a month. The album took almost four times longer to produce than the last. She felt as if she were starting her career all over again.

Karen Choemer, writing for *Newsweek*, characterized Wynonna's new album as "confident, stirring and refreshingly unpredictable;

it moves from sultry romantic pop to sassy Memphis soul to yee-hawing Southern rock. Wynonna can sing like a dream. She's got the most exhilarating voice in country today—not just pretty, but full of depth and dimension."

On the flip side of all her talent, Wynonna is the irresponsible, bratty prima donna who excuses herself by saying she is trying to find herself and to redefine her relationship with her mother. That really doesn't excuse her thoughtless behavior toward colleagues and servants.

The year started out propitiously. Wynonna and Arch finally decided to marry, but as with everything involving the Judds, there was high drama, tension, conflict, changes, confusion, and fighting. At first, they were going to get married during the Christmas holidays, around the time of Elijah's first birthday, December 23. However, that plan didn't work out, so the marriage was set for January 1996, with the ceremony to take place in Ryman Auditorium.

Friends said that Naomi really pressured Wynonna to marry. Arch was the father of her grandchild, and she felt he should be married to the mother of her grandchild. Beyond that, Wynonna had received a lot of negative mail from her fans, but she dug in her heels back in October and said she would marry when she was ready.

Wynonna said she wanted to be sure she was ready for marriage and that she and Arch had both gone through extensive premarital counseling. The numerous sessions demonstrated to her just how much they needed help. They were not ready to be parents, an all-consuming endeavor. How could they take on the additional burden of marriage? She looked forward to having a family; touring and performing were not the only important things in life. Nevertheless, she would go back on the road to promote her album *Revelations* and perform. As she told *People* magazine reporter Tony Scherman, "I want people to know I'm back. I'm out there touring like my hair is on fire. I'm stomping and snorting, ready to get on that bus and kick butt. And I'll tell you what. I'll be on the road until they put rhinestones on my walker."

The usual Judd conflict erupted as soon as Wynonna announced again that she was ready for marriage. Naomi started to take charge, and Wynonna insisted that it was her wedding, not Naomi's. Wynonna yelled that the wedding was off, jumped on her Harley-Davidson, and disappeared for a day.

When she returned, she decided she was still too fat to be a bride and did what she had done several times before. She entered the Nashville Baptist Hospital, where they sucked out some of the fat by using the liposuction technique. To her shock, she discovered a week after that procedure that she was pregnant again with their second child. Wynonna was now due to start her new tour in the middle of March. The tour would last many months. The doctor advised her to spend only two months on the road so she would have time to properly care for herself and the baby during her pregnancy.

As noted earlier, Wynonna and Arch had been to counseling and had consulted the guru Deepak Chopra for advice. Everybody was advising marriage for the sake of their firstborn, Elijah, and now, with a second one on the way, the children. Finally, Arch proposed again, and this time, Wynonna said yes. Arch says he wrote out the proposal, and rehearsed it, and even called his future sister-in-law, Ashley, for her advice.

Regardless of the constant battling, Naomi has a great influence on Wynonna, who knew that Naomi didn't like the idea of her being an unwed mother, particularly since she had been faced with that issue herself and insisted on marriage before the child, who turned out to be Wynonna, was born. Still, Wynonna wanted everybody to know that she made her decision to wed Arch out of faith, not fear. She thought about it and prayed a long time, she says, and was convinced it was the right thing to do. The new baby already had a name, even though the child was not due until July. The baby would be named after her grandmother, Pauline Grace, if a girl and after grandfather Samuel Glen if a boy.

Wynonna and Arch were finally married on Sunday, January 21, 1996, in the Wallace Chapel of Christ Church in Nashville. It seemed as if Naomi's hepatitis might recur, which worried Wynonna. The illness had been in remission for some time, but Naomi had been sick during the weeks before the wedding.

The man who was to walk Wynonna down the aisle and give her away was Michael Ciminella, who came in from his home in Belgravia Court, Louisville, Kentucky, to do so. As mentioned earlier, almost a year before, he had revealed he was not Wynonna's natural father. After her natural father, Charlie Jordan, got Naomi pregnant, she apparently talked Michael into marrying her. For the first thirty years of her life, Wynonna did not know about Charlie Jordan, just as he did not know about the wedding and had not been invited because Wynonna still thought of Michael Ciminella as her father.

Predictably, with this volatile family, tensions rose as the wedding approached. The ceremony was called off in a fit of frustration or anger several times before Sunday, January 21, arrived. While tabloids hired helicopters to circle overhead and a phalanx of reporters and photographers surrounded the small chapel of Christ Church on Old Hickory Boulevard in Nashville, the wedding party and guests gathered at 3:00 P.M. and the ceremony got under way at about 4:00 P.M. The star was neither the bride nor the groom in their cream-colored outfits but their one-year old son, Elijah, who kept crying for his mother. Thus, Wynonna, now thirty-one, and Arch Kelley III, forty-five, exchanged vows, while a really emotional participant, Naomi, cried. As the couple left the church to the cheers of friends and fans, they waved and smiled and climbed into a 1952 Cadillac and headed for the reception, another family affair, since it was held at Naomi's restaurant, the Trilogy.

The two hundred guests cheered the new couple and enjoyed the caviar, pasta, shrimp, salmon, and sushi as Wynonna and Arch danced together to the strains of "Tennessee Waltz." Then the party dissolved into happy talk, champagne, and food for the next four hours until Arch and Wynonna made it back into that 1952 Cadillac and headed for the $2,000-a-night Presidential Suite at the Opryland Hotel.

If Wynonna's off-again, on-again marriage proved a strain for Naomi, Ashley brought stress to her mother when she said she would appear nude in front of the cameras for her role as Marilyn Monroe in HBO's *Norma Jean and Marilyn*. Witnesses on the set described Ashley arriving in a robe and announcing to the crew, "Hi, I'm Ashley, and I'm going to be nude for the next twelve hours. I'm not embarrassed, and I hope you won't be, either." Then, as she stepped forward and dropped the robe, she said, "This is my body."

The media released the story about Ashley's nude scene before she could alert her mother. Naomi is quite straitlaced and religious and deplores vulgarity or obscenity in her presence. Ashley offered the excuse that the role was about Marilyn Monroe, but Naomi didn't understand why her daughter would take such a role. Even at the beginning of Ashley's career, she refused to do a nude scene in her very first movie, the 1992 Christian Slater film *Kuffs*, so why now?

While Wynonna awaited her next baby, Naomi was easing back into entertainment with a new talkshow idea. She taped some pilots in Los Angeles and then went back to the farm to meditate and pray. She decided that the ideas for the show were ill conceived and they would require further work. Meanwhile, she prepared for a special on the Family Channel called *Very Personal With Naomi Judd*, with Fran Drescher, Tim Allen, and Jane Seymour.

The January day that Arch and Wynonna got married was a happy one that they would look back upon fondly. As Wynonna carried her second baby to almost the end of her term, the central problem became her weight. By the time her first child, Elijah, was born, she had soared up to 275 pounds. She then trimmed back with the help of some cosmetic surgery to 150 pounds several months before the wedding. Unfortunately, she was pregnant by the time of the wedding and gained weight rapidly. She had almost doubled her weight during her second pregnancy and now weighed in at 300 pounds.

Several weeks before the new baby was due, Wynonna began serious contractions, and Arch rushed her to the hospital. Thus began one of the most torturous experiences of Wynonna's life; she endured eighteen hours of labor. Finally, the doctors decided to deliver the baby by C-section, which they did at 4:00 A.M. on June 21. Happily, they were able to deliver a nine-pound, four-ounce baby girl, but they were concerned she might have problems with her lungs or a weakened immune system. She was named Pauline Grace Kelley.

After giving birth to Pauline, Wynonna could not endure the experience of having another baby. An added disappointment was that the doctors would not let Wynonna breast-feed Pauline because she was taking blood-pressure medicine required by her weight, which the doctors said could adversely affect her milk and her child's health.

The month following Pauline's birth, Wynonna lost almost seventy pounds as the result of her third liposuction operation. Her weight bothers her because it doesn't feel comfortable, she hates the fat jokes she hears when people think she's out of earshot. In her usual way, she told the cosmetic surgeons to remove the fat, as they did twice in 1995. Naomi objects to her daughter's having any kind of unnecessary surgery, but Wynonna's flippant attitude is that she has more money than God and she'll do whatever she pleases, except that she also doesn't want to displease her mother.

This latest cut, suck, and tuck session did not accomplish the desired result; Wynonna was too overweight. She was still left with an excess of more than sixty-five or seventy pounds, which her five-foot-five-inch frame could not comfortably carry. Once she reached 150 pounds, she would have to struggle to keep the weight down. It would mean curbing her voracious eating habits and, in her mother's mind, achieving inner serenity.

Naomi brought Wynonna to Deepak Chopra's very upscale weight spa in La Jolla, California, but it didn't work. Chopra apparently told Wynonna that she still had too many internal conflicts and that when she was depressed or upset, she turned to food for emotional sustenance. When she settled this inner turmoil, she would be able to control her eating. Naomi agrees. She has great faith in Chopra and belongs to the board of directors of his health spa.

In the months following her marriage to Arch in January, the couple became notorious for fighting in public. Wynonna's staff has sided with her because they don't want their territory compromised by the man they ridicule as a boat salesman, suggesting he doesn't know anything about the music business. Arch accompanied Wynonna on her tours because she wanted to bring the children with her and she trusted him to take care of them. She didn't have time to do so herself when she was traveling and performing. Consequently, Arch feels like a glorified nanny or bellhop who looks after kids and luggage. He doesn't like the role. After they had been officially married for nine months, Wynonna banished Arch to a small cabin away from the main house. She freely admits that they need postmarital counseling since the premarital sessions didn't work.

Wynonna seems determined to keep Arch from assuming many husbandly duties. She also has publicly humiliated him. A recent incident took place at the party after the Country Music Association Awards when Wynonna literally ignored her husband and flirted outrageously with country singer Michael Bolton, with whom she sang a duet during the televised portion of the awards program. Her behavior made Bolton uncomfortable, but he still took her with him in his limo when they left the awards show, leaving Arch to ride home with Naomi and Larry. That, apparently, was not the end of the Michael Bolton connection. Since then, he has dined with Naomi and Larry and has been dating Ashley.

In 1996, Ashley's next film, *A Time to Kill,* appeared. In it, she plays the wife of a white lawyer in the South defending a black man accused of murder. In 1993 the first film Ashley appeared in, *Ruby in Paradise,* generated a lot of excitement at the Sundance Film Festival. She had been attending acting classes at Playhouse West, waiting until she removed the braces from her teeth, and when that happened, she began to audition. A self-assured woman, she called on the Triad theatrical agency and convinced them to sign her. They agreed to do so with the provision that they only had to place her in one role. She was offered the role in Christian Slater's *Kuffs* but turned it down because of the nude scene required but talked her way into another role on the same film so she could immediately join the Screen Actors Guild. Later, she got roles in *Star Trek: The Next Generation,* and then the TV drama *Sisters,* after which she left TV roles behind to make her film debut in *Ruby in Paradise*. The movie won the Grand Jury Prize at the 1993 Sundance Film Festival.

In August, Wynonna gave a concert for thirty-nine hundred fans—a thousand short of a sellout—in Boston. Critic Jeffrey B. Remz described it as a ninety-minute show in which to her audience Wynonna could do no wrong. The concert was more soul and rhythm and blues mixed with gospel. It featured what she called her theme song, "What It Takes," which has the lyrics "I like to make it my own way." Remz concluded: "No matter what the style, Judd, a warm, gritty, go-your-own-way singer, keeps rolling."

She once told an Internet chat-room audience that it has always been her fantasy to ride up and down the aisles at one of her concerts on her Harley, and she occasionally calls her fans Wynuts or Ajuddfans. She has come a long way as an artist since she and her mother had to break up their act, and she feels she's still learning and making progress. Wynonna now feels that the most important part of her show occurs when she communicates with each member of her audience despite her strong fears of performing and sense of vulnerability.

In early March 1997, Larry and Naomi announced that they could no longer find anybody to run their Trilogy restaurant the way they wanted. Ironically, the restaurant was thought to be one of Nashville's best new restaurants, but it had gone through chefs at a prodigious rate. The most recent one, Debra Desulniers, announced that she was leaving for a chef's job in Branson, Missouri. Desulniers was the third chef at the Trilogy during its fourteen months of existence. Part of the problem may have been that the restaurant didn't have a clear vision of what it should do and be.

Retired entertainment celebrities often want to be affiliated with a restaurant when they are no longer in the limelight. For aging celebrities, a restaurant means a party every night and a continuation of those good old days when they were active in their fields and spent nights as the center of attention.

The Trilogy was run in an inconsistent manner. Sometimes it

was open for lunch; at other times it wasn't. Sometimes, but not always, it had music during the dinner hour. It offered well-produced, good corporate banquets, receptions, and parties, but the quality of the day-to-day business of serving meals varied. A successful restaurateur knows one has to be there all the time, when meat and groceries are delivered until closing time, when the day's receipts are counted. It is more than a full-time job, which is not the kind of schedule that most celebrities have in mind who just want to drop by and have a good time.

Meanwhile, Rysher Entertainment, Quincy Jones, and David Salman, who were producing the *Naomi Judd Show*, decided in their own minds that the time wasn't ripe or the elements of the show weren't balanced correctly. They decided to postpone the Naomi Judd talk show and perhaps do it at some future time.

Among the many things Naomi was doing with her life was not relaxing and resting, as instructed by her doctors for the past seven years. She was continuing her speaking engagements, working on a book, trying to get a TV talk show launched, making special appearances and engaging in other projects, such as creating the Naomi Judd Education and Research Fund to help find a cure for liver diseases.

In the spring of 1997 people in the country-music business speculated that Naomi might rejoin her daughter, Wynonna, in creating again their special brand of music. Everybody knows that Naomi hated leaving the business because of her hepatitis C infection five years earlier. She was also terribly bored despite the excitement of opening a restaurant and finishing her cookbook. She gives lectures around the country about how she's getting the upper hand over her hepatitis, but that is pretty weak tea compared to performing in front of thousands of fans.

When asked about a reunion tour, Naomi is vague in her reply. She says that if she and Wynonna ever did that, it would happen because the time was right. In February 1998 that time looked as if it might be near. Naomi announced that she believed she was cured of her hepatitis C; her system had been clear of it for at least the last six years. This could be the beginning of a Naomi-Wynonna reunion, if Wynonna could endure it.

In the meantime, Wynonna has been having difficulty. Her last record-album sales fell off significantly, and her concerts have not drawn the kind of sold-out crowds she and her mother enjoyed. Whereas the singing Judds would play to sold-out audiences of twenty thousand, Wynonna was only drawing four thousand fans.

Most album producers believe Wynonna is too skittish, insecure, and lazy. She no longer does the work a good album requires, even though she did so on her first two albums. It took almost a year and a half for her to produce her third one, *Revelations*.

Wynonna may also not want a reunion tour with her mother. She has struggled hard to establish her solo career and reinvent herself. She does not want people to think she needs her mother to rescue her.

June brought the sad news of the death of Wynonna and Ashley's paternal grandfather, Michael Ciminella, who died in Ashland at the age of eighty-three. He had founded the Ashland Aluminum Company in 1947 when he moved to town. At about the time she heard the news, Naomi made another appearance in Boise, Idaho, lecturing about positive thinking and faith in God, with the proceeds going to the Naomi Judd Education Research Fund.

In June, 1997 the Naomi and Wynonna Judd Charity Memorabilia Auction in Nashville auctioned off their artifacts to benefit the fund. The most sought after item was bought by Helen Berger of Tacoma, Washington, and Ann Gorham of Omaha, Nebraska, who jointly paid $8,600 to have dinner with the two singing Judds. Wynonna's Wurlitzer jukebox went for $5,000; a diamond ring of Naomi's, for $1,000; a day on the road with Wynonna, $4,350; Wynonna's acoustic touring guitar, $1,800; and her motorcycle helmet, $310. Naomi's mink coat was withdrawn from the auction when nobody would meet the minimum opening bid of $5,000; it was not a mink-coat type of crowd.

By the summer of 1997 the eighteen-month, tumultuous, fight-punctuated marriage was over between Wynonna and Arch, according to their friends. She had thrown him out of the house.

Now in 1998, Naomi is on the bookshelves and on TV talk shows promoting her new book, *Naomi's Home Companion*, filled with recipes, advice, observations about life, and the conviction that what is wrong with America today is the decline of the family, which is due to families not sitting around the kitchen table to have a meal together at least once a day. This observation is even true of families with only a single parent. Naomi tells of how she always gathered her two daughters around that table even if the fare was as meager as fried bologna sandwiches. This meal brought the family together in good times and bad. The one thing Naomi wouldn't do when she appeared on the Rosie show was gossip about her daughter Wynonna and country star Michael Bolton, even when Michael appeared on the show and cooked up some food described in Naomi's book.

Naomi also says that women need to plan "significant days" in their lives when they pamper and nurture themselves. She believes that they should simplify their lives and focus on what truly makes them happy and what is meaningful.

So much attention has been focused on Naomi and Wynonna and their high-octane emotions that everyone seems to assume that the twenty-nine-year-old Ashley has been the serene and centered member of the family. She was certainly the one in the background during those years when her mother and older sister were on the road building their careers.

Along the way Ashley has had her share of love relationships, including the two most notable with Matthew McConaughey and singer Michael Bolton. She is widely adored in Hollywood because she is a classic brunette beauty who is also intelligent. Scripts are now being offered her regularly, and life seems, finally, to be good to the smallest and the least-known Judd.

Ashley has purchased a 180-year-old farmhouse in Nashville, close to the farms her mother and sister own. The restoration she has in mind is different from most. In keeping with her dedication to books and reading, she wants the remodeled house patterned after C. S. Lewis's *Chronicles of Narnia*, with cubbyholes, secret passages and the like.

There are times now when Ashley is depressed and realizes that her Judd childhood in an all-female, poverty-stricken home was not as bright and cheery as she has tried in the past to pretend it was. Even when her mother and sister were winning awards and topping the country-music charts, Ashley was still in her teens, still in school, and still trying to figure out what her life was all about. She didn't have a lot of help from mama or sis.

No one was more stunned by Ashley's descent into deep depression than her mother; she never realized how life and loneliness had affected her youngest daughter. The effect it had on Naomi was another troubling aspect for Ashley. Whatever happened and however any of them felt, Ashley understands that her mother as a single parent had struggled through deprivation and abuse to provide the best she could for her two daughters. Even so, it hurt. The time she spent with Michael Bolton helped, even though the romantic part of that relationship has cooled. They are still good friends.

The death of Princess Di produced a strong reaction in Naomi, whose birthday is the same as Diana's. Naomi called for a boycott of tabloid newspapers that support the paparazzi and buy the intrusive photos they take. The photographers buzzed Wynonna's wedding, ambushed her grandson when he was out playing, and eavesdropped on Naomi and her family when they went out to a public place. She says the boycott has to start with the tabloid buyer because "the buyer is at the top of the food chain here." She likens paparazzi and tabloid publishers to the lying tobacco company executives, junk-bond salesmen, and those people who cheat senior citizens out of their pensions. She once came close to suing a tabloid, but her two daughters talked her out of it. Still, she is disturbed that the American public seems to idolize many celebrities who are immoral and who ridicule the public for its morality.

Meanwhile, Naomi is pleased about the success of her cookbook, which isn't exactly a cookbook. It contains eighty-five of her favorite recipes, designed to get the family to gather around the kitchen table, but there are also jokes, tales of good times and bad, and observations about being a single mom, all leavened with tips on God, love, charity, and inner peace. It's less of a cookbook and more of a Naomi book. In some ways, that's been true of the Judds, who are not Naomi, Wynonna, and Ashley as much as they are Naomi plus two.

Nicknames often reveal what people think of each other, and with the Judds this may be particularly true. Each of them has nicknames bestowed upon her by the other two. Naomi is the Queen of Everything, while Wynonna is variously the Princess of Quite a Lot, Sweet Tater, The Countess of Hip, or Hurricane Wynonna, depending on her mood of the moment. Ashley is the Queen of the Screen or Sweet Pea. Ashley is known to others as the Littlest Judd, the Third Judd or the Nonsinging Judd.

Interestingly, Ashley's nickname for herself is Ballbuster. Some who know the family history think of her as Ashley the Abandoned because from the time she was in high school in Nashville her mother was always on the road. Today Ashley is a fast-rising movie actress who launched her career in 1993, ten years after her sister and mother turned professionals, and, like her mother, is very much in control of her life. She is also very demanding and flip, like her sister. She becomes soft and withdrawn only around her mother and whoever is her current boyfriend.

Since her Malibu cottage burned down, she has been living on her Tennessee farm near Naomi and Wynonna, where she is exhilarated by the peace and space it offers for walking and roaming the woods. "It's truly in the genes" is what this eighth-generation Kentucky woman says about the mountains and the woods, and besides, her mother is nearby at last. Ashley says her mother is "ridiculously supportive and nurturing," which is what Ashley has always longed for, and Naomi is also an "absolute force to be reckoned with," which is what Ashley and Wynonna have both become. The relationship between Naomi and Wynonna is different. Someone once described them as two cats with their tails tied together and thrown over a clothesline.

Wynonna continues to pursue her singing career, and her two children mean more and more to her. Her newest album, *The Other Side*, is touted by people in the business as her best solo production so far. Naomi is always looking for things to do and, after finishing her cookbook, worked on recording inspirational tapes based on her experiences. They are designed to help women find spiritual roads to happiness—all in keeping with her personalized license plate, FAITH 1. Ashley continues to pursue a successful acting career while taking pleasure in shocking others by talking openly about sex and sexual positions but keeping her own romances private. She, her mother, and her sister continue to bond, bellow, and brawl and probably always will.

To quote Wynonna, "We put the fun into dysfunctional."

Sources

Books

The Judds by Bob Millard
Love Can Build a Bridge by Naomi Judd
Country Music, USA by Bill C. Malone
In the Country of Country by Nicholas Dawidoff
Country Music Culture by Curtis Ellison
All American Guide to Country Music by Frank and Patricia Eichenlaub
Deep Thoughts From a Shallow Mind by Doug Cdrca
Cash: The Autobiography by Johnny Cash and Patrick Carr
The Comprehensive Country Music Encyclopedia by Dwight Yoakam
Definitive Country by Barry McCloud
Country by Peter O.E. Bekker
The Southern Appalachians by Jerome Doolittle
The Recording Industry Sourcebook
Three Chords and the Truth by Larry Leamer
Country: The Music of America by Julie Mars
Nashville's Unwritten Rules by Dan Daley
All Music Guide to Country by Michael Erlewine
Bluegrass: A History by Neil Rosenberg
Bluegrass Breakdown by Robert Cantwell

Magazines and Newspapers

The Tennessean (various)
Nashville Banner (various)
National Geographic, February 1977
National Enquirer (various issues)
Star (various issues)
Atlanta Constitution—119 stories
Boston Globe—32 stories

Charlotte Observer—58 stories
Christian Science Monitor—3 stories
Denver Rocky Mountain News—70 stories
Miami Herald—75 stories
Newsday—61 stories
Philadelphia Inquirer—86 stories

San Francisco Chronicle—30 stories
USA Today—86 stories
Washington Post—51 stories
Saturday Evening Post,
   January–February 1996
People, May 22, 1995
People, February 14, 1994
People, January 10, 1994
Entertainment Weekly, December 3,
   1993
Entertainment Weekly, October 8,
   1993

People, March 1, 1993
Entertainment Weekly, February 26,
   1993
Entertainment Weekly, April 10,
   1992 (multiple stories)
People, December 9, 1991
Nation, August 15, 1987
Life, February, 1986
Time, January 13 1983

Video Tapes

America's Music—The Roots of Country, 3 video tapes, Turner
   Broadcasting
The Judds—Across the Heartland
Clips of various Judds on the Nashville Network

Direct Interviews

Former teachers, lovers, band members, and others

Index

269